60b
9

CAMBRIDGE STUDIES IN RUSSIAN LITERATURE

Andrey Bely:
a critical study of the novels

CAMBRIDGE STUDIES IN RUSSIAN LITERATURE

General editor HENRY GIFFORD

Andrey Bely:
A critical Study of the Novels

J. D. ELSWORTH

*Senior Lecturer, School of Modern Languages
and Modern History, University of East Anglia*

CAMBRIDGE UNIVERSITY PRESS

CAMBRIDGE

LONDON   NEW YORK   NEW ROCHELLE
MELBOURNE   SYDNEY

Published by the Press Syndicate of the University of Cambridge
The Pitt Building, Trumpington Street, Cambridge CB2 1RP
32 East 57th Street, New York, NY 10022, USA
296 Beaconsfield Parade, Middle Park, Melbourne 3206, Australia

First published 1983

Printed in Great Britain at
the University Press, Cambridge

Library of Congress catalogue card number: 83-1793

British Library Cataloguing in Publication Data
Elsworth, J.D.
Andrey Bely. – (Cambridge studies in Russian literature)
1. Bely, Andrey – Criticism and interpretation
I. Title
891.73'44   PG3488.E/

ISBN 0 521 24724 1

Contents

Preface

Two chapters of this book have appeared in substantially the same form before: chapter one in *Forum for Modern Language Studies*, vol. xi No. 4, 1975 (also in *Studies in Twentieth Century Russian Literature*, edited by C.J. Barnes, Scottish Academic Press, 1976), and chapter three in *Russian Literature*, vol. iv No. 4, 1976. Some overlapping material has also appeared in *Andrey Bely. A Critical Review*, edited by G. Janecek, Lexington, Kentucky, 1978, in *Andrey Bely. Centenary Papers*, edited by B. Christa, Amsterdam, 1980, and in *Poetry, Prose and Public Opinion of Russia 1850–1950, Essays Presented in Memory of Dr N.E. Andreyev*, edited by W.J. Harrison and Avril Pyman (forthcoming).

All translations in the text, unless otherwise indicated, are my own. Where the purpose of a quotation is as well served by an English translation as by the original, I have used a translation only. Where the intention was primarily to show features of Bely's Russian that are lost in any translation, I have left the quotation in the original but attached as accurate an English rendering of the sense as I could contrive.

I have incurred many debts in the course of work on this project. It is a matter of deep regret to me that it was not completed and published before the death of Dr N.E. Andreyev, who first led me to the subject and was always tireless in his advice and encouragement. I owe a great debt also to Professor Dame Elizabeth Hill, who directed my doctoral research. In the course of many visits to Russia I have profited greatly from the conversation of Professor D.E. Maksimov, and also of A.V. Lavrov and S.S. Grechishkin, who have shared their knowledge with unstinting generosity. I am grateful to N.K. Kotrelyov for allowing me to use his vast bibliography of the Symbolist period. It also gives me pleasure to acknowledge a great bibliographical debt of many years' standing to V.A. Skorodenko. I am indebted to the British Council and the British Academy for assistance towards research in the Soviet Union, and to the University of East Anglia for generous provision of study leave.

The indispensable support and forbearance of my wife, Bente, have not been taken for granted, and I wish to record my especial indebtedness to her.

Norwich, 1982 J.D.E.

Introduction

This book is concerned with one aspect of the work of a complex and prolific author. Besides writing novels, Andrey Bely was a poet, a theoretician of the Russian Symbolist movement, a philosopher of the history of culture, a literary critic, a voluminous memoirist and a copious correspondent. His published bibliography lists over six hundred items, of which more than forty are separate books,[1] and there lies in various archives a quantity of unpublished material that is probably equal in volume. Only gradually is his work being studied, only gradually is the unpublished work becoming available. There is no prospect of a definitive edition of Bely's works, and no imminent likelihood even of a definitive biography. Equally this book makes no claim to be a definitive study of his novels.

Any one of Bely's separate capacities would have been sufficient to secure him a permanent reputation. Much of his poetry is strikingly original, showing great rhythmic inventiveness and constant evolution. His verse memoir, *First Encounter*, from 1921, is widely regarded as one of the highest poetic achievements of the early twentieth century. Yet as poetic spokesman of his generation, Bely is inevitably overshadowed by Blok. As a memoirist, on the other hand, he has no rivals. His *Reminiscences of Blok*, upon which he embarked as soon as he returned home from his friend's funeral in August 1921, went through several stages of revision and expansion to emerge as three volumes of memoirs, covering the period from his childhood to 1912, which are essential reading for anyone interested in this era of Russian culture. His theoretical writings are often, to say the least, opaque, yet we know that he could hold spellbound any of the audiences that came to hear him lecture on the most diverse topics, from poetic rhythm to Apocalypse; and if he never silenced the scepticism of a professional philosopher such as Berdyayev, still he was much more than a dilettante and enjoyed in his own day great popular standing as a thinker and a teacher. He was also a highly competent musician, and in his later years turned himself into an efficient painter in water-colours. It is perhaps on account of his versatility, as much as anything else, that he might be said typically to embody the aspirations of his generation. For the unifying quest of the second generation of Russian Symbolists, those who, like Bely, came to maturity at the turn of the twentieth century and dominated its first decade, was a vision of a re-integrated human personality, and the dream of creating what they thought of as a new organic culture. This same concern informs every aspect of Bely's own work and makes it all the more hazardous to detach one such aspect from the rest.

Nevertheless it is as a novelist that Bely has achieved the greatest lasting fame. It was with an experimental prose work, called a *Symphony* that he made his literary debut in 1902, and in the realm of prose there is no one to overshadow him. His second and best-known novel, *Petersburg*, was the single most influential prose work to appear in the immediate pre-revolutionary period, and the principal progenitor of early Soviet experimental prose. Not only is Bely the most innovative prose-writer of the first third of the twentieth century, but it is also true to say that the novel form provided him with the best vehicle for embodying his complex view of human culture and the proper function of art. Bely's novels are the core of his achievement.

However, they are not easy to approach. The author of the first book on the subject asserted that it was inappropriate to consider Bely's aesthetic and cultural theories, since all that was required to reveal the meaning of the novels was 'the eyes of an unprejudiced connoisseur of art'.[2] I beg to differ. The aesthetic system of Bely's novels, the ideas underlying both form and content, do not easily yield themselves to simple observation. That is why the first part of this book is devoted to an examination of Bely's ideas. The first chapter summarizes the theory of Symbolism as Bely developed it during the first decade of the century, while the second examines his debt to anthroposophy, the teaching of Rudolf Steiner, whose pupil Bely became in 1912.

The groundwork for this book was done in the 1960s, in the preparation of a doctoral dissertation for Cambridge University. At that time the study of Bely was still very much in its infancy. No work of his was published in the Soviet Union between 1940 and

1966, and what little was written about him was mostly inaccurate and abusive. In the West the serious examination of his legacy had begun in the 1950s with books by Maslenikov and Mochul'sky, and a number of further contributions appeared in the first part of the 1960s. The last fifteen years, however, have witnessed a great upsurge of interest and output both in Russia and the West. Very little of the present text remains in the form it took originally. It has been completely re-written to take account of the large amount of valuable research done by others in the meantime, and also to accommodate my own changed understanding of its subject.

After the theoretical first part, Bely's novels are taken, in chapters three to nine, in chronological order of composition. I have in all cases used the first book-form publication of the novel as the basis for discussion. Each of these chapters sets out to be a coherent description and interpretation of the novel in question, while the development of Bely's ideas and techniques is traced from one to another. I attempt to touch upon every important aspect of each novel, though I have also tried to avoid repeating similar statements about similar features; in this process many features, such as the internal ramifications of imagery or the patterns of alliteration, are merely indicated and not treated with the detail that is devoted to them in more specialized research articles. If some recent specialized research on Bely has run the risk of failing to see the wood for the trees, I may be thought to have erred in the opposite direction. At all events I have attempted in each case to relate all the observed features to the central theme, in the hope of showing how the novel functions as an aesthetic whole. There is much more to be said about every aspect I touch upon, and I have no doubt that the chart of Bely's development as a novelist could be drawn in other ways as well. However, this is the first attempt to draw it at all.

Bely's career spanned an equal period on either side of 1917, but he belonged to the pre-revolutionary world in a way in which he could never belong to that which replaced it. It is as a representative of Symbolism that he has received much the greatest attention, both in Russia and in the West. Critical response to his first three novels began to be formulated in the periodical press of the time, and they have continued to attract a substantial amount of comment and exegesis. *Petersburg* has been the subject of more research than all the other novels put together. It has been translated into a dozen languages and has had many separate studies devoted to it. Most recently it has become the only novel of Bely's to be re-published in Russia since the year after his death, as both main redactions of it have appeared in fine scholarly editions. (His other novels and works in different genres are available mainly in Western reprints of earlier editions.) Of the two English translations of *Petersburg* the second is a model of accuracy. *The Silver Dove* and *Kotik Letayev* have also been translated into English and a few other languages. Critical literature on *The Silver Dove* is still not particularly extensive, though some interesting essays have appeared. *Kotik Letayev* has fared particularly well at the hands of American Slavists, and recent studies have provided material of high quality on its language and structure.

Bely did not emigrate after the revolution, though he spent two years in Germany, mainly in Berlin, from 1921 to 1923. His works continued to evoke critical discussion in the first decade or so of the Soviet regime, and several of the critical works dating from this period are in no way superseded. His new works, however, received less and less attention, and by the time his last novel appeared in 1932 he was perceived as a bizarre survival. He attempted to accommodate himself to the new political and cultural climate, and made obeisance to Marxist ideas in some of his writings. He allowed quite serious distortions to enter the final version of his memoirs, presumably in the hope of making palatable to the new readership as much as possible of the ideas and aspirations of his own generation. But this all availed him very little. Marxist critics were not taken in by the introduction of pseudo-Marxist notions as illustrative metaphors, and the unacceptable idealism and mysticism of Bely's outlook were constantly emphasized in the few reviews his later work received. Paradoxically the critics of the emigration were taken in more easily. In its cultural conservatism the emigration was not naturally sympathetic to Bely the innovator anyway, and every hint of a concession to the Soviet regime was liable to be read as total capitulation. So it came about that Russian critics of both camps disdained his later works. But it would be a mistake to attribute the virtual silence towards his late novels exclusively to political and historical factors. They came to assume an increasingly esoteric character, requiring an effort of adaptation from the reader that very few are willing to make. That is the principal reason why even Western students of Russian literature have still paid little attention to them. *The Baptized Chinaman* and *Notes of an Eccentric* elicited a modicum of response at the time, and have been studied in certain aspects since, but *Moscow* and *Masks* have been given only the most cursory and partial attention. I have attempted here to suggest a way of reading them that is consistent with the rest of what we know about Bely, and to rescue them from complete oblivion.

One thing that this book does not attempt to do is to relate Bely's novels to his biography. They are all based to a substantial extent upon events from his own life, and in many cases the information about prototypes is readily available in his memoirs. In a full study of his life and works there would be a place for a consideration of his autobiographical sources, and of the way in which the raw material of experience was transformed into the plots of his novels; but without extensive biographical details the simple assertion of identity would serve no purpose. He claimed, for instance, that the carpenter Kudeyarov in *The Silver Dove* was based in part upon D.S. Merezhkovsky,[3] but that assertion cannot be properly understood without a full account of Bely's developing relations with Merezhkovsky over a considerable period. I have outlined Bely's biography in another book,[4] though not in the detail that would be needed to satisfy this purpose properly, and I saw no reason to repeat that material here.

PART I

1

Bely's theory of Symbolism

The essays that comprise Bely's theory of Symbolism were written and published between 1902 and 1912. They cannot be said to represent a homogeneous body of writing; they vary both in philosophical approach and in style. The earliest essays were written under the clear and confessed influence of Schopenhauer's aesthetics. Later Bely turned to Kant, and between 1906 and 1908 devoted much effort to the study of contemporary German neo-Kantian philosophy. Around the end of 1908 he renewed an interest in occultism that had been in abeyance for some years, and attempted a fusion of neo-Kantianism and theosophy. By no means all the essays, however, are written in a recognizably philosophical style. He noted himself that a number of them were written in what he called an 'Argonaut' style,[1] a lyrical, highly metaphorical style that seeks to persuade by other means than rational argument. This, though, is a feature that is not restricted to certain isolated works, but pervades very many of the essays at one point or another. It is not at all uncommon for a staid philosophical argument to break off without warning into a passage of a visionary nature. Furthermore Bely made no attempt to work out a consistent terminology for his ideas, and created needless confusion by his use of variable synonyms and his tendency to allow a single word to assume conflicting meanings.

Bely's tendency directly to contradict himself has perhaps been exaggerated; what seem to be contradictions are mostly attributable to vagaries of terminology. But it is certainly the case that the expression of his views was sometimes affected to the point of distortion by his relations with other members of the movement. In the hot-house atmosphere of Symbolism, where existential commitment to ideas went so deep that a personal quarrel and a philosophical disagreement could hardly be distinguished, much was expressed immoderately in the heat of the moment. And Bely was one of the most immoderate. Just at the point of Symbolism's

7

greatest popularity, in the years following the abortive 1905 revolution, Bely was involved in a lengthy feud with the Petersburg group, with Blok, V. Ivanov and G. Chulkov. The movement's popularity led to a spate of imitations and a certain debasing of its values, and Bely mixed his justified opposition to this trend with his personal and philosophical altercations with the Petersburg Symbolists. The result was a series of essays whose inordinately polemical tone does more to obscure than to clarify the issues at stake.

Bely's essays are also incomplete. He wrote in his memoirs: 'There were articles, addresses, conversations devoted to every point of my literary theory; but I never compressed it into paragraphs.'[2] During the years in question he published in the periodical press over 130 separate essays (not counting short notices of books); some 80 of these were re-published in the three volumes *Symbolism, Arabesques* and *The Green Meadow*,[3] along with a number of new works, and, in the case of *Symbolism*, an extensive commentary. Yet despite this quantity of output Bely did not succeed in putting down the entire theory as he envisaged it. For one thing the periodical press demanded fresh articles far more frequently than a writer could be visited by fresh ideas, and there is in consequence a large element of repetition. Bely displays a tendency to start afresh each time he sets pen to paper, to re-formulate in new terms ideas that have been expressed before. Furthermore the essays often bear the marks of having been written in haste; this is true even of some that were written expressly for inclusion in the collected volumes. A prime example is the most ambitious philosophical essay of all, 'The Emblematics of Meaning', a hundred pages in length, written expressly for *Symbolism*, and completed, on Bely's admission, in a week.[4]

The intrusion of a poetic manner into Bely's philosophical arguments leads to another problem. Often his arguments are conducted less in accordance with logic than through verbal association. A given word may be defined in the terms of one argument and then transferred, complete with its definition, into another context, where it acquires, or implicitly presupposes, another definition. The two (or more) definitions may be logically quite unconnected with each other, yet the word continues to be used – in a poetic rather than a philosophical manner – with all the implications acquired through either definition intact. Conversely the transitions may be made not through the gradual extension of the meaning of one word, but through the telescoping of the meanings of several words. Words which may be established as synonyms in a specific context sometimes continue to be used as synonyms in other contexts. The overall result of the consistent use of these devices is the destruction of perspective by a process of reducing concepts to two one-dimensional series of overlapping or inter-changeable notions, which two series then face each other as interchangeable antitheses.

A final objection that has rightly been raised against Bely's theoretical writings is that the procedure, acceptable within reason, of employing generally understood shorthand references to known arguments is taken to an unacceptable extreme. The commentaries to *Symbolism*, as well as some of the essay texts themselves,[5] abound in single-sentence references to complexes of ideas that are taken as familiar and used as a basis of further argument. It sometimes becomes impossible to follow, let alone to judge, the details of Bely's reasoning.

Thus there are a number of valid and substantial criticisms that can be raised against Bely's theoretical writings. It does not follow from this, however, that they are intrinsically uninteresting or unworthy of study. The purpose of this chapter is to show that behind all the infelicities that beset Bely's theory as formulated there lies a consistent and distinctive vision of the general tele-ology of culture which is essential for an adequate understanding of the rest of his work, and is also intrinsically important as an episode in the history of ideas in Russia.

Behind Bely's theory in the period prior to 1912 lie two fun-damental philosophical influences and a number of secondary ones. The greatest debts are not always the most clearly acknowl-edged. Vladimir Solov'yov and Nietzsche exercised upon his thinking an influence so pervasive that its limits are difficult to define. With thinkers whose influence was more localized or tem-porary there is less problem in indicating the particular points of contact. Bely's early attachment to the aesthetics of Schopenhauer is a case in point; his prolonged engagement with the neo-Kantians, in particular Heinrich Rickert, leaves a distinct imprint upon the form of his argument for several years; his fluctuating relations with Merezhkovsky are reflected in his chang-ing views about the degree of affinity between Symbolism and the social democracy movement. The quest for influences is not an end in itself, merely a way of establishing perspective. Behind all influences lies a specific manner of experiencing the world that is peculiar to Bely. Fedor Stepun has described his thought as 'exercises on a flying trapeze under the big top of his lonely ego'.[6] While this may suggest a degree of solipsism that would preclude almost all communicative value, it is clear that in one sense the remark is just. All Bely's works, both theoretical and literary, spring from an original intuition to which all the tools of science and philosophy that he employed were made subservient. The most striking feature of this manner of experiencing the world is Bely's conception of it as a duality, or series of dualities, that he is concerned to reconcile. This is expressed in the foreshortening of perspective through argument by extended synonyms, which, in terms of imagery, is also a feature of the novels. Bely's theory of Symbolism is an attempt to prove that it is in Symbolism that the reconciliation of all dualities is to be found.

Bely's premise is that European civilization is undergoing a crisis, which expresses itself in man's accentuated awareness of certain fundamental dualities. 'Never before have the basic contradictions of the human consciousness been in such sharp conflict in the soul.'[7] This quotation is taken from an essay written in July 1910, 'The Crisis of Consciousness and Henrik Ibsen'.[8] In that essay Bely enumerates five such contradictions from which men suffer: between consciousness and feeling; between contemplation and will; between the individual and society; between science and religion; and between morality and beauty. In the context it becomes apparent that the first of these, the duality of consciousness and feeling, is a statement of the general problem, of which the others are particular aspects. It is an opposition for which many different formulations can be found in Bely's essays: 'consciousness and experience', 'consciousness and life', 'feeling and reason', 'intellect and feeling'.[9] The fundamental conception is of a division in man between a rational and an intuitive response to the world, and a sense that while each is valid, there is no way of connecting them, so that man is faced with an impossible but inevitable choice. In describing the effects of the crisis he describes as 'cripples' both those who have made such a choice, elevating to hegemony one of their faculties while neglecting the other, and also those who fail to make a choice and vacillate between the two.[10]

Just as the conflicting human faculties may be known by various names, so may the attitudes to which the resulting 'cripples' resort: empiricism, positivism or determinism on the one hand, decadence or individualism on the other.[11] In the terms of 'The Crisis of Consciousness and Henrik Ibsen' the positivist pole is seen in an outlook involving trust in abstract reasoning, in traditional morality, in the will to action as applied directly to empirical reality, and in the conclusions of the natural sciences. The pole of decadence is expressed in reliance upon feeling, contemplation and beauty, and in the habit of making a fetish of the fortuitous experience. On the one hand is a false coherence of experience accepted by those who have not realized the existence of the crisis, on the other is the abandonment of coherence by those who are aware of the crisis but cannot resolve it.

Bely's argument can be illustrated by the example of the conflict of contemplation and will. A mechanistic world-view, an understanding of the world in terms of scientifically established causal relations, leads to an understanding of the human will as wholly controlled by objective external forces. The positivist fails to make this inference, whereas the decadent sees the implication, and takes refuge in a contemplative attitude to the world, where the will is thought not to come into play at all. Bely's argument about the nature of contemplation, however, is designed to show that neither of these attitudes is an adequate response. Man's experience of the external world is not a passive reproduction of a pre-existent reality, it is an active transformation of it through the prism of feeling. Every cultural period is marked by its common manner of transformation, which is its 'style'. Furthermore it is possible for any individual to possess a distinctive 'style'; it is just as possible to speak of Nietzsche's style as it is of Assyrian or Gothic style. In such a creative process one may speak of the will to contemplation. Schopenhauer was therefore mistaken in asserting that the will is suppressed in artistic creation. What has happened is that instead of being naively applied to empirical reality it is transferred to the reproduction of reality in 'the images of artistic and intellectual creation'.[12] These images in turn become an influence for the changing of empirical reality. The will to action has proceeded by an indirect route, and, given this understanding, the conflict between contemplation and will has been overcome. Out of the thesis and the antithesis Bely has produced a synthesis; this is a typical example of the form his arguments take.

In discussing the conflict between the individual and society, Bely takes issue with Marxism. He does not name it, but speaks of 'economic materialism'. He sees this doctrine as asserting the complete dependence of the individual upon society; the individual consciousness is regarded as being determined by the class conflict in society. The concept of class ethics, which the doctrine deduces from this dependence, Bely considers irreconcilable with individual ethics, indeed tantamount to a denial of ethics. In an earlier article, 'The Idol with Feet of Clay',[13] he had denied that statements about ethics could properly be made at all within the framework of Marxism. Invoking Kant's distinction of the spheres of nature and of freedom, he had argued that the part of Marxist doctrine that examines economic relations as an object of scientific research is concerned with the sphere of nature, while the moral imperative deduced from the conclusions of this research belongs in the sphere of freedom. According to Kant, no such transition from nature to freedom is possible. In 'The Crisis of Consciousness and Henrik Ibsen' Bely offers a general epistemological criticism of the doctrine. It declares the abstract categories of the reason to be the product of economic conditions; yet from an epistemological point of view the very method of 'economic materialism' is determined by those categories.[14]

If the doctrine of 'economic materialism' is nevertheless accepted, Bely sees that ethics come to be statistically determined: the majority is right. But he considers that truth has never been an attribute of the majority; it is born in the minority, indeed in the single individual. To Bely the very notion of a majority opinion is suspect. He claims that the expression in words of any conviction is to some extent a distortion of it, since the words can never completely render the complexity of motives that underlie the conviction. The coincidence of any two opinions is based upon their verbal formulation, which in neither case is wholly adequate to the content. Any agreement is necessarily a compromise. The agreement of the masses consists of an abstraction from a multitude of individual convictions, by which each individual conviction, robbed of its real motives, loses in force. Bely sees such quantitative argument assuming an ever increasing significance in contemporary society, to the detriment of the individual.

Bely's attitude to Marxism has been more fully described by N.A.Valentinov than it ever was in print by Bely himself. In the years 1907–9 Valentinov fulfilled the role of Bely's Marxist mentor, and he has left an account of conversations he had with Bely about Marxism and other subjects. Bely was sympathetic to Marxism as he understood it, but his understanding of it was original and aroused the anger of an orthodox social-democrat such as Valentinov. Bely viewed Marxism as a doctrine of the coming Apocalypse, a vision of the transformation of man and human society, akin but inferior to that of Vladimir Solov'yov. When Valentinov objected that the two were wholly incompatible and that it was impossible to make a transition from Marx to Solov'yov, Bely responded that the opposite transition, from Solov'yov to Marx, as a transition from the general to the particular, was nonetheless possible. Bely interpreted the idea of revolution, which appealed to him, as 'explosion' (*vzryv*), insisting that 'explosion' was a spiritual act. Marxist doctrine, with its reference to economic relations, could provide no explanation of such an act, whereas Solov'yov's account in terms of cultural crisis and psychic changes does provide an explanation.[15] In 'The Idol with Feet of Clay' Bely explicitly stated that Marx's theory of historical necessity was incompatible with the freedom required to perform the act of creativity that Marx yet demanded of man.[16]

This account of Valentinov's also casts light upon the way in which Bely responded to the thought of others. He mistrusted the actual verbal formulations of thoughts, and sought to penetrate beyond them to some underlying attitude, where he could discern similarities not evident on the verbal surface. He might have said that for all their difference in formulation Marx and Solov'yov had a similar 'style'. This feature of his thinking goes some way to explain a peculiarity of his reading habits which is also reported by Valentinov. He recalls being told by Bely's friend Ellis (L.L.Kobylinsky) how Bely would read the first fifty or seventy-five pages of a book with great attention, but then gradually adapt the author to suit himself, so that he had the impression of understanding the whole train of thought and having no need to read the rest.[17]

Bely's distinction between positivism and decadence operates both as a general critique of prevalent habits of thought, and as an explanation of the historical role envisaged for the Symbolist movement. The terms refer to the dominant trends in Russian thinking in the decades prior to the rise of Symbolism, and it is evident that Bely regarded Symbolism as providing their synthesis in a historical sense. It will be seen that in other contexts, in his novels, there are other sets of opposites that stand in very similar relationships to each other. Stepun spoke of Bely as constantly poised between the poles of chaos and crystallization.[18] This is a happy formulation, and one which brings to mind another pair of terms: Nietzsche's concepts of the Dionysian and the Apollonian. The area of experience that Bely designates as 'feeling', where reside the 'motives' for convictions, whose verbal formulation is always inadequate – the impulse that precedes all form – is clearly a close relation of Nietzsche's Dionysus.

Bely's concern is with the world created by human thought; he knows no other. It is telling that in his discussion of the conflict between the individual and society he makes no mention of the social reality in which such a conflict would normally be assumed to take place. It is in the conflict between a determinist attitude that sees the individual as subject to the objective facts of society, and a decadent attitude that sees the individual as essentially unrelated to society, that Bely finds the problem. The solution to the crisis of culture lies therefore in the transformation of habits of thought: 'The transformation of the reality outside us depends on the transformation of the reality within us.'[19] From this he infers the need for a transformation of the self, an idea which carries further loud echoes of Nietzsche, and declares this transformation to be the ultimate task of culture.[20] 'We must forget the present; we must recreate everything from the beginning; and for this we must recreate ourselves. And the only slope we can clamber up is ourselves. At its summit our ego awaits us.'[21]

The changes in Bely's philosophical approach meant that he attempted to construct more than one basis for his theory. In his collected volumes he included essays from the earlier, Schopenhauerian period on the grounds that Symbolism could be reached from various starting-points. By far the fullest such undertaking, however, stemmed from his study of neo-Kantian epistemology, and it is appropriate to begin the exposition of his detailed argument there.

The status of epistemology as the only discipline capable of guaranteeing the meaningfulness of an argument is described in the article 'On Scientific Dogmatism.'[22] In ancient times, Bely maintains, the subject-matter of philosophy was the whole of reality. As the individual sciences developed, however, each usurped as its own subject-matter a particular area of reality, gradually diminishing the realm of philosophy. The result of this process is that in the present century philosophy finds itself with no subject-matter at all. Each science, however, has its own specific method, which limits and determines the validity of its conclusions. The conclusions of one science are not applicable to another. Thus an overall picture is only to be gained through epistemology, as a discipline that correlates scientific methods.

This analysis of the present situation of philosophy was common to all branches of neo-Kantianism. Bely was familiar with the work of many representatives of the movement, both in Germany and in Russia, but he was particularly drawn to the Freiburg school, founded by Windelband. This school was distinguished by an affinity to Fichte, expressed in its positing of a supra-individual ego and in its insistence on regarding cognition as an act.[23] It is principally to the work of Heinrich Rickert that Bely refers. Since, however, he cannot be said to follow Rickert very exactly, but rather to select and transmute such parts of his argument as suit his own purposes, it is as well to outline the relevant parts of Rickert's epistemology separately, before going on to expound Bely's own ideas.

Rickert defined his philosophy as transcendental idealism. It is idealism because no being is assumed other than that which can be a content of consciousness; Rickert expressly abandoned the metaphysical dualism of immanent and transcendent being. It is transcendental because, in contrast to subjective idealism, it points beyond the content of consciousness to a transcendent task. Rickert maintained that all judgements, in that they aim at truth, acknowledge a transcendent imperative (*ein transzendentes Sollen*), beyond which nothing can be posited. Owing to the logical primacy of duty (*Sollen*) over being, he found the final ground of all immanent being neither in that being itself, nor in any transcendent being, but in a transcendent ideal, which it is the task of the cognizing subject to realize: 'The object of knowledge is thus for transcendental idealism not given, either immanently or transcendentally, but set [as a task to be performed] [*aufgegeben*].'[24]

Transcendental idealism does not conflict with empirical realism, the basis of the sciences, because it is concerned not with the content of judgements, but with their form. He explains the concept of form by pointing to the element of affirmation in the judgement 'colour is'; affirmation alone distinguishes the idea of a colour that is from the simple idea of a colour. The concept of being therefore acquires meaning only through affirmation (or negation), and affirmation, being that part of a judgement that does not refer to its representational content, is the form of the judgement.[25]

Empirical realism regards the truth of a judgement as dependent upon the coincidence of its form with the form of reality. For transcendental idealism, however, there is no independently existent reality whose form the form of judgements could reflect. Rickert therefore regards the form of reality as the product of the act of judgement: 'The epistemological centre of gravity lies therefore not in the form of the already made judgement, but in the act of judging, in the affirmation that *gives* form and founds reality.'[26] Since every individual empirical subject is a part of reality it cannot be assumed that individual acts of judgement form reality; such an assumption would make reality dependent on one of its parts. Rickert therefore posits, purely as a logical necessity, 'the judging consciousness in general' (*das urteilende Bewusstsein überhaupt*); this is not to be regarded as corresponding to any reality.[27]

All sciences assume a coherent world, existing in one time and one space, and subject to the law of causality. Rickert insists that its coherence is part not of the content of knowledge, but of the form. It is therefore necessary to find the forms of imperative whose acknowledgement gives rise to and justifies the concept of a coherent world. Rickert draws a distinction between constitutive and methodological forms, taking as examples the concepts of causality and law of nature. Each causal relationship, he argues, is individual and unrepeatable, whereas the concept of a law of nature is an attempt to express what different causal relationships have in common. Causality is a constitutive form, law of nature a methodological form; the latter implies a relationship between the general and the particular, which can be thought of only as a logical relationship, never as a real one. Rickert considers that all forms that refer to the general are methodological forms. Moreover he considers that any world of concepts created by methodological forms is an interpretation by the empirical subject, indeed is anthropomorphism.[28]

Bely follows this part of Rickert's argument in asserting the inadequacy of science as the foundation of a world-view.[29] Rickert, however, goes on from this to admit that epistemology is not concerned with answering questions about the essence of reality. He argues that once the concept of objective reality has been clarified it becomes evident that questions about its essence are scientifically unwarrantable. This statement of Rickert's provokes Bely to declare that epistemology confers upon existence an order which is devoid of meaning. Rickert is evidently not unaware of the limitations of his philosophy, for he goes on to say that the only way of approaching the 'ontological problem',[30] which is left unaccounted for after the solution of the problem of objective reality, is to endeavour to experience as much as possible of the content of reality. He adds, however, that a single essence of reality will not be discovered by this route either; on the contrary, the variety of reality will become all the more evident.

Rickert warns, furthermore, against the danger of regarding concepts as possessing the character of reality. The very process of reducing reality to concepts is in some measure a distortion of the variety of reality. This fact he regards as a further reason, besides the formal aspect of all judgements, why knowledge cannot be an exact representation of reality. All knowledge, he concludes, is a transformation of reality. By this assertion Rickert is acknowledging that there does exist a reality independent of the knowing subject. He regards the geological fact of the earth's existence before there were men to perceive it as a demonstration of the existence of some such reality.[31]

Thus Rickert establishes the ethical basis of epistemology: 'It follows from our concept of cognition that the final basis of knowledge is conscience.'[32] He considers that this discovery determines the task of philosophy in the present age. Philosophy is no longer the one all-embracing science it once used to be; it has been ousted from that status by the individual sciences. 'Philosophy leaves the whole of *being* to the individual sciences, in order to inquire everywhere after *meaning*.'[33] Philosophy is a science of values.

Rickert was at pains to show that his transcendental idealism could coexist with empirical realism, and that its conclusions were therefore not in conflict with those of the sciences. Every scientific judgement has two aspects: as regards its content it relates to being and is correctly understood as realistic; as regards its form it is to be understood as idealistic. But sciences themselves are concerned only with immanent reality and are right to give attention only to the content of the judgement. Objective reality in the sense in which it is understood in natural science is not threatened by transcendental idealism.

Bely's attitude to reality is a problem many of his commentators have faced. It has been noted – both by critics on the basis of his work, and by memoirists on the basis of personal acquaintance – that he seemed to perceive reality as somehow unstable. This view has been well expressed by Stepun: 'Bely's being and his art are only to be properly understood if one imagines that throughout his life he saw and described all glass balls in the moment of their transformation into skulls, and all towels in the moment of their transformation into winding-sheets.'[34] This, however, is a statement about Bely's psychological make-up, rather than about his philosophy. There is doubtless considerable truth in the suggestion that objective reality was not a thing he ever took for granted, though Stepun's implication that what he saw behind it was purely spectral is certainly at odds with his own view. But the theoretical issue is essentially separate from this. In his memoirs Bely criticized himself in retrospect for not starting out with a definition of what he understood by reality. Instead of doing so, he explained, he used the term 'reality' (*deystvitel'nost'*) to describe what was understood by it in other philosophies, so that his theory appeared to be a rejection of reality, when it was in fact a rejection of various interpretations of reality.[35] This was indeed a way in which he sometimes operated, but at other times he expressed a clear view which is fundamentally in accord with Rickert's. Bely does not, any more than Rickert, deny the independent existence of objective reality, thought of as simply a series of objectively existent phenomena, which cannot in themselves be altered by human thought. And he is similarly content to surrender these phenomena to the individual sciences. But he considers that while the phenomena themselves are given, the relationships between them are the product of human thought, and the scientific approach, which operates with the concept of causality and sees relations in the aspect of necessity, is not the only approach possible.[36] He is not content with Rickert's agnostic attitude towards the essence of reality. If knowledge means knowledge of the meaning of life, he declares, then science is not knowledge; it is the systematizing of ignorance.[37]

The fundamental problem which, in Bely's view, Rickert's epistemology leaves unsolved, is again a duality: the duality between the form and the content of knowledge. Neither constitutive nor methodological forms are capable of imparting meaning. The application of methodological forms can have only relative significance: the conclusions reached by any given science are valid only within the terms of its specific method. Constitutive forms, however, being the forms of the particular, are not susceptible to ordering in the way that methodological forms are. Bely therefore concludes that all contents of consciousness, where they are not given relative significance by the application to them of methodological forms, are chaos.

In one of the notes to *Symbolism* Bely speaks of his route 'from Kant to Rickert and beyond'.[38] In his memoirs he reports that when Rickert was told of his views he clearly dissociated himself from them.[39] The point at which Bely can be seen to part company with Rickert is where he picks up and develops the idea of experiencing reality.[40] What was merely a laconic aside in the original becomes the kernel of Bely's argument. It is through experiencing reality, he maintains, that we make the otherwise chaotic contents of consciousness meaningful: 'experiencing them, we pass these contents through ourselves, as it were; we become an image of the Logos, organizing chaos'.[41] Clearly the human faculty that performs this process is that which he calls 'feeling'. The order thus conferred upon the contents of consciousness is not logical; Bely insists that here it is proper to speak not of cognition, but only of creation. The idea that creation has primacy over cognition is probably the idea most frequently encountered throughout Bely's theoretical works.

The dichotomy between the form and the content of knowledge is for Bely yet another way of expressing the duality which is the fundamental characteristic of the crisis of the European consciousness as he sees it. Returning to the terms of his distinction between positivism and decadence, it may be seen that the content of knowledge, which is objective reality, is the material of positivism, and the form of knowledge, which is a subjective reaction to that reality, is the material of decadence. Just as in historical terms this duality is resolved in Symbolism, so in philosophical terms it is resolved in the symbol.

The symbol as an epistemological concept is derived from Rickert's concept of value. Bely argues that all concepts philosophers have placed at the pinnacle of their systems – Kant's thing-in-itself, Fichte's ego, Schopenhauer's will or Hegel's spirit – are reducible to the concept of value. This concept itself Bely declares to be not further reducible, and he equates it with the concept of the symbol, which thus becomes the limit of all possible formation of concepts.[42] All philosophical systems are expressions of value; their significance is not theoretical, for theoretical significance belongs to epistemology alone, but is symbolic.

This symbolic nature is not peculiar to philosophy. All human creative activities – science, philosophy, art or religion – are ways of 'symbolizing human creation'.[43] This assertion makes clearer what Bely means by symbolic significance. It is particularly important that what is symbolized is 'human creation'. All products of human cultural activities are symbols of the act of creation, externalizations, one might say, of an internal process.[44] This process of symbolization is the process of the creation of values. 'Cognitional value consists in the creation of idea-images, the cognizing [*opoznaniye*] of which forms objective reality itself; cognitional value is to be found in the creative process of symbolization.'[45] Cognition, then, is a subsequent stage. Meaningful objective reality, the world men inhabit, is brought about by these two successive processes, which consist, we can now see, in the application of 'feeling' and 'consciousness' respectively.

By 'objective reality' here Bely clearly means something substantially different from that humanly irrelevant world that is consigned to the sciences. Yet this objective reality at the end of the process can have an important feature in common with the unformed reality man originally faces. If it becomes static, it once again becomes hostile. This explains Bely's attitude to concepts and dogmas. Rickert had warned against regarding concepts as corresponding exactly to reality, since they distort its variety. Bely rejects concepts on different grounds; to him their application is stasis. 'An abstract concept definitively crystallizes past acts of cognition; but the aim of humanity is to create the objects of cognition themselves ... An abstract concept ends the process of the subjugation of nature by man.'[46] Dogmas, similarly, are no longer creative: 'any conclusion offered to us in the shape of a dogma is in itself the empty shell of value'.[47] This rejection of any notion of objective truth is another feature of Bely's argument for which he seems to be indebted to Nietzsche.

The act of creation which the symbol represents is the process of passing objective reality through experience and thus endowing it with meaning. Bely points to the Greek derivation of the word to justify his own usage of it in the meaning of 'an organic conjunction' of one thing with another.[48] The symbol is the fusion of form and content, and the duality between form and content, in the epistemological meaning of those words, is the most concise expression of the central duality underlying the crisis of European culture.

At the same time, this definition is in effect the starting-point for Bely's discussion of the artistic symbol. A clearer definition of the artistic symbol reads: 'The symbol is an image, taken from nature and transformed by creation; the symbol is an image which combines in itself the experience of the artist and features taken from nature.'[49] It can easily be seen that 'the experience of the artist' corresponds to epistemological 'form', and 'features taken from nature' to epistemological 'content'. While art does not enjoy theoretical pride of place in Bely's philosophy, since its symbolic nature is shared by all other human creative activities, it is nonetheless to art that the greater part of his attention is devoted. Artistic creation is the way of fusing form and content with which Bely was most closely concerned, and the interest of his epistemological theory lies mainly in its function as an introduction to his aesthetic theory.

This fusion of form and content, of experience and objective reality, is present, according to Bely, in all art. For all art is symbolic, not only that which calls itself Symbolist. Classical and Romantic art differ only in the precedence they give to objective reality and inner experience. In his essay 'The Meaning of Art' Bely enumerates algebraically eight possible ways in which 'b' – objective reality – and 'c' – inner experience – may be combined to form 'a' – the symbol. Every symbol is a unity, and the separate elements of objective reality and inner experience are 'means of manifesting artistic creation', means, that is to say, of creating the symbol.[50]

These elements, however, do not stand in an equal relationship in the symbol. In art, Bely asserts, the world of appearances (*vidimost'*) stands in a subordinate relationship to inner experience. This might be expressed differently by saying that what is important in the symbol is not so much the 'features taken from nature' as the manner of their transformation through the experience of the artist. This is what Bely understands by style. The artist's creative experience is expressed in artistic form.

There are two essays in *Symbolism* devoted specifically to the problem of artistic form.[51] In them Bely propounds a gradation of existing art forms very much along the lines of Schopenhauer's, with music at one extreme and architecture at the other. He uses a system of classification in terms of time and space. Temporal and spatial elements are found to be present in inverse proportion to each other. Music is the supremely temporal art, where 'time is expressed in rhythm' and 'space is expressed . . . by means of misty analogies'.[52] Sculpture and architecture stand at the other end of the spectrum, where 'for rhythm in the proper sense is substituted the so-called harmony of form'.[53] Time and space are present embryonically, as it were, in the art forms dominated by the other: 'It may be said that in music we have the potentials of space, in architecture the potentials of time.'[54] This conception makes it possible for Bely to reject all normative theories of genre and posit an infinite variety of possible genres between the two extremes. Poetry stands at a kind of mid-way point. The poetic image 'grows on to' musical rhythm, 'restricts rhythmic freedom and, so to speak, burdens it with [elements of] the world of appearances'.[55]

When Bely originally formulated this theory of the gradation of art forms in 1902 he accompanied it by a prophetic utterance to the effect that all art forms were moving towards music, as the most perfect. This evolutionary conception is not taken up again in the later essay (written in 1906), but the status of music as the highest art remains unchanged, and is declared in terms still reminiscent of Schopenhauer: 'Music has to do with reality itself, abstracted from appearance.'[56] What seems to be a statement of a metaphysical dualism is, however, modified by the following sentence: 'It represents the succession of experiences without seeking for them a corresponding form in appearance.' Thus 'reality itself' is implicitly equated with 'the succession of experiences'. Although this identification is nowhere clearly argued, it is in fact the nearest Bely comes to a definition of reality. It is expressed elsewhere as 'the totality of possible experience'.[57] The justification for regarding music as capable of expressing reality in this definition comes through an extension of the notion of time. Bely invokes Kant's definition of time as 'the form of inner sense'[58] and reaches a position where the temporal element in art is equated to the artist's inner experience, his creative transformation of chaos. This is what Bely understood by Rickert's epistemological concept of form, and he transfers essentially the same meaning to the notion of aesthetic form. The element of time is present in poetry in rhythm, and it is therefore rhythm above all that Bely examines in his attempt to discover the creative experience which has given form to chaos and is symbolized in the work of art. Despite the Kantian form of the argument, however, it appears that behind this idea lies once more the Dionysian 'spirit of music' derived from Nietzsche.[59] By a similar use of Kant's definition of space as 'the form of outer sense', Bely comes to identify the spatial element in art with the world of appearance (i.e. the sense-data of outer sense), so that another way of expressing that fusion of form and content which is the artistic symbol is to speak of the fusion of temporal and spatial elements.

This identification is only possible as long as 'content', in the context of the aesthetic discussion, is taken to have the same meaning that it has in the epistemological argument. This is, indeed, the meaning it has traditionally had in literary criticism: a part of objective reality. It is with reference to this meaning that Bely describes the division into form and content as merely a methodological device for studying 'the given artistic unity'.[60] But the word 'content' has the same duality of meaning in Bely's aesthetic argument that the term 'objective reality' has in his epistemological discussion: it refers at different times both to the original unformed material and to the finished product of human creative activity. In this second meaning Bely seeks an alternative definition of it. He finds that there are two ways of looking at it, which cannot, at the present stage of knowledge, be connected: '... we have to regard the content of art now as *form*, now as *meaning*'.[61] The sense in which it can be said that the form of art is also the content of art may be extracted from Bely's discussion of the nature of the symbol. What is meant is that the creative action of transforming objective reality, which is what the symbol symbolizes and which is given in the artistic form, is itself the content of art.[62] Art is about that creative action, not about the phenomena used as a means to express it (content in the conventional sense). When Bely then speaks of the content of art as 'meaning' (*smysl*), he is referring to the meaning of such creative activity in general. The question to which this statement is properly the answer would be: what purpose does such creative activity serve at all? Bely's answer to the question of meaning is that the meaning of all art is religious.

Bely's assertion of the religious significance of art may appear at first sight to contradict his insistence that art is not to be regarded as subordinate to religion.[63] But this contradiction vanishes if it is borne in mind that Bely regarded any dogma as 'the empty shell of value'. The religious significance of art does not consist, therefore, in reference to any established religious dogma, and no religious dogma may claim the allegiance of art. Indeed in one passage Bely asserts that in religion there can be no dogmas.[64] Art appears irreligious, in that it 'seeps beyond the limits of eroded religious forms', but its religious nature lies in the fact that it 'creates a different, living form which has not yet been found'.[65] The essence of religion, in Bely's view, lies in the creative activity that gives coherence to human experience. But this does not, of course, explain what is meant by speaking of the meaning of art as religious, since at this point the argument is tautological. The concepts of religious and creative activity are identified and each explained in terms of the other.

Bely's real grounds for asserting the religious nature of man's creative activity are to be found in another conception of religion, one which is derived from Vladimir Solov'yov. This provides an alternative set of terms for the epistemologically based argument and serves to link the historical and philosophical aspects of Bely's theory. Bely's attachment to Solov'yov is different in nature from all the other philosophical affiliations of his early period. Direct references to Solov'yov in his theoretical works are surprisingly few, and in an essay of 1907 Bely spoke of Solov'yov's system as having 'nothing to say'.[66] Yet it is known that Bely had frequent meetings with Solov'yov in the autumn of 1898, saw him again shortly before his death in the summer of 1900, and spent the autumn of 1900 deeply absorbed in the study of both his philosophy and his poetry. Apart from the fact of personal acquaintance through his friendship with Solov'yov's brother's family, Solov'yov was associated for Bely with his most intimate mystical experiences. His first meeting with him was preceded by a vision of

the advent of Antichrist and the end of world history, the theme
which Solov'yov himself developed in his *Tale of Antichrist* of
1900.[67] The study of his work was inseparable from the mystical
elation of that period of Bely's life. Despite the absence of overt
references and the later coolness towards Solov'yov's metaphysics,
there is therefore no reason to doubt that the similarities between
Bely's theory and Solov'yov's system are attributable precisely to
Bely's knowledge of Solov'yov. It is clear that Solov'yov's basic
conception of the nature of the universe and the meaning of history
became fundamental to Bely's own outlook.

According to Solov'yov's cosmology the differentiated, phenomenal world is the product of the splitting of the prime being, the
Absolute or God. God required the world in order to manifest his
love. The unifying principle of the phenomenal world is the
'world-soul' (*mirovaya dusha*), which is the common subject of all
creatures and contains both divine and natural principles. But it is
not bound by either, and, being free, is able to assert itself
independently of God. This, at some stage, it did, thereby losing its
participation in the divine principle and becoming wholly a part of
the natural world. Thus by a voluntary action of the world-soul God
and the world became alienated, and all creatures became subject
to decay and death.

The historical process, which begins with the appearance of man,
is not different from the cosmological process, but is a new stage in
it. It is marked by the reunification of the world-soul with the divine
Logos. This reunification takes place in the human consciousness,
and is most perfectly manifested in Christ. The world-soul, as it now
appears, linked with the Logos, is also termed Sophia, the Eternal
Feminine. Sophia has another function as the true cause and aim of
creation. She therefore contains the potentiality of the reunification
of the differentiated phenomenal world, and at the end of the
historical process will reappear as the Kingdom of God.

Solov'yov thus sees the historical process as the process of
reuniting the world with God. This is to be achieved by man, but not
by individuals – by mankind in general. He maintains that the
human individual acquires significance only by regarding himself as
the hypostasis of something higher, mankind in general, which
Solov'yov identifies with Sophia. Just as in the cosmological process
the world-soul is the common subject of all creatures, so Sophia is
the universal subject of the historical process.[68]

Sophia is barely mentioned by name in Bely's epistemologically based argument, but there are concepts in his theory that correspond to both principal functions of Sophia in Solov'yov's philosophy. Bely's concept of the supra-individual ego is certainly not thought of, like Rickert's, as posited out of logical necessity, but not existent, but bears a close resemblance to Sophia in Her identity with mankind in general, the subject of the historical process. This resemblance is indeed essential. Theory of knowledge, by revealing that all philosophical and religious systems possess symbolic value, but not the character of exclusive truth, frees man for unlimited creation.[69] It is only the belief that in the act of creation men realize not only their individual ego, but also the common supra-individual ego in which they all participate, that allows a process so deeply rooted in subjectivity to be seen as possessing a universal teleology. This teleology is itself essential if Bely's notion of 'creative activity' as the essence of culture is to have an ultimate justification. Solov'yov's notion of Sophia's ultimate manifestation as the Kingdom of God provides the goal of the process that is culture.

Bely's 'creative activity' is religious because it is the way of overcoming the duality between the ego and the world. In neo-Kantian terms the duality was between the form and the content of knowledge. Translated into the terminology of Solov'yov this same duality is the central metaphysical problem: the split between God and creation. The agent that performs the process of reunification is the Logos. Bely's use of this term has in common with Solov'yov's the view of the Logos as present in the human consciousness, and while he could clearly have derived it from many another source besides Solov'yov, there seems little purpose in his using it at all, unless it is with implicit reference to a complex of meaning such as it acquires in Solov'yov's philosophy. If the word is understood in this sense then the full religious meaning of 'creative activity' in Bely's system becomes clear: 'creative activity' is the manifestation of man's striving towards unity with God.

By the end of the decade Solov'yov's ideas had been overlaid in Bely's thinking by many others, most recently by some aspects of theosophy. In this situation it is not to be imagined that Bely subscribed to Solov'yov's philosophy in any dogmatic sense. Even so undoctrinal an assertion as the statement that man's creative activity is the manifestation of his striving towards unity with God might seem to Bely, by this time, too dogmatic. For the idea of God as understood in Solov'yov's essentially Christian philosophy, or, for that matter, as understood in an exclusive sense in any religious system, is specifically rejected. In 'The Emblematics of Meaning', in which Bely combines neo-Kantian epistemology and theosophy, the idea of God is replaced by the concept of the Symbol (with a capital letter). Of this Symbol it cannot be said either that it exists or that it does not exist, but it can be expressed by means of a symbol (with a small letter), defined as 'an image which manifests the Symbol'.[70] In this terminology God is a symbol with a small letter. Just as the epistemological part of his argument results in positing the concept of the symbol as that to which all philosophical systems can be reduced, so in the theosophical part the Symbol is posited as the common value to which all religious systems ultimately refer. Such a statement as that man is an image of the Logos cannot then be read as revealing any specific doctrinal allegiance, but must be seen as one possible metaphorical expression of a truth that is finally ineffable. It can, indeed, equally truthfully be stated in reverse: the metaphor 'Logos' is an expression of man's creative activity.

The direct impact of Solov'yov's ideas is more clearly evident in some of Bely's earlier, more metaphorical and visionary essays. A good example is the essay 'The Apocalypse in Russian Poetry',[71] in which he argues that the task of all poetry is to express the unity of universal truth, to create the image of the Eternal Feminine (i.e. Sophia), while the task of religion is to embody in life what art has created in images. This idea of the relation between art and religion, the idea of art as 'theurgy', remains essential to Bely's views even when they are later expressed somewhat more staidly. He sees in art an active force for the complete transformation of reality, inasmuch as it prepares men for the transition to a new form of community. Art as it exists in the present world is only 'a temporary measure ... a tactical device in humanity's struggle with fate'.[72] The situation of struggling with fate and being defeated Bely calls tragedy, and he holds this situation to be 'the condition [*usloviye*] of aesthetic creation'.[73] He compares art to a bomb, and the evolution of art forms to the path of a bomb from the hand that throws it to the wall of the prison it is to destroy. The ensuing explosion will destroy both the prison – the world seen in the category of necessity – and the bomb – art.[74] Thus art will only achieve its true aim when it ceases to exist.

The idea that artistic creation is a step towards religious creation is one that Bely shared with many of the other Symbolists. There was, however, both disagreement and unclarity about the nature of the relationship between them and the manner of the transition. In Vyacheslav Ivanov's theory the necessary linking ideas are: that the symbol gives rise to the myth, as the expression of a collective mystical intuition, and that a transition is imaginable from present-day theatre to a kind of rite (*deystvo*) or mystery-play (*misteriya*) in which the audience would participate as the chorus of ancient Greek drama. The original religious nature of dramatic action would be revived, and this new theatre would be the focus for the expression of the myth-oriented, collective self-awareness of a new religious community.[75]

Bely has no disagreement with Ivanov over the assertion that myth has its origin in symbol,[76] or that the new religious community they both envisage will express itself through myth. Apart from the general objection that the Petersburg Symbolists were spreading imprecise and insufficiently substantiated ideas, his public wrangle with Ivanov was centred upon two main items of disagreement. One of these is fundamental and will be discussed in the closing section of this chapter. The other is Bely's rejection of the idea that the theatre could become a focus of all art forms, or that the experimental theatre of Meyerkhol'd and Komissarzhevskaya could be seen as a first step towards the creation of mystery-play.[77] When the dust began to settle, however, it became clear that Ivanov's opinion on the latter point was not far removed from Bely's. He did not see in the modern theatre that 'dawn of the new myth-making' that Bely had attributed to him, and did not consider that a change in the form of drama could bring about the change in the hearts of men that was needed.[78] There remains nonetheless a basic difference in their views here, for while Ivanov sees the theatre, or a development of it, as the arena for the expression of myth, Bely looks for this to the nature of language itself.

These are alternative attitudes to the communicative function of art. Bely's theory of Symbolism regards artistic form as essentially dynamic in nature, and rests upon the assumption that the good reader is guided by the form of the work back to the artist's original creative process, which he then re-enacts. This is crucial for the theurgic conception of art, for religious creation is necessarily collective and must presuppose that art is effectively communicative. But his awareness that art forms are nonetheless part and parcel of the given world leads him to demand of the artist that he should ultimately give up art and 'become his own form';[79] instead of creating works of art, that is to say, he must actively create his new self. This idea underlies his brochure *The Tragedy of Creation* (1911),[80] in which he speaks of Tolstoy's departure from Yasnaya Polyana as the rejection of art as a form of the given world in favour of a spiritual act that transcends it. The theme of the rejection of art plays quite an important part in Bely's work,[81] but it is difficult to reconcile this idea of the artist's self-transformation with the belief that the communicative, mythopoeic function of art has yet to be fulfilled.

The idea that men who overcame their present dualism would then be able to create a new kind of human community is present in Bely's thinking in one form or another throughout the decade, indeed throughout his life. It is an idea that can be traced back both to Nietzsche's conception in *The Birth of Tragedy* of a new myth-oriented culture, and also to Vl. Solov'yov's notion of 'integrated life' (*tsel'naya zhizn'*). In the early years of the century it is closely associated with the ideas of imminent apocalypse that Bely also shared with Solov'yov. In 'The Apocalypse in Russian Poetry' the idea of the religious function of art is combined with an apocalyptic vision expressed in images drawn from the Russo-Japanese war. After the failure of the 1905 revolution, however, the swift expectation of the end of history gave way to a somewhat more patient eschatology, though the ideas of apocalypse – or 'explosion' – and the new community continued to be associated with each other.

No idea of Bely's is surrounded by quite as much confusion as that of the new community, because it was the one most directly affected by the fluctuations of his relations with others. It was an idea he took in a literal and existential fashion, and he was incapable in this issue of separating his theory from his experience. It was an idea also of great importance to Merezhkovsky and to Ivanov, and it was Bely's relations with them that largely coloured his expressed views. Bely's fundamental notion is close to Ivanov's: that individuals who develop individually to the point of awareness that they partake in a common subject, Sophia, can unite through that awareness in a community that demands no sacrifice of individual freedom, and in which the link between the members is not mechanical, but organic. The route to this religious community is by way of myth, which is seen as a collective form of symbolic creation. After Bely's return from Paris in the spring of 1907, however, he quarrelled with Ivanov in the course of his attack upon the Petersburg Symbolists. His violent rejection of what he regarded as imprecise thinking and dangerously undisciplined mysticism in Ivanov led him to use Ivanov's term '*sobornoye tvorchestvo*' ('oecumenical creation') as a term of abuse. This inevitably obscured the essential similarity between Ivanov's notion of '*sobornost*'' (oecumenicity) and the idea of '*obshchina*' (community), as Bely preferred to express it.

Until the end of 1908 Bely was close to Merezhkovsky and Gippius, and in some of his essays adopted Merezhkovsky's view that the Symbolists and the socialists were engaged in fundamentally the same struggle. In the essay 'Social Democracy and Religion', based on a lecture delivered in Paris and dedicated to Merezhkovsky, he argued that while the social democrats founded their plans for constructing an ideal state upon economic statistics, their impulse for wishing to transform existing society was essentially ethical, and therefore religious. The successful creation of a socialist state would release men's energies from the petty concerns that largely absorb them now, and lead to the formation of free communities. The socialist state would then have to choose between the alternatives of imitating its forbears and repressing these new growths, or allowing itself to be carried along by the new movement and ceasing to exist.[82]

The basic distinction between the form of social organization known as the state and the new community envisaged is the distinction between a mechanical and an organic system of relationships. It owes much to the distinction between State and Church that is made in *The Brothers Karamazov*, and in referring to it Bely sometimes uses Zosima's words, '*Budi, budi*'. The idea that the two types of system can move towards the same end (which is contrary to Dostoyevsky's conception) is supported less by argument than by quasi-prophetic utterances. It is, however, consistent with Bely's own rejection of Marxist theory, for what he is asserting is that the real motives of the Marxists are not what they believe them to be, and that their actions and aims are therefore not invalidated by their false theory. During the years

1905–8 Bely was hostile towards Dostoyevsky's ideal of humility and his rejection of revolution, regarding them as negative attitudes that would prevent the realization of the new religious community.[83] Around the end of 1908, however, Bely's views changed considerably, and he gave up his support of the social democrats and of Merezhkovsky. Soon he was speaking of Dostoyevsky in quite other terms, seeing him as a religious prophet.[84] His disaffection with social democracy is evident in his support of *Vekhi*.[85] After 1908 the topic of the new community ceases to be a major theme in Bely's theoretical writing, but it is clear both that he came to a view of political revolution almost indistinguishable from the one he had criticized in Dostoyevsky and Berdyayev,[86] and that the idea of 'obshchina', shorn of its political aspect, remained an integral part of his thought.

A fundamental place in Bely's thinking is occupied by his theory of language. Language it is that makes possible the original act of creation with which all human culture begins. In the first place it is man's weapon for subjugating nature, for rendering harmless the hostile surrounding world by imbuing it with meaning. Man's original act in relation to the external world is the act of naming; by naming a thing, man asserts its existence; without this act neither the world nor the ego would exist. Cognition follows upon it: 'The process of cognizing is the establishment of relations between words, which are subsequently transferred to the objects corresponding to the words.'[87] The word itself is a symbol; man fuses in it the two incomprehensible elements of space, the objective world, and time, the subjective experience. The Greek 'logos' is no less important to Bely in its original meaning than in its theological sense.

The act of naming, being the creation of individual words, is prior to grammar and the logical relations it expresses. Bely puts forward a chronological sequence in which cultural activities follow from the original act: 'The word gave birth to the figural symbol – the metaphor; the metaphor appeared as something actually existent; the word gave birth to the myth; the myth gave birth to religion, religion to philosophy, philosophy to the [abstract] term.'[88] At the end of this process stands the concept; communication by means of concepts refers men to what has already been created, whereas the purpose of a living community is to create the objects of cognition. Truly abstract terms, by which

Bely means the language of epistemology which is (or strives to be) entirely devoid of psychic content, he compares to crystals, which carry no infection. His venom is reserved for the word of common usage ('*khodyacheye slovo*'), under which he includes the language of all sciences but epistemology and mathematics, which is half term and half image, which is not living but pretends to be, and makes a mockery of man's creative striving.

At the end of the process of the word's development men are left with a language consisting entirely of terminology, which, they realize, is not capable of expressing all they have to express. It is at this stage that Tyutchev's famous dictum, 'a thought once spoken is a lie', is true. It is not, however, true of the living word: 'But the living, spoken word is not a lie. It is the expression of the inner-most essence of my nature; and since my nature is nature in general, the word is the expression of the innermost secrets of nature.'[89] At the end-stage there arises a new cult of the word. It is a mistake, Bely asserts, to regard the cult of the word as a cause of decadence, or as itself a decadent phenomenon. It is, on the contrary, a reaction against decadence and the harbinger of a new cultural renaissance. It is clear that at the end of the word's development, as Bely sees it, man finds himself in a situation very similar to that at the beginning; he is surrounded by a hostile and meaningless world, which he has to set about taming.

In the second half of 'The Magic of Words' Bely attempts to show how figures of speech, which are the 'organic principle' of language and contain 'the whole process of creative symbolization',[90] develop and function, and thereby to demonstrate the fundamentally mythic nature of language. The basis of his argument, which in large part is derived from Potebnya, is that the difference between epithet, simile, synecdoche, metonymy and metaphor is a difference of degree, not of kind. By taking as examples two objects – the crescent moon and the horn of an animal – and two epithets that may be applied to either – 'white' and 'sharp' – and combining them in a number of different ways, he displays all the gradations from simple adjective by way of compound adjective to metaphor. The result of this process is the creation of a mythic animal; the moon becomes the external image of a heavenly bull or goat, which is itself hidden from men's eyes.[91] The creative act accords to this an ontological being, independent of man; the process by which it was created is reversed, and the end-product comes to be regarded as the cause. This is how the transition is made from poetic to mythic creation.

The process Bely outlines here, whereby something that is a product of human thought comes to be regarded as an independently existent cause of objective phenomena, is a process he also observes elsewhere. Discussing in 'The Emblematics of Meaning' systems of objective idealism, he argues that the naive mind transfers to the objective world the requirement of human thought that cognitive principles be purposively related to each other:

thus the norm of cognition becomes the object; and there arises the doctrine of ideas, as objective essences independent of the principle of our perception of reality; one more step, and the naive consciousness endows these essences with individual qualities of our nature; or else these essences become the bearers of physical forces; and so a world of gods is formed.[92]

Once the provenance of any such system is made conscious it cannot, of course, be accorded the character of objective truth, and this is essential to Bely's argument. Similarly, with mythology, he rejects any suggestion of objective truth:

When I say 'the moon is a white horn', I do not, of course, with my consciousness assert the existence of a mythic animal, whose horns I see in the sky in the shape of the moon; . . .

Nevertheless in this instance he leaves the door open to a kind of subjective truth. The quotation continues:

but in the deepest essence of my creative self-assertion I cannot help believing in the existence of some reality, the symbol or representation of which is the metaphorical image I have created.[93]

'The deepest essence of my creative self-assertion' is not a particularly felicitous piece of terminology, but in the general context of Bely's theory it is not too difficult to see what he means. He is referring to that area of the human mind (which he had not ventured to name by anything more precise than 'feeling' or 'experience') where the original act of creation takes place, preceding cognition. It is with that area of the mind that man may be said to believe in his myths; subsequent translations of them into forms appealing to the consciousness are distortions. And it is communication at that level that is the prerequisite for the new community. In this way art, by exploiting the natural mythic propensities of language, may actively prepare the way to the new community.

In his article on Potebnya's *Thought and Language* Bely introduces Potebnya's notion of the word's 'inner form', by which is meant the evocation through the word's sound (phonetic form) not only of the image of an object, but simultaneously of a presentation associated with the object. An example is:

a window, as a frame with glass panes, arouses the presentation of an act: the window as a place towards which one looks.[94]

The inner form is fluid and varies between persons and occasions. There are cases in which it stems directly from the word's phonetic form: where there are several words derived from a single root, each word of preceding derivation may be called the inner form of the subsequent one. It is the inner form of words which gives language its essentially symbolic nature, which the scientific use of language seeks to eradicate. This notion of 'inner form' provides a more persuasive argument for the inherent symbolism (in Bely's sense) of language at an advanced stage of development than is given in 'The Magic of Words'. Every word possesses, at least potentially, an unlimited number of transferred meanings. This indicates the way in which a modern poet might approach the task of rejuvenating the language's metaphorical – and mythic – capacities. Indeed it summarizes some of the essential devices that Bely himself uses in his novels from *Kotik Letayev* onwards.

The specific nature of Bely's theory of Symbolism can perhaps best be appreciated by a brief comparison with the ideas of Vyacheslav Ivanov, his main rival as theoretician of the movement. The issue on which their understanding differs most importantly can be summarized by juxtaposing Bely's statement that the word is already a symbol with Ivanov's statement that reality itself is a symbol.[95] In Ivanov's view the artist's task is to reveal the hidden, but real essence of things; in Bely's the artist, in common with other creative humans, creates an order that is not present in raw nature. This is what Ivanov called 'idealistic symbolism' (in contrast to his own 'realistic symbolism'),[96] and it was in vain that Bely sought to defend himself against the appellation,[97] just as it was in vain that Ivanov protested it was not meant for him.[98]

Yet Bely insisted that his symbols were no less real than anybody else's. His basis for doing so lies in his belief that the essentially subjective process of endowing the objective world with meaning is performed not by the empirical subject, but by the Logos acting through him. On the other hand he then undermines this tenet by speaking of the relationship of Logos to world-soul as a symbol, to which Ivanov replies that it is not a symbol, but a real event.[99]

Speaking a little later of Bely as a poet, Ivanov makes a remark that could equally well be made of his theory, when he writes that Bely 'wishes for realism but cannot overcome idealism'.[100] He was not alone in noticing that all Bely's protestations of realism do not at any point reveal a belief in an objectively existent God. Berdyayev wrote: 'A. Bely deifies only his own creative act. There is no God, as Being [*Sushchiy*], but the creative act is divine, God is created, he is a value in the process of creation, what is to be, not what is.'[101] He went on to speak of Bely's tragic illusion that one could arrive at the Absolute without setting out from the Absolute. Stepun has also observed that there is no evidence in Bely's work of an awareness of any transcendent reality.[102]

This judgement is surely correct. Whether constructed in the terms of a Nietzschean rejection of objective truth, or in those of an 'omnivorous'[103] theosophical acceptance of all possible forms of truth,[104] Bely's arguments do not reveal a metaphysical dualism such as is traditionally attributed to the Symbolists in general. Despite the importance that the person of Christ had for him, and the value he attached to the mystical traditions of the Eastern church,[105] his was not a traditionally religious temperament. The separation of the immanent and the transcendent, and the clear distinction between knowledge and faith, were contrary to his view of the world. The religious impulse coexisted in him with a rigorous rationalism. They are never quite resolved in his theory of Symbolism, with its ambiguities about the status of the human creative act.

One area in which Bely's theoretical work is known to have been influential is that of the analysis of verse rhythm, in which his pioneering essays provided one of the stimuli for the Formalist movement. By and large, the Formalists adopted and developed his methods without feeling any need to adopt anything of the premises on which they were based. Bely held that the analysis of a poem's rhythm could reveal the form of the creative act, the poet's 'creative agitation' (*tvorcheskoye volneniye*). Although in his own essays he did not proceed from the analysis to any attempt at description of creative processes, he maintained that to draw such connections must be the task of a future science of aesthetics:

at the basis of future aesthetics must be laid the laws of creative processes, connected with the laws of the embodiment of these processes in form, i.e. with the laws of literary technique.[106]

Underlying this somewhat utopian demand is the assumption, more commonplace now than when Bely was writing, that the analysis of the structure of cultural products may ultimately reveal the laws by which man creates his symbolic world. Yet Bely would have been aghast at the idea that all his analyses reveal might be the structure of the human brain. Such an inference, in keeping with the Kantianism that he constantly sought to overcome, would seem to him to solve the problem of the immanent and the transcendent by denying the latter altogether. He fought to avoid the conclusion, which Ivanov and others were ready to draw from his theory, that the human symbolic world had no absolute objective validity. While much important twentieth-century thought has started from the acceptance of this conclusion, Bely retreated from it and took sanctuary in the doctrines of Rudolf Steiner and the belief that the inner and outer worlds are identical.

2

Bely and anthroposophy

It is not hard to understand the appeal of anthroposophy to those who had responded to Vl. Solov'yov's idea of creating an integrated culture.[1] It is a uniquely comprehensive doctrine that proposes to reconcile the spiritual and the material, to answer all questions and resolve all contradictions. Without rejecting scientific thought it overcomes materialism and re-asserts, on a rational footing, the spiritual nature of man and the universe. An added appeal to educated Russians must have been the fact that Rudolf Steiner had a high opinion of Solov'yov and extensive familiarity with Russian religious thought, as well as with the whole tradition of Western philosophy.[2]

Bely's introduction to this doctrine did not entail the rejection of anything he had previously believed; he never ceased to regard himself as a Symbolist. Of the other major Symbolists only Maks Voloshin took much sympathetic interest in anthroposophy; Vyacheslav Ivanov had a passing flirtation with it, while Blok, with his abhorrence of abstraction and generalization, remained totally unmoved by it. But many other Russians of Bely's generation, including a number of his personal friends and former 'Argonauts', became followers of Rudolf Steiner.

Bely had first read H.P. Blavatskaya's *From the Caves and Jungles of Hindustan* in 1896 and acquired an interest in ancient oriental philosophy that preceded and led to his later preoccupation with Schopenhauer.[3] His first detailed acquaintance with the doctrines of modern theosophy came in 1901, but he conceived no great liking for it at that time, and avoided theosophical circles until 1908. It was towards the end of that year that he began to take a serious interest in it, and this is reflected in some of his essays, particularly 'The Emblematics of Meaning'.[4] The commentary to the *Symbolism* essays is especially full of references to occult traditions. In 1909 he published an essay, 'The Seven Planetary Spirits', which is unambiguously theosophical in content.[5]

However, his attitude to theosophy was by no means uncritical. He wrote of Blavatskaya's works as an example of confusion and fantasy mixed with genuine talent and perceptiveness.[6] In a fuller comment he expressed the view that theosophy as it then existed bore little relation to what he imagined it ought to be: since it completely disregarded problems of methodology its conclusions were quite bereft of epistemological value.[7] Bely evidently read some of the works of Steiner, whom, like most people, he did not at that time distinguish clearly from other theosophists, as early as 1909. His published references, however, show no special enthusiasm for his work.[8] His eventual meeting with Steiner in the spring of 1912 was only in part brought about by sympathy for Steiner's writings: it was immediately occasioned by a recurrence of the occult experiences that he had been undergoing for some time, and which he hoped Steiner might be able to explain.[9]

There is nothing fortuitous in the fact that it took a personal meeting with Steiner to turn Bely from an interested, but critical, reader into a prospective disciple. The spread of anthroposophy cannot be explained without reference to its founder's personality. Many people who met Steiner had the impression that he understood them better than they understood themselves.[10] He had a gift for instilling trust in others that is attested by memoirs of him and is evident in the way his followers speak of him. Berdyayev, a more critical observer, put the matter differently, speaking of Steiner as a man who 'convinced and hypnotized not only others, but himself as well'.[11] Whatever the nature of the influence, there is no doubt that Bely fell swiftly and lastingly under the spell of Rudolf Steiner's personality.

Steiner objected to the intellectual sloppiness of the official theosophists no less strongly than Bely. He was concerned to establish the tenets of the theosophical tradition on the basis of the methods, or an extension of the methods, of scientific investigation. He was not willing to accept them, or anything else, as revealed truth, but sought to apply to them the same criteria of verification that are applied in scientific experimentation. His conviction that nothing need or should be excluded from the realm of thought, and the opposition to Kant that is entailed in that, must have appealed to Bely after his long struggle with Kant and neo-Kantianism.

Anthroposophy does not regard itself as a system of dogma. The cosmology that Steiner puts forward, in all essentials identical with that of other theosophists, is an immensely complex doctrine about spirals of cosmic evolution through seven planets, seven races on each planet, seven sub-races of each root-race, and about the gradual development of individual egos through these stages by way of innumerable incarnations governed by the law of karma. There are spiritual forces governing these processes at their various stages, and almost infinite interrelations between the system's various parts. It is summarized in Steiner's *Occult Science: an Outline*.[12] To the sceptical it may appear as a doctrine of infinite tedium. To those of a more traditionally religious cast of mind it appears as fundamentally un-Christian in its disregard of the idea of grace and its lack of transcendence. Though complex, it is a perfectly clear and unmysterious system, and can presumably be memorized by anyone with the necessary patience and strength of memory. But to memorize the system is not to understand anthroposophy. Steiner held that his system was neither speculative philosophy nor a matter of faith, but an object of knowledge. Knowledge of its truth was given to him through direct perception – not, of course, sensory in nature – of the spiritual world. He also held that it was possible for anyone, with practice, to develop the faculty of spiritual perception that was given to him, and thus to experience directly, with no less certainty than is given by the senses, the truth of what his system expounded. His teaching explains how to attain the various degrees of heightened perception, or stages of initiation, as well as describing what is revealed at each stage. To understand anthroposophy is not to know with the rational mind what the teacher has said, but to attain the faculty of perceiving its truth. Steiner frequently argues in his books in terms of normal and deficient perception, where, for example, the world as seen by modern science is as seen by the colour-blind.

Bely was undoubtedly one of Steiner's most gifted pupils. Even if his philosophical training left doubts in the mind of Berdyayev,[13] it was considerably superior to that of most anthroposophists. His perception of the physical world as transparent,[14] and his accessibility to occult experience, equally marked him out as a promising acolyte. It is evident that the organization consisted of a small number of people with great intellectual and occult talents, and a much larger number of followers who were able to do little more than memorize their lessons. Bely complains of this in his memoirs of Steiner.[15] For those the doctrine tends to become precisely the matter of faith that it is supposed not to be: they are sustained by their faith that knowledge is available, although they have not attained it, in much the same way as Pisarev believed that natural science would in due course explain everything that was at present mysterious. But Bely went well beyond this schoolroom approach. In the years following his introduction to anthroposophy he underwent an intense and at times painful process both of study in the conventional sense, and also of occult meditation. His 'intimate biography' records his progress in these matters.[16] There is no reason to doubt the psychological reality of the mystical insights he experienced. Difficulties arise, however, from the translation of such experiences into literature. The objection is often raised against the works of Steiner himself that they are rationalistic and boring; to which the retort is that it is only the verbal surface that creates that impression, while the actual experience to which it leads is dynamic and vivid, and involves the entire personality. Esoteric literature requires to be read in a frame of mind that precludes a normal critical response. The critic faces a quandary, since to disregard that requirement is clearly in some sense to misread, while to observe it is to forego criticism. The critic who is not an anthroposophist has to tread a delicate course between these two positions. This problem is inevitably relevant also to Bely's works in anthroposophical vein, though in the end there are probably no more than a couple of works of his where the problem becomes really acute.[17]

Steiner's cosmological system is preceded, both logically and chronologically, by works of an orthodox philosophical nature. The philosophical premises which justify the method of supersensory perception, or spiritual science, are expounded in works from the 1890s, of which probably the most important are *The Philosophy of Freedom* and *Goethe's World Outlook*.[18] In *The Philosophy of Freedom* Steiner argues that it is possible to overcome the division into spirit and matter, or ego and world, upon which all dualistic systems depend, by examining the nature of thinking itself. He accepts that in thinking about the world man inevitably adds something, by way of conceptualization, to the pure matter of observation, and that knowledge in this sense is therefore not a pure reflection of reality. But he considers that an area of certainty can be attained by thinking not about any particular content of consciousness, but about thinking itself. Even though one cannot observe one's thinking at the same time as performing it, but can only think about observations already made of previous thinking processes, the essential fact remains that here alone the subject and the object of the thought are qualitatively the same. The condition of thinking about thinking is an exceptional one, since in the normal process of thought the thinker's attention is directed to the object, not the process; it is a condition which becomes, under the name of meditation, the essential first stage of spiritual science.

We cannot know anything about thought without first thinking. This is a case where the assertion of the primacy of creation over cognition can correctly be made. It is only in the case of thought about thought that man reflects upon something that he has himself created. Nevertheless Steiner argues that thinking is not subjective. There must be thought before there can be concepts. 'Subject' and 'object', being concepts, are the product of thought, and it is therefore false to say that the individual subject thinks. Since thinking is beyond subject and object, is neither subjective nor objective, the application by the thinking subject of a concept to the object is a process performed not by the subject, but by thinking itself. Steiner thus reaches a position where thought acquires an independent existence and man, in the act of thinking, participates in a universal process.

It is an accident of the human organism that perception and thought are separate processes. But it is a mere prejudice to regard the world as immediately perceived as being complete in itself, and thought processes as therefore exterior to it. On the contrary, nature brings forth thought in the human mind with just the same necessity as it produces the flower of a plant. The complete plant is not the plant as seen in one particular moment, as men necessarily perceive it, but the plant living through its entire growth-cycle. Men know this cycle not by mere perception, but by thought. The whole reality is given only by the combination of the two. For this whole dynamic reality Steiner uses, somewhat confusingly, the term 'concept' (*Begriff*). It would be perfectly possible, he argues, for a spirit to receive percept and concept simultaneously. In our present condition it is the process of thought that restores to man the unity with the cosmos that is disrupted by the separation of percept and concept.

The ability to combine these two simultaneously is the feature Steiner emphasizes in Goethe. Schiller objected that the *Urpflanze* was an idea and could not be perceived, but Goethe remained convinced that he actually saw it. In this sense his attitude was consistent with the true meaning of Platonism, which has been misunderstood in the mainstream of Western thought. The misunderstanding has led to that division of object and idea that Steiner seeks to overcome. By 'idea' he means the same as by 'concept'. When he speaks of the 'ideal' world the word is therefore not to be understood as an antonym to 'real' (as it is in the 'mistaken' Platonic tradition). The ideal is not perceptible in the same sensory way as the physically real, but it is available to super-sensory perception, and is no less objectively existent. Steiner's philosophy can therefore be called 'concrete idealism'.[19]

This is not the place (nor is this author qualified) to offer a philosophical criticism of Steiner's argument. There would in any case be little point in demonstrating flaws in it as philosophy, because it is in one sense artificial to separate it from the esoteric parts of his doctrine. There can be little doubt that Bely, like others of his followers, was first drawn to Steiner by other things than his philosophical writings, and there is no historical sense in taking them separately as though his followers required first to be convinced of them before proceeding to the rest. On the contrary, the predisposition to accept them was most probably present before they were read. In Bely's case it is not possible to establish in what order his study of Steiner was pursued, nor is there any great need to do so. There is ample textual evidence in *On the Meaning of Cognition*[20] to show that he was, by the time of its writing in 1916, abundantly familiar with Steiner's epistemology. What is important here is to show the way in which the adoption of Steiner's views influenced Bely's own philosophical outlook.

The fundamental premise of the crisis of European culture retains both its central position in Bely's thinking and very much the same definition. It is generally indicated by other pairs of terms, such as: myth and thought, or faith and knowledge. Using this latter pair Bely expresses the problem with an aphoristic neatness: 'knowledge without faith is abstract; and faith without knowledge is a fairy-tale'.[21] Most frequently Bely employs the terms East and West. These were scarcely used in the theoretical works of the earlier period, but had appeared in much the same meaning as early as the *Second Symphony* (1902),[22] and had supplied the title for the projected trilogy of novels, of which *The Silver Dove* was to be the first.[23] His preference for these terms is directly associated with the way in which he now approaches the crisis. The theosophical doctrine of evolution through successive spirals is accompanied by a theory of recapitulation: at each stage the organism must first recapitulate at its new level the sum of all previous evolution, before it can advance to the fulfilment of its present destiny. The whole of the past is therefore constantly present.[24] This principle operates at all levels: it has been observed, for instance, in the mind of the child in *Kotik Letayev*.[25] In his theoretical works Bely is concerned with its operation in cultural periods. The culture of the present contains all the cultures of the past. Bely's concern with cultural history in this sense provides a major element of his writing in the later period, from his notes on his visit to Sicily, Tunis and Egypt in 1910–11, to his unpublished *History of the Development of the Spiritual Soul*.[26] The notions of East and West are thought of not in a geographical sense, but as shorthand designations of ideal attitudes whose interaction can be seen to give specific definition to particular cultural periods. Nevertheless they correspond, of course, to attitudes conventionally associated with Oriental and Occidental culture. This understanding makes possible for Bely the assertion that the ancient Persian prophet Zoroaster is Western in his 'humane clarity and assertion of the personality', while Kant is 'the founder of China'.[27] The task of culture is the re-unification of these two principles – which may also be expressed as the re-unification of pre-Socratic and post-Platonic philosophy.[28] This is the task that Bely sees for anthroposophy.

Steiner's conception of the non-subjective character of thought provides the solution to the problem of the status of the human creative act, that beset Bely's theory of Symbolism. Bely speaks of the realization that: 'it is not I who think the thoughts: they think me...'[29] and that 'thought and nature are the same'.[30] But the realization of this truth entails a radically new way of thinking. Most people, in studying philosophy, do nothing but memorize the conclusions of other philosophers and the manner in which they establish transitions from concept to concept. But these transitions and conclusions are merely the foam on the surface of thought, which is itself subliminal, dynamic.[31] True participation in the thought of another requires immersion in this original process. It is not difficult to see how this idea relates to the notion of 'rhythm' in Bely's earlier writings, and indeed that term retains its central importance in the later work too.[32] Its affinity to the Nietzschean concept of the Dionysian is made abundantly clear in such an assertion as 'Reason is Dionysus.'[33] This Dionysian current, then, which is the essence of both nature and thought, has to be brought to consciousness without being rendered static and lifeless. Such is the desired fusion of 'Western' conscious thought with 'Eastern' inchoate experience.

All forms of abstraction must be dispensed with. The world as given is anterior to all formation of concepts, and therefore none of the concepts we customarily use are truly applicable to it: 'the world proper is non-material, forceless, non-numerical, causeless, fortuitous, non-existent, non-possible, non-true, non-real etc...'[34]. Bely acknowledges that man is not at present capable of imagining such a world, but insists 'only this world is given'.[35] Abstract convictions about the nature of reality are not rejected out of hand; Steiner's system accords relative validity not only to the conclusions of individual sciences within their own methods, but also to all actual and possible outlooks upon the world. He enumerated twelve possible types of *Weltanschauung*, seven possible 'moods' and three possible 'tones'. Complete meaning emerges only from the combination of them all. Bely arrives at the figure of 63,504 as the number of 'nuances of a single abstract thesis', and thus reaches the conclusion that any abstract assertion in the terms of only one such 'nuance' represents 1/63,504 of real dynamic meaning.[36] It is possible that this meticulous arithmetic is intended as an elaborate joke; but humour, it has to be admitted, is not a strong point of anthroposophy.

The process of true cognition, which is to restore the unity of nature and thought, consists of three stages: imagination, inspiration and intuition. Imagination is the state in which one becomes aware of spiritual realities, inspiration that in which one perceives the relations between them, and intuition that in which one becomes united with them. The progress through these stages, which is a task for the future, upon which even the greatest minds have yet properly to embark, is the path of initiation. Initiation is a process that leads both inwards and outwards simultaneously. The candidate reveals deeper and deeper levels of spirituality within himself, at the same time perceiving their correspondence with the real spiritual forces that govern the universe. He thus comes to know by his own experience the truth of the occult history of the universe that is described in the earlier chapters of Steiner's *Occult Science: an Outline*. These three stages of initiation are described in the later parts of Bely's *On the Meaning of Cognition*. In keeping with the doctrine of spiral recurrence he also offers two cosmic parallels of the process. On the one hand these three stages – described as the stages of 'immediate given-ness', the division into world and thought, and the re-unification of world and thought in reality proper – are said to reflect the three stages of the creation of the universe – which Bely describes in terms which could well be an expression of Vladimir Solov'yov's cosmology: '(1) the creation in God of man and the world, (2) the separation of man and the world from the divine bosom, (3) the uniting of man and the world in human activity that transforms the world and returns man to the Deity'. On the other hand they are a re-enactment of the birth, crucifixion and resurrection of Christ.[37]

The figure of Christ occupies a central place in Steiner's cosmology. This is true in a geometrical sense in that the earth is the fourth of the seven planetary stages of evolution, while Christ appears at the turning-point of the fourth of earth's seven phases. More important, though, certainly for Bely, is the role attributed to Christ in the initiation process. The essential recognition of the divine, the higher Ego, within the individual ego, is also spoken of as the meeting with Christ, or as the birth of Christ within the individual.[38] The path of initiation in all mystical traditions has involved a symbolic 'death' of the old man in preparation for the 'resurrection' of the new. Steiner, indeed, while accepting the crucifixion as historical fact, regards the Gospels as less a historical record than a traditional account of the typical life of an initiate.[39] This path through crucifixion to resurrection is also the path of the initiate into anthroposophy. At the same time, given the centrality of Christ to all evolution, and the identity of the inner and the outer, it is clear that the cosmic parallel of the redemption of all creation is equally apposite to either of the others. In Bely's theoretical works these parallels sometimes appear as little more than non-obligatory metaphorical illustrations of the argument; but there is no doubt that they are meant with complete literalness. The earlier Symbolist idea of the transformation of the self, that owed more to Nietzsche than to the theosophical tradition,[40] finds its ultimate formulation here. If there is one theme that unites the whole of Bely's work, this is it.

Anthroposophy retains the theosophical teaching of the evolutionary succession of different human races, each of which has its appropriate and appointed task. In his use of this idea, Bely insists upon the original character of anthroposophy as a theory of universal culture. He employs here the concept of the 'individuum', meaning an indivisible complex of many parts, and argues that human culture cannot be understood unless humanity as a whole is taken as one such 'individuum', as it is in anthroposophy. Without that understanding he considers that the concept of race degenerates into a purely biological notion.[41] This conception of the succession of racially defined cultures opens the door to the idea of detrimental influences emanating from creatures or spirits that have failed to attain their appropriate level of evolution. Within the general evolutionary optimism of Steiner's system, this is the principal source of evil. Such forces may, like any other spiritual force, be found in the culture of the present. In some of his articles Bely associates certain contemporary cultural developments with 'barbarism' in this sense.[42] In the *Moscow* novels this idea provides the source of one of the principal strands of imagery.

Bely's attitude to the revolutions of 1917 is coloured both by the ideas of apocalypse that had meant so much to the Symbolists, and by the contrast of Dionysian 'rhythm' and static forms that he had developed through anthroposophy. His initial reaction, however, owes more to the idea of crucifixion in its anthroposophical guise. The sense that Russia as a nation was undergoing a kind of Golgotha, fulfilling a messianic mission, can be found in Bely's poetry immediately after his return from Switzerland in the early autumn of 1916. Here it is based upon the nation's suffering in the world war, which Bely regarded as an unqualified manifestation of barbarism. However, it also underlies his long poem *Christ is Arisen*, which was written in the spring of 1918, and is clearly associated with the revolution. If the war is Russia's crucifixion, then the revolution is her resurrection. Bely's only public pronouncement of a theoretical nature dating from the time of the revolution is his brochure *Revolution and Culture* of 1917.[43] This is based upon a contrast of culture, as an evolutionary process expressed in forms, and revolution, as that which destroys all forms and makes culture temporarily impossible. The evolution of forms is attributed to an inner spiritual force that is never itself embodied in form; and the ultimate aim of that force is revolution. It is the duty of the artist to surrender himself to the current of revolution, which Bely also expresses in terms of anthroposophical initiation. He uses Marxist ideas as explanatory metaphors in his argument that the new relationship that will come to exist between the artist and his forms cannot at present be imagined, just as socialists cannot imagine precisely what will happen after the revolution.

This conception of revolution as an upsurge of the Dionysian force that destroys all static forms led Bely into further altercations with Vyacheslav Ivanov, whose more realistic understanding of political events he attacked in *The Siren of Learned Barbarism*. He accused Ivanov of being too deeply entrenched in an abstract manner of thought to be able to understand the spiritual nature of what was taking place; indeed he reached the extraordinary conclusion that Ivanov failed to understand the revolution because his thinking was essentially Marxist in nature.[44]

Bely's religious enthusiasm for the revolution was short-lived, however; it waned as he began to realize that the bolsheviks actually were in control of it, and would not allow its progress to be determined by any force but their own rationalism. His writings during his stay in Berlin in 1921–3 reveal his reconsidered attitude: 'A consequence of the sociological sophism of the Marxists is the monstrous famine of a land of many millions.'[45] He had envisaged the destruction of the state and all its institutions, which he had described as 'the premature solidifying of music'.[46] Even after his return to Russia he continued at first to express the view that revolution as he envisaged it had still not come about. If regarded in terms of a materialistic understanding of history it becomes merely another stage of evolution, the substitution of one set of forms for another, but: 'Revolution is certainly not the revolution of forms; it is law, as such, exploded – for all time.'[47]

Revolution and Culture is the only work of Bely's after 1912 that takes up the theme of the eschatology of art in terms similar to the theory of Symbolism. It is a re-statement of the idea that at a certain point the artist must give up the creation of art in order to transform his own soul. It is a theme which for a time he took with complete literalness, and which becomes a chapter both in his biography and in his development as a novelist.[48] It is not, however, typical of Bely's approach to theoretical questions in his later period. Far greater attention is devoted to his theory of language.

In his earlier essays on language Bely had based his argument upon the distinction between its abstract and metaphorical uses, distinguishing, that is to say, between two kinds of symbolic referent. In his later studies he concentrates upon the distinction between language as a system of references and language as a physiological process. He adopts from Wilhelm Wundt the idea that language is originally derived from mimic gesture. Imitation in sound is said to be a late form of communication through mimicry. Every word is an organized combination of sounds, where each sound is produced by muscular actions that may be called gestures.[49] In anthroposophical doctrine man responds to the forces at work in the universe with all the organs of his body; these physiological linguistic responses are thought of as the expression of the pre-conscious, Dionysian level of man. Bely's interest in this aspect of language is undoubtedly connected with the development, under Steiner's guidance, of the art of 'eurhythmy', the expression in dance movements of what is believed to be the inner essence of the sounds of language. Bely now finds the genesis of myth not, as earlier, in a progression from epithet to metaphor, but in the original phonetic properties of words: 'The root of a word is a metaphor in itself; and it has no need of figural elucidation; the root of a word is the metaphor of all subsequent metaphors arising from it; and myth is the sum of all myths blossoming from the sum of metaphors.'[50]

The human creation of language is the creation of reality. From an original state in which men perceive no separation between self and world, they develop to one in which that differentiation is made and experienced as terrifying. The sounds that are produced as a result are the beginning of cognition, the beginning of the creation of reality. As in 'The Magic of Words' Bely finds contemporary language in a critical state. The connection between sound and meaning has been lost as a result of the loss of faith in the identity of nature and spirit. Its two poles are seen in the work of epistemologists at one extreme and Futurists at the other, meaning without significant sound, and sound without meaning.

The relationship Bely now envisages between thought and meaning is illustrated in *Glossolalia*, a work that occupies a half-way stage between theory and poetry, and which Bely sub-titled 'a poem about sound'. He writes in the introduction, in a manner by now familiar:

It would be utterly perverse to see in *Glossolalia* a theory, proposing to prove anything to anybody. *Glossolalia* is an improvisation on a number of acoustic themes; I put forward these themes in the way in which they develop in me the fantasies of sound-images; but I know: behind the figurative subjectivity of my improvisations is concealed their non-figurative, non-subjective root.[51]

Glossolalia is an attempt to depict in sounds the cosmology of anthroposophy. It represents the four stages of evolution, of which the planet Earth – the state of solid matter – is the fourth; Bely speaks of them as the four days of creation. The dominant characteristics of the three preceding planetary epochs were: on Saturn an immaterial state of warmth, on Sun a gaseous state and on Moon a fluid state. Humanity has evolved through these conditions, at each new state recapitulating those passed. On Earth man therefore has the task of recapitulating, at a level appropriate to Earth existence, the previous three stages, before advancing further, into areas of increasing spirituality. It is to this recapitulation that the greater part of *Glossolalia* is devoted. It is accompanied in the first place by the identification of certain sounds with the spiritual conditions of which the various planetary states were reflections. Cosmic development is then pursued from stage to stage through the parallel of the development of one sound or combination of sounds from another. From the sounds available at each given stage are derived both mythological names, as illustration of the direct development from sound to myth, and existent words in a variety of languages, to illustrate their subliminal retention of phonetic, or mythological meaning.

At one point Bely describes the significance of sounds in the present stage of the Earth's evolution. Some of the definitions that appear here are of obvious relevance to acoustic patterns in some of the novels. There is not supposed to be anything dogmatic in Bely's identification of sound and meaning: 'When I assert – 'a sound is such-and-such': I am not attaching anything to the assertion, but drawing sketches; and at once I cast them aside and the sounds flow.'[52] Its truth is to be perceived at a different level of consciousness from that where dogma operates. If it persuades, then it is thanks to the form in which it is expressed, and dependent upon its context. It can, though, by that same token, be used again in a similar context, and there is justification for seeking parallels in the novels, while there would not be any sense in looking for them in travel notes or book reviews.

The fullest theoretical exposition of Bely's ideas about language in the light of anthroposophy is contained in the essay 'Aaron's Rod'. Here he discusses the ways in which all levels of language operate in poetry. The deepest level of all is rhythm:

it is the earth-centre of sounds, and this centre is molten; it seethes and bubbles; it pulsates with flame, like the heart, dissolving forms within and hurling out sounds in the thrusts of its modulations; if the thoughts of poetry are its head, if the images are its nerves, the vowels its lungs; if the combination of consonants reminds us of the connective tissue. . . , then the rhythm is the dark blood that heats the organism.[53]

The idea of poetic rhythm as the outward expression of the Dionysian impulse still underlies this conception. Bely goes on to argue that the metrical norms of poetry are developments from, and rigidified forms of, an original rhythm. Their canonization is a process of increasing artificiality, whereby the distance from the rhythmic impulse to the embodied form becomes ever greater. He begins to lay emphasis upon rhythmic prose as the form in which the greatest subtlety of rhythmic variation is possible, and which may thus represent the closest approximation of form to impulse.[54] It is worth noting that in his conception of possible rhythmic forms in literature Bely allows a similar unbroken spectrum to that which he had posited in his earlier classification of art forms in terms of time and space.[55]

Bely's new conception of the metaphorical nature of sound itself has an effect upon his conception of the role of metaphor in the more traditional sense. He speaks of it as:

at once the axis of literary forms and the limit of the daytime consciousness of the surface of the subliminal lands beyond consciousness;. . .everything that stands above metaphor is penetrable in thought; everything that lies below metaphor is the element of night. . .[56]

He then comes to distinguish poets on the basis of their use of metaphor. Tyutchev is a poet whose poetry is founded upon metaphor; while expressing the awareness of the threshold and the chaos beneath, his poetry does not conquer the chaos. Pushkin, on the other hand, is a poet whose poetry is rich in metonymy and meaningful sound. Bely defines metonymy as 'the transference of images, their relational replacement one by another', and argues that cognition itself takes place on a metonymic principle.[57] While Tyutchev's metaphoric poetry leaves chaos chaotic, Pushkin's is able to penetrate the nocturnal side of life with the clear light of wisdom. In other words, Pushkin's poetic forms are more adequate to the original Dionysian impulse.

These ideas had a clear effect upon Bely's own writing. The rhythmic quality of his prose becomes increasingly evident with time. The transition from a basically metaphorical style to one based upon metonymy and phonetic effects can be clearly seen at about the time he wrote 'Aaron's Rod', that is to say, between *Kotik Letayev* and *The Baptized Chinaman*. It will be necessary to return to these questions in the discussion of Bely's later novels.

There is an inherent paradox in all Bely's theoretical writing. It is designed to express a view of the relationship between man and the world and of the nature of human culture, that by its own definition is not expressible in analytical language. This paradox was already clearly visible in 'The Magic of Words', where Bely acknowledged that the myth he derived from descriptions of the moon was not believed with the conscious mind, but nevertheless was somehow believed with 'the deepest essence of his creative self-assertion'. Whatever that term may be taken to mean (it is merely one of many ways of expressing the Dionysian sub-conscious), it clearly does not refer to the level of the mind with which one reads and understands an analytical essay such as 'The Magic of Words'. The replacement of the analytical understanding by the Dionysian understanding cannot be brought about by persuasion on the level of rational conviction. Evidently that is why Bely's arguments so often turn into utterances of a poetic, rather than a philosophical nature. He was well aware of this limitation of philosophical, discourse, and did not seek to be a systematic philosopher. It is perhaps there, as much as anywhere, that the influence of Nietzsche is to be found. It is probably also a principal reason why he spoke disparagingly of Vladimir Solov'-yov's metaphysical system.[58] It was noted in Chapter I that Bely's theoretical essays tend to be highly repetitive. While this is in part attributable to the pressures of publication in the periodical press, it has more to do with Bely's tendency to make of each essay a fresh and complete act of communication with his readers. He assumes no previous acquaintance with his ideas, no shared premises or ready formulations, which would tend to reduce the act of communication to the re-iteration of a fixed dogma. The tension between the language of philosophical discourse and the language in which real insights are conveyed becomes even more acute as his views on language develop. *Glossolalia* occupies an important place here, as a work which fully realizes the tendency of theory towards poetry, but is not definable as either. It exemplifies the breakdown of a genre division between two different kinds of discourse. It also exemplifies the basic problem of esoteric writing in its ostensible imperviousness to criticism. On the one hand Bely is not asserting that certain sounds necessarily and always possess certain meanings, while on the other he is asserting that the attribution of specific meanings to them does possess more than subjective and occasional validity. His claim that it is senseless to criticize his knowingly false etymologies on the basis of philological science is logically supported by the belief that scientific method is not a route to any truth worth knowing. His work can be criticized only from a standpoint that it specifically rejects. The attempt to establish a mode of discourse in which esoteric insights can be conveyed leads to a situation in which all other forms of communication are precluded.

What, in the end, is the relation between the theory and the novels? From the argument above it appears that the theory needs the novels more than the novels need the theory. It ought to be through works of literary art, such as the novels, that the outlook described in the theoretical essays is actually communicated to the reader. If that communication were unproblematical it would take place of itself, simply by virtue of the artistic form, and there would be no need of the theory to prepare it. But the theory exists precisely because it is not unproblematical, because readers are not, in fact, able to derive from the literary text alone all that the theory says it should convey. The theory is designed to prepare the reader, to teach him how to read. Just as Steiner's doctrine is designed to lead his pupils from deficient to 'normal' perception, so Bely's theories of art, particularly in his anthroposophical period, are designed to train readers to read in new ways. And his novels increasingly come to embody principles of construction which need the guidance of his theory if they are to be understood.

To say that is not to set up the theory as a criterion of judgement for the novels. Nor is it to accept the premise that in approaching the novels through the theory the reader will change his perception except in the sense that he may learn to understand a hitherto unfamiliar artistic system. He may understand that system, as he may understand the theory, without undergoing the spiritual transformation of which they both speak. Bely's copious theoretical writings are so obviously available as a tool for interpretation that it seems simply perverse to disregard them. The relation between them and individual novels will be seen to fluctuate. It is by no means a constant simple relationship of programme and execution, although it acquires more of that character towards the end of his career. At all stages of his career it is true to say that similar concerns underlie both his theoretical and his artistic writing, and therefore that the two taken together are in the end more readily comprehensible than either taken in isolation.

PART II

3

The Silver Dove

It was not until the end of the decade of Symbolism that Bely turned to the writing of novels. Up till 1909 he was known as a poet, a theoretician of the Symbolist movement, and the author of four experimental prose works which he entitled 'Symphonies'. It was with his *Second, or Dramatic Symphony* that he made his literary debut in 1902 (his *First, or Heroic Symphony*, though written first, was not published until 1904).

The appearance of the *Second Symphony* almost coincided with the publication of Bely's first theoretical essay, 'The Forms of Art', in which he declared that all art forms were evolving towards music.[1] In a brief and cryptic preface he wrote of the *Symphony*'s possessing three meanings, or aspects: the musical, the satirical, and the philosophical or symbolic.[2] The musical aspect he sees as stemming from the task of expressing a series of moods, which are linked to each other through a basic mood, or key. By 'mood' Bely evidently has in mind something more than a subjective emotional condition, but it is not readily clear precisely what. In the introduction to the *Fourth Symphony*, however, he writes of his attempt 'to delineate as clearly as possible certain experiences which underlie, as it were, everyday life and essentially cannot be embodied in images'.[3] It then becomes easier to see that these experiences are that which he refers to in his theoretical works as 'inner' or 'mystical' experience, which is the true ground of communion between men and eludes embodiment in language understood purely as a referential system. Bely's conception of music is derived both from the Schopenhauerian notion of its ability to give direct expression to absolute reality, without mediation through the world of appearances, and also from the Nietzschean idea of its Dionysian quality, its relation to the unindividuated common core of experience. It is this inter-subjective inner experience that he designates by 'mood'.

The 'satirical' aspect of the *Second Symphony* lies quite unproblematically in its satirical representation of 'certain extremes of mysticism'.[4] Like the other three *Symphonies* it possesses a rudimentary plot, concerned, in this case, with the illusory eschatological aspirations of characters resembling Bely's Moscow acquaintances of the time. There seems to be no reason why the plot element of a *Symphony* must necessarily be satirical; certainly the *First Symphony* has nothing much of satire in it. If one were to extend the description of the three aspects of the *Second Symphony* into a definition adequate for all four, it would be necessary to replace the word 'satirical' with a more general notion such as 'representational'. When Bely then asserts that the third meaning – the symbolic – emerges from the fusion of the other two, this turns out on examination to be a rough and ready formulation of the idea he will develop at much greater length later, that the symbol is the fusion of form and content.

While the 'satirical' or 'representational' aspect involves the depiction of the people and objects of the phenomenal world, the 'musical' aspect reveals a different set of relationships between them than that which pertains on the phenomenal plane. The symbolic meaning derives from the juxtaposition of the phenomenal and the non-phenomenal, of the individual and the unindividuated, or of time and eternity. However, when Bely claims at the end of the preface that symbolism is attained through the fusion of all three aspects in a single passage or verse of the *Symphony*, one must protest that most of the formal, musical properties cannot be perceived in a single short passage, and that the symbolic meaning can really only emerge from the whole work.

Since the traditional forms of continuous narrative prose derive their continuity from the depiction of an objective reality which is itself seen as spatially and temporally continuous, the requirement of depicting a reality whose coherence lies beyond space and time leads to the creation of a prose which is discontinuous. In order that the reader's attention should be drawn to the higher coherence, expressed in the symphonic form, it is necessary to disrupt the customary expectation of coherence on the phenomenal plane. The basic structural principles of the *Symphony* form thus involve dis-integration at one level, and re-integration at another.

The discontinuity of the prose is evident at a glance. The text is divided into short sections of from one line to seven, consisting either of a single sentence or a small number of simple sentences. In the *First* and *Second Symphonies* these sections are numbered, a practice that was dropped in the last two without causing any substantial change. These short sections then form the basic units of longer passages, averaging perhaps a page in length, at the end of which the numbering (where it is used) recommences at 1. The visual impression combines with the lack of complex syntactical relationships to produce an impression of separate entities juxtaposed by chance, rather than a coherent world. Consecutive motifs frequently depict people or things that possess no evident relationship to one another; and the fortuitous nature of the juxtapositions is even clearer at the level of the longer sections where abrupt changes of material become the rule. Viewpoint is also conspicuously volatile, with rapid alternations between 'long shots' and details. The discontinuity of phenomena is supported by the pervasive thematic contrast of time and eternity. The sun and the sky stand in opposition to the kaleidoscope of the streets; awareness of the contrast is part of the inner experience of some of the characters; and the theme appears also in a parodic form, as where a customer's cry, 'The bill' (*schot*), evokes a series of cognate words to do with counting and leads back to the idea of individuation.[5]

The disruption of the normal perception of relationships is enhanced by the eccentric use of conjunctions:

A poet was writing a poem about love, but had difficulties choosing a rhyme, but dropped a blot of ink, but, turning his gaze to the window, took fright at the boredom of the heavens.[6]

The repetition of 'but' to introduce the second and third coordinate clauses, where normally one would expect (in Russian as in English) 'and', destroys any sequential or causal relationship between the clauses, and sets the three clauses introduced by 'but' into an identical relationship to the main clause but no identifiable relationship to each other – as though they were alternative, mutually exclusive readings. In other places Bely will deliberately disrupt an apparently coherent time sequence by breaking off to tell us: 'That was yesterday.... But today...', and a little later, while the reader still remembers that example: 'But that was on the following day... But now...'.[7]

The division of the text into short sections is a device that Bely undoubtedly adopted from Nietzsche's *Also sprach Zarathustra*. Clearly this is a device that not only disrupts automatic perception but also draws the reader's attention to the constant recommencement of the short paragraphs and thus, in the same way as the lines of verse, to the rhythm. Elena Szilard has attempted to show precise similarities of rhythmic structure in *Zarathustra* and Bely's *Symphonies*, and has certainly succeeded in demonstrating that such features as rhythmic parallelisms and cadences can be perceived as playing similar roles in both cases.[8] That is not to say that the *Symphonies*, any more than *Zarathustra*, are written in a prose of sufficiently regular rhythm to be equated with any verse metre. Rhythmic prose in that sense is something to which Bely came later. What matters here is that the sections are for the most part short enough for their rhythmic shape to remain in the memory as the reader passes from one to another; the reader thus becomes aware of a general rhythmic movement in the longer passages, that confers an overall structure to replace the logical structure normally expected of prose.

G. Janecek has argued that the 'symphonic' structure is based not upon the aspects of words most apparently musical, namely sound and rhythm, but upon their semantic, morphological and syntactic properties.[9] What has just been said about rhythm constitutes a certain qualification of that assertion. While it is true that rhythm as a system of constant and readily perceptible recurrences – as in poetry or music – is not in evidence in the *Symphonies*, the fact that the reader's attention is immediately drawn to the rhythm of the prose prepares him to perceive the 'symphonic' repetitions and modifications of those elements that are so used. E. Szilard has also demonstrated that there are significant recurrences of rhythmic units in positions where they acquire something of the function of a refrain, and serve to reinforce the structural unity, and therefore separateness, of the individual sections. She has also shown that assonance has quite an important part to play.[10]

Nevertheless it is true that these features could not in themselves create a 'symphonic' form, which requires the systematic recurrence and modification of larger elements, theme and imagery. In the introduction to the *Fourth Symphony* Bely describes in some detail how the structure operates, and although his instructions have been shown not to reveal all that is claimed for them,[11] the basic principle is not difficult to discern. The parallel with the form of symphonic movements rests on the way in which themes, initially established separately, are then divided, merged, reduplicated, repeated with modifications, reversed – indeed developed in most of the ways familiar from symphonic music. Images appear and re-appear in different contexts, in relation to different themes, so that their connotations constantly shift and expand. This allows for the creation of new and unsuspected relationships; characters may share experiences, indeed may not always be ultimately distinguishable from one another; apparently unrelated phenomena may suddenly be thrown into each other's orbit by the repetition of an image that the reader remembers from an earlier context.

Memory, indeed, is at the heart of the matter. Not only are great demands made of the reader's memory, if he is to perceive the complexities of the form and the relationships it establishes, but the process of straining to recall something on the edge of oblivion is ultimately what the *Symphonies* are about. The phenomena of this world are not separate from the world of eternity, but are its replica, and men have the innate capacity for recognizing this because they can recall the knowledge of it from the spirit's existence before birth. This Platonic idea of anamnesis, which is later to play so prominent a role in *Kotik Letayev*, appears most clearly in the *Third Symphony*, where the parts are so arranged that the hero's experience alternates between the chemistry laboratories of Moscow University and a dream world where he is a child and his acquaintances appear in roles derived largely from *Zarathustra*.[12] Ultimately he escapes through madness and suicide back to the eternal world thus glimpsed. This somewhat mechanical juxtaposition has no exact equivalent in the other *Symphonies*, and involves too concrete a depiction of the world of eternity to be aesthetically convincing; what emerges is a privately mythologized alternative reality that strikes the reader as precious.[13] But the idea that phenomena can remind men of the noumena they have forgotten underlies the whole conception, and is seen in the *Second Symphony* in the way in which images can re-appear in the thematic contexts of both time and eternity. It is the musical form that makes this recollection possible.

The great importance of memory in the appreciation of these works also affects the question of their evaluation. The whole is only as memorable as its parts, and if memory falters the effect is lost. The *Second Symphony* is among Bely's most enjoyable prose works because the wit and the satire of the individual parts make them worth remembering, so that the task of recognizing their ramifications is pleasurable and rewarding. In the *Fourth Symphony*, on the other hand, Bely was so intent upon delineating experiences that are not fundamentally susceptible to embodiment in images that he saturated the work – in any case the longest of the four – with totally metaphorical landscapes, synaesthetic colour adjectives and imagery of shadows and snowstorms. As a result the words do not evoke sensory impressions that the memory can retain and the reader is wearied beyond all hope of reward.[14]

Each *Symphony* is divided into three or four parts; the Russian word for 'part' (*chast'*) is also used to designate the movements of a piece of music, and it is evident that 'movement' is the meaning Bely intended. The change from one movement to another, corresponding to the change of tempo and often of key between the movements of a symphony, is usually marked by a readily perceptible change of location and atmosphere. However, while the movements of a symphony may sometimes repeat some thematic material, for the most part they do not, and the cohesion of the whole is secured by the relatedness of the keys in which the movements are written, with the customary return in the final movement to the key of the first. Bely experimented with different kinds of contrast between the 'movements' of his verbal 'symphonies', but in all cases was constrained to maintain thematic links between them. It is hard to see how else, in a literary work, he could have established its unity. As a result some critics have been inclined to see the several parts of his *Symphonies* as constituting not several movements, but one single movement, in which a single range of thematic material is used in very many different ways.[15] This ambiguity shows the limitation of the experimental form. Bely tells in his memoirs how the *Fourth Symphony* made clear to him once and for all the impossibility of symphonic form in literature; the contrapuntal system and the plot pulled the work in opposite directions, and the form was unable to satisfy the two kinds of demands that its author was making of it.[16]

It is natural, then, that in the desire to find a form that could adequately embody a plot, Bely turned to the novel. It is a general feature of Russian literature between the two revolutions that writers moved away from the lyrical forms that had been typical of the decadents and the early Symbolists towards forms capable of expressing social experience and three-dimensional historical reality. Blok is seen escaping from the confines of lyricism to the historical themes of his third book, and into drama and auto-biographical epic (*The Rose and the Cross, Retribution*). A similar shift has been documented between the first and second editions of Remizov's novel *The Pond*, written in 1902–3 and 1911 respectively.[17] In this general process experimental prose forms gave way to forms that owed more to the earlier tradition of the novel. Nevertheless, in Bely's case the technique he had developed in his *Symphonies* for creating an alternative set of relationships, a second level of meaning, through recurrent imagery, was taken over directly into his novels. The experience of writing the *Symphonies* imparted to Bely's novelistic technique some of its most original and distinctive characteristics. At the same time it would be a mistake to imagine that he turned his back on the symphony form for ever. His autobiographical poem *First Encounter*, written in 1921, achieves this form more clearly and convincingly than any of the works which claim it in their title; and as plot later began once more to wane in importance in his novels, features of the symphony form came back into greater prominence. Bely himself spoke of *Kotik Letayev* as his 'fifth symphony'.[18]

The small number of other prose works Bely wrote in the first decade of the century are of little intrinsic interest. The longest of them, 'Adam', has been impressively analysed as an experiment in narrative viewpoint, but there is little evidence that the experiment brought results.[19] In the configuration of the main characters it carries some anticipation of *The Silver Dove*, but since both are based to a large extent on Bely's own experience with Blok and his wife in 1906, there is no great significance in that. The same relationship is transparently exploited in the little story 'The Bush', which is distinguished by the attempt Bely made to imitate the language of the mediaeval *bylina* – an attempt that was not repeated, although faint echoes of it can be detected in *The Silver Dove*.[20] The characters in Bely's short prose works tend to be drawn principally with a view to their allegorical exploitation, and the dialogue acquires a somewhat laboured secondary meaning of which the speakers are evidently unaware.

It would be hard to find in these occasional pieces any real anticipation of the novels that were to come.[21]

The Silver Dove occupied Bely throughout the year 1909[22] and was first published in the last issues of *The Scales*, which ceased publication at the end of that year. The same type-setting, with only the pagination changed, was used for the first book-form edition, published by Skorpion in 1910. The first four chapters re-appeared as volume 7 of Bely's collected works in 1917, but the only other complete edition of the novel came out, in two volumes, in Berlin in 1922.[23]

In a preface to the Skorpion edition, which was reprinted in the incomplete edition of 1917, but not thereafter, Bely explained that the novel was the first part of a planned trilogy, to be entitled 'East or West', and that most of the surviving characters would be encountered in the second part. This was used to justify the fact that their fates were not brought to completion in *The Silver Dove*. But the trilogy did not come about. The intended second novel developed into *Petersburg*, which contained in its first edition a few casual references to *The Silver Dove* that were later removed. Bely's third novel, *Kotik Letayev*, bears no resemblance at the level of plot to either of its predecessors. Yet a deeper thematic link continues to exist between all three – and indeed between all Bely's novels – and in his correspondence he continued to refer both to *Petersburg* and to *Kotik Letayev* as continuations of his trilogy long after it was clear that the superficial links had vanished.[24]

In turning to the novel form Bely introduced into his work many features of the realistic tradition which had been absent from his earlier prose. The action of *The Silver Dove* takes place in an environment which is historically identifiable and temporally and spatially continuous. The temporal sequence of the action is entirely straightforward. Local uncertainties about the length of time elapsing are due to such uncertainties in the mind of the hero. It is perfectly clear that the overall action occupies a period of about three months, from June to September. The dialogue lacks the studied transparency it often possessed in the early stories; either the characters are aware of what they represent, and speak of it coherently, or, if they are unaware of it, their symbolic significance is rendered by other means than dialogue.

Yet were *The Silver Dove* to stand or fall by its realism, it would be a failure. Although the environment is recognizable, it is not in a realistic sense convincing. As Stepun has written, what is convincing about the novel is its atmosphere, while the characters representing the concrete, historically developed Russia fail to come to life.[25] They remain essentially two-dimensional, forming a stylized backcloth against which the spiritual drama of the hero is enacted. The presence of realistic features does not turn *The Silver Dove* into a realistic novel, but it does to a substantial extent account for its greater success. The novel bears witness to Bely's growing endeavour to relate his ideas about the crisis of culture to Russian historical reality and to clarify the particular role that Russia was to play.

The wider cultural and historical significance of characters and action is rendered in the first place through the grouping of characters in relation to specific places. The action of the novel takes place in three locations: the village of Tselebeyevo, the neighbouring estate of Gugolevo, and the town of Likhov. Geographically speaking, Tselebeyevo lies between the other two, with Gugolevo to the West of it and Likhov to the East. On the realistic plane this arrangement is of no significance; what is important is that Gugolevo represents that aspect of Russia's cultural heritage that Bely attributes to the West, and Likhov the aspect that he regards as Eastern in nature. Tselebeyevo is the meeting-point of these two conflicting tendencies, the melting-pot, one might say, of Russia's future. Each of the major characters except the hero, Pyotr Dar'yal'sky, belongs to one of the three places. In Gugolevo lives Katya, Dar'yal'sky's fiancée, with her aged grandmother, Baroness Todrabe-Graaben, and their servant Yevseich. Katya's uncle, Baron Todrabe-Graaben, the articulate representative of the West, comes to stay with them there. The sect of the 'doves' hold their meetings in Likhov, in the house of the merchant Yeropegin (but only in his absence, since his wife's membership of the sect remains hidden from him). The leader of the 'doves', however, the carpenter Kudeyarov, lives with a woman called Matryona in Tselebeyevo. In Tselebeyevo there also live a number of other characters: the priest, Father Vukol, and his wife, the deacon, the shopkeeper Ivan Stepanych and his son Styopka, and several negligible minor characters. Dar'yal'sky's friend Schmidt, an elderly mystic who offers astrological interpretations of the mysteries tormenting Dar'yal'sky, also lives there in a rented summer cottage.

The plot concerns the movement of Dar'yal'sky from West to East. He has spent the last two summers in Tselebeyevo with Schmidt and only on his recent engagement to Katya Gugoleva has he gone to stay on the Gugolevo estate. Hardly has this come about (a few days before the novel's action begins), when Dar'yal'sky becomes aware of the mysterious attraction of the peasant-woman Matryona, whom he glimpses in the village church. He succumbs to this attraction, leaves Gugolevo, and goes to live with Matryona and Kudeyarov. Kudeyarov not only connives at their cohabitation, but initially encourages it; the intention is that Matryona shall become pregnant by Dar'yal'sky and give birth to a child of the spirit, the 'doves'' Messiah. After a while Dar'yal'sky comes to realize that Matryona is entirely in Kudeyarov's power, and that he, in his attachment to her, is therefore in Kudeyarov's power too. The spell is broken, and Dar'yal'sky plans to return to Moscow. The 'doves', however, cannot afford to let him go, since he knows too much about them; they take him to Likhov – where he believes he can catch the train – and murder him.

The cultural and historical significance of East and West is conveyed in part directly through the relevant characters, but in different ways. The conventional means of the realistic novel: objective depiction, narration of genealogy, elucidatory comment from the narrator, are used principally in the description of the representatives of the West. This is entirely appropriate, since it is the old Russia of the nineteenth-century novel that Bely's West connotes – a static bureaucratic Russia with an exhausted tradition of thought. The chaotic East of *The Silver Dove* is by definition formless and without genealogy, and therefore, unlike the West, cannot be described by conventional means. It can only be evoked, and its evocation is effected through a network of symbolic images. This is what produces the novel's atmosphere.

The representative function of Gugolevo is made immediately clear by direct comment from the narrator. Following the scenes in chapter three (in which Gugolevo first figures as the scene of the action), where Yevseich, the typical lackey, is described, and the daily ritual of the taciturn Baroness's morning tea depicted, there comes a passage from the narrator:

And you too, old and dying Russia, proud and petrified in your majesty, do you not likewise, every day, every hour, in thousands of chanceries, offices, palaces and estates, perform these rituals, the rituals of ancient times? But, O sublime one – look around you and drop your gaze: you will realize that beneath your feet an abyss is opening: you have but to look, and you will tumble into the abyss. . .(p.90)[26]

But the West would be inadequately represented by two women and a servant whiling away their lives on an isolated estate. It acquires an active spokesman in Baron Todrabe-Graaben, who is mentioned twice in the first chapter, but does not appear until the fifth, called from St Petersburg by his mother to help solve the problems created by the departure of Dar'yal'sky to the 'doves' and the theft of her jewels. Several pages are devoted to a description of the Baron, his father and uncles, and his past life (pp.211–19). The overriding feature of all male members of the Todrabe-Graaben family is their extreme eccentricity. In the futility of their activities and their escape from serious problems into witticisms they embody decay. The Baron's eccentricity appears to be the last kind of self- assertion open to him in view of his knowledge that he belongs to a declining culture. He asserts in conversation with Dar'yal'sky that Russians are dying out, and only Mongols and Negroes increasing, and that the Mongols will take over the country. He tells Dar'yal'sky that his talk of the ineffable is merely a demonstration of his inability to express himself coherently, and calls on him to return to the West, where, as a member of the intelligentsia, he belongs (pp.232, 256).

The Baron's extreme prognostications reflect the helplessness of the decaying Western culture in face of the incursions of the chaotic East. Gugolevo, safe, as it seems, in its age-old ritual, does not even notice that it is being superseded – or pretends not to notice:

but those sitting here do not know the new Russia, neither the songs of the new Russia, nor the words that stir the soul behind the linden-tree; the lads, and the song, and the words of the song – why, distant they sound, those words and those songs, in the distance the lads are singing; and never shall those words and those songs reach this quiet haven, never shall those lads find their way into this garden; but that is an illusion: both the words and the song itself are here, and the lads are here: long already the song has been poisoning this air, filled with the sounds of old, and making the Baroness's dark eyes dilate with terror; the Baroness learned all this long ago; both herself and Russia she condemns to perish as victims of this fateful struggle; but she pretends to be deaf and dumb: as though she knew nothing of those new songs. . . (p.94)

The incursions of chaos take a variety of forms. The tranquillity of Gugolevo is first disturbed by a minor revolt among the peasants on the estate, who gather to complain about the steward's behaviour. Among their remarks is heard:

Why take our hats off? Soon it'll all be ours anyway. (p.108)

No sooner are the peasants dismissed than General Chizhikov arrives, a familiar figure in the district, of whom it is not known, however, whether he is who he claims to be, or General Skobelev, or the robber Churkin, or Count Gudi-Guday-Zatrubinsky – or simply Matvey Chizhov, an agent of the secret police (p.111). The only thing ultimately learnt about him is that he uses the opportunity to steal the Baroness's jewels (p.183). With him comes Yeropegin, the Likhov flour merchant, who avenges himself on the Baroness for an ancient affront by demanding from her a debt she cannot pay (p.116). Yeropegin's assault is the only one withstood, as the Baron ultimately dissuades him from pressing his dishonest claims (pp.192–3). Those two are followed by a fellow-student of Dar'yal'sky's, one Chukholka, whose principal characteristic is his habit of mixing all kinds of incompatible ideas into an incoherent whole.

These arrivals are all symptoms of disintegration, as are the rumours of uprisings in the neighbourhood and of the priest of a nearby village who brought all his parishioners out on strike (pp.158–9). They and the sub-plots to which they belong are loosely linked to the main theme of chaos by unobtrusive devices. The chief representative of chaos is the sect of the 'doves'. They have no actual affiliation with the *sitsilisty* (socialists), whose influence is perceptible in the peasant's remark, but affiliation is not impossible: its desirability is discussed by two members of the sect (p.61). Yeropegin is not a member, but is unwittingly connected with the sect, as both his wife and mistress are members; and it is in his house in Likhov, the sect's meeting-place, that Dar'yal'sky will ultimately be killed.

Although Tselebeyevo is the main scene of the action, it is made clear from the very beginning of the novel that the chaotic element is not indigenous to the village, but comes from elsewhere. At the end of the first section, a description of Tselebeyevo, comes a passage about the road. Ever since it was built it has exerted a magnetic influence upon people, who go willy-nilly along it, never to return; and from the town of Likhov, to which the road leads, come rascals and drunkards to make merry in the village. This image of the road is developed later in the same chapter:

The road ran past there – past, past – ran beyond the village – ran away up the slanting slope of the plain and was lost at the very sky, because here the sky bent low to the village (there, beyond the boundary, and, it seemed, beyond the sky, was the fine town of Likhov). And a gnarled bush could be seen there, but from the village it seemed like the dark figure of a traveller, wandering solitary towards the village; the years passed, and still the traveller walked and walked: he could not reach human habitation, but all the time threatened the village from afar. (p.26)

In this way the mysterious quality of the road becomes fused with the image of the bush, which represents a threat. The same combination of images recurs towards the end of the first chapter, where it is first explicitly stated that the road leads to the East (p.37). The expression *tyomnaya* (or *tyomnen'kaya*) *figurka* recurs throughout the novel as a leitmotif, often referring to the bush, but in the last chapter referring to a sinister and unidentified figure that follows Dar'yal'sky. Having been carefully prepared, it brings with it each time, even if they are not mentioned, the ideas of the road to Likhov, the East, and a nameless threat.

Before anything concrete is learned about the 'doves' they are linked with the image of the bush. The carpenter Kudeyarov is first seen standing outside his hut, gazing down the road on the lookout for an expected visitor. The figure of Abram, the beggar who plays a leading part in the sect, eventually separates itself from the figure of the bush:

the road led far: the distance was clear, and there was no one; no, there was someone, surely someone was approaching the village; that was not the bush – there was its dark figure; and there beside it was another figure, also dark... (p.26)

The simple fact that the figure of Abram has to be explicitly distinguished from that of the bush implies an affinity between them, and, by extension, between the 'doves' (on whose behalf he has come) and the vague threat.

The nature of the sect is made clearer in the second chapter, where one of its meetings in Yeropegin's house in Likhov is depicted (pp.62–71). What takes place during their rite is not described from the viewpoint of an external narrator, indeed it is not really *described* at all. By a concentration of acoustic effects –

alliteration, assonance and rhythm – combined with imagery of light and colour, but very little that evokes any precise sensory image, Bely attempts to recreate in the reader the state that is attained by the 'doves'. It is prose, as Mochul'sky has said,[27] of a hypnotic quality. The 'doves' attain a condition where: 'it seems there exists neither time nor space, but wine, blood, the dove-blue air and sweetness. . . ' (p.70). They cannot hear their sentinel Ivan Ogon', who clamours for admittance, despairing of his lonely task of warding off the unseen enemy. Bely heightens the effect by this late introduction of an external viewpoint. Were Ivan to enter, the narrator explains, he would find no one there, for they are walking in heaven, conversing with the angel; the 'doves' overcome the categories of time and space, their individualities are submerged. Is this the mystics' longed-for union with the Absolute, or is it primordial chaos?

The 'doves' have another aspect. At the beginning of Chapter 2, before the meeting is shown, but after the emergence of Abram from the domain of the bush, he and Kudeyarov are seen walking to Likhov, discussing the sect's affairs. It transpires from this conversation not only that they believe they have found in Dar'yal'sky the man to father Matryona's child, but also that Kudeyarov has ambitions for the sect of a less spiritual nature. He hopes Dar'yal'sky will still marry Katya and put the 'doves' in possession of her inheritance, and that Yeropegin's money, too, will fall to them on his death (pp.48–9). At this point Kudeyarov mentions only that the herbs he is sending the merchant's wife appear to be doing her husband no good; but gradually it becomes apparent that Kudeyarov is systematically poisoning Yeropegin through his unsuspecting wife. When Yeropegin returns home he immediately begins to feel ill on drinking the tea into which his wife has put the herbs (p.72). But this is not sufficient for Sukhórukov, the Likhov coppersmith who is the most criminally inclined member of the sect. When Yeropegin, becoming suspicious of his wife's activities in his absence, discovers the appurtenances of the sect, Sukhorukov persuades his mistress, Annushka Golubyatnya, to poison him properly (pp.200–1). He is last seen paralysed but still in possession of his faculties, muttering the sounds 'o-t-r', which his wife takes to be the beginning of her maiden name, Otrygan'yeva, but which the reader realizes to be the beginning of a different word – *otravili* – 'they have poisoned me' (p.314).

It is not immediately clear what qualifies Dar'yal'sky to be the mediator between the East and the West. He goes to the East and perishes, but in what sense is he representative of the West? He is a member of the intelligentsia, which in the eyes of Baron Todrabe-Graaben makes him a 'man of the West' (p.256); but clearly Dar'yal'sky does not represent the decaying West of the Baron. The answer must be culled from the information given about his past life. Dar'yal'sky is a poet, and has published a book of poetry about goddesses, who some say are only peasant women with their clothes off (p.7). He dreams of the future of Russia in terms of Ancient Greece (p.102) and with his Russian blacked boots and Theocritus in his pocket he symbolizes their unity.[28] The idea of Ancient Greece as the ideal civilization, where men's various faculties were not in conflict with each other, is one of the constant undercurrents of the Symbolist movement.[29] The West lives by reason alone, the East by feeling alone. Dar'yal'sky is searching for a new religion, which will reunite the various strands of life.[30]

It is one of the tenets of Bely's theory that artistic and religious creation are different not in kind, but only in degree. Both partake of that fusion of spirit and matter that is the nature of the symbol, only while art embodies it in images, the task of religion is to embody it in life.[31] The ultimate aim of art is only achieved, therefore, when art is transcended. Dar'yal'sky, as a poet who has abandoned poetry for the creation of a way of life, is fulfilling Bely's injunction to artists. The principal theme of *The Silver Dove* is the problem of the formulation of religious experience and the creation of a new religious community. The West of the Todrabe-Graabens has lost sight of the task entirely. Its fulfilment by the Tselebeyevo clergy is reduced to a matter of routine. The 'doves', on the other hand, take the task up. The climax of their activity comes in Chapter 6; during a rite in which Kudeyarov, Matryona, Dar'yal'sky and the carpenter's labourer take part, a dove seems to emerge from Kudeyarov's breast. It has the beak of a hawk, and tears open the breast of each of the other three. They fall as though dead, but from their bodies comes a mist-like substance which forms into the image of an ethereally beautiful youth:

the dove-child, born of rapture and arisen from four dead bodies, as the oneness binding their souls... (p.265)

As the trance passes, the image disappears, and the blood that flowed turns back into spilt wine.

The ultimate symbolic image, the religious cult-figure, is always denoted in Bely's writing by the word *Lik*, which is the traditional word for a face depicted on an icon. It is used here too. What the four 'doves' have created is the passing image of the cult-figure that should bind their souls into a true religious community. What is wanted of Dar'yal'sky and Matryona is its lasting creation in the flesh. The birth of the dove-child would signal the redemption of the world through the real reunification of spirit and matter that is foretold, but not enacted, in the artistic symbol.

Thus the central issue of *The Silver Dove* is the most contentious issue in the theory – and no less in the lives – of the Symbolists themselves. Dar'yal'sky is a member of this generation of the Russian intelligentsia, that looks not to the old West, but has absorbed the lessons of its latest rebellious spirits. Bely had written of this in his essay of 1907 'The Present and Future of Russian Literature'; with the collapse of the utopian faith in progress, he had argued, the constant religious message of Russian literature appeared in a new light:

Our route lies in joining the earth with heaven, life with religion, duty with creativity; in the light of this new unification the individual approaches society and the intelligentsia the people in a new way.[32]

Russian literature has always had its roots in the people, and 'the first Russian Nietzscheans, with Merezhkovsky at their head, went to meet the religious ferment of the people'.[33] It is in this specific sense that the novel treats, as Bely himself noted, among others, the traditional conflict of intelligentsia and people,[34] and it is in this sense that its hero represents the link between East and West.

The two sides of Dar'yal'sky are expressed in particular through his relationships with the two women, Katya and Matryona. Katya represents quite a different aspect of the West from that embodied in her uncle. She is characterized mainly in negatives: she does not talk, she seems hardly to hear what is said to her, it is not certain that she even thinks. She has no practical accomplishments and is not impressed by clever conversation. Yet although she does not need to articulate it she has a profound feeling for nature and art (p.81). If articulate expression is the only criterion of understanding, then clearly Katya has little to recommend her. But in fact what emerges from the depiction of her is a pure spiritual quality, uncontaminated by the life around her, a pure potentiality.

Katya and Dar'yal'sky are not seen together until after Dar'yal'sky has begun to respond to the attractions of Matryona, and his behaviour has begun to create tension between them. It is clear that Katya represents to him an ideal that he cannot now attain without first deserting it:

Katya! There is in the world only one Katya; travel the whole world, you will not meet her again: you will pass the fields and spaces of our far-flung land, and further: you will be in thrall to dark-eyed beauties in foreign parts, but they are not Katya; you will go to the west from Gugolevo –straight, straight on; and you will return to Gugolevo from the east, from the steppes of Asia: only then will you see Katya. (p.98)

Katya cannot be said to understand Dar'yal'sky or to appreciate what she represents for him. She worries about his past life like Kitty reading Levin's diaries, and interprets his preoccupation on a rather primitive level. After his desertion of her it seems likely that she will marry a new suitor; presumably there is nothing else left open to her than to follow the customs of her class. Her strength is in her emotional directness and certainty; she overcomes her misgivings about Dar'yal'sky's past and tells him:

'I will take you however you are. . .' He dropped on to his knees in the damp grass, in the nettles and she kissed his burning forehead sadly. And so he rose from the ground, girded round by the strength of her love for the battle to come. (p.127)

But his sense of mission, as of a knight taking leave of his lady (intending eventually to return), is a part only of his experience, not of hers.

Articulate expression is certainly not a feature of Dar'yal'sky's relationship with Matryona, either. Indeed they have nothing to say to each other at all. She represents for him the recollection, or semblance, of a female figure of whom he has dreamt, but whom he has never met. This thought passes through his mind even during his final explanation with Katya:

he remembered that unique one, whom he had never met, not even in Katya. Katya he loved, but she was not that dawn: and that dawn was not to be met in female form.

But on reflection he decides:

it was possible to meet her, but her countenance would be sullied by the earth; suddenly there stood before him the image of the peasant-woman of yesterday: she, perhaps, would be his dawn... (pp.125–6)

Matryona might be the flawed earthly embodiment of the highest ideal. The ambiguity inherent in this underlies the whole of Dar'yal'sky's relationship with her and with the 'doves'.

At times it seems Dar'yal'sky has found in her 'his soul's sacred homeland', and that she is 'a dear sister, not yet wholly forgotten in the dreams of life'. They are bound by something other than love: 'the undeciphered immensity of a mystery that crushes you'. The hold on his soul is all the greater for Matryona's physical ugliness: her pock-marked face, sagging breasts, protruding stomach, and the manure on her feet. It is her eyes, seeming to contain the blue ocean in which Dar'yal'sky flounders, that exercise power over him. If she rolls her eyes so that the whites are seen instead, the spell is broken and she becomes just a lascivious peasant-woman (pp.162–4).

The ambiguity of the 'doves' is expressed in a number of other ways, besides the characterization of Matryona. One example is Kudeyarov's face, which seems to consist of two independent, self-contradictory halves. It is frequently referred to with the expression *razvody kakiye-to*, which not only supports, through its etymological root-meaning of 'leading apart', the idea of the face consisting of two halves, but also carries implications of chaos by suggesting a random pattern of lines in place of the form one expects of a face. Yet in the scene of the 'doves'' rite in Likhov, his face seems to become 'the Countenance of the Spirit' (p.67). Abram, the beggar, has a stick with a tin dove as its knob; it is said to be a mixture of walking-stick, shepherd's staff, and club (p.27). The insignia of the sect is similarly ambiguous: it consists of a large piece of red silk on which is embroidered a human heart at which a white dove is pecking; but the dove has the beak of a hawk (pp.59–60). This insignia is realized, as it were, in the scene of the dove-child. There is a distant, but distinct analogy with the holy family in the Kudeyarov household: Kudeyarov is himself a carpenter, while Matryona, who is not legally his wife but is generally supposed to be so *de facto*, is expected to conceive not by him. In the breaking of bread and drinking of wine that precedes the rites in Kudeyarov's hut there is, similarly, a recognizable analogy with the Last Supper.

Imagery of light is very extensively used in connection with the 'doves'. Its principal connotation is not enlightenment, but rather a reference to the beginning of Genesis: light as that which is first created out of the void of darkness. The carpenter himself, arriving at the 'doves" meeting in Likhov, is said to emerge from primeval darkness. Much is made, at that meeting, of the contrast between the brightness inside the bath-house and the darkness outside. The 'doves', it seems, are themselves recommencing the world's creation from nothing. Kudeyarov, in moments of ecstasy, himself emits rays of light. This occurs during a scene in which he lays hands upon Matryona, and the rays he emits are compared to the threads of a spider's web (pp.235–7). Shortly afterwards Dar'yal'sky becomes entwined in a glistening spider's web which seems to embrace all things and remains in his soul if he closes his eyes. He cannot tell whether this is the transfiguration of the world, or its perdition. He comes to the conclusion that he is caught in the web by which Kudeyarov binds Matryona to himself.

Another series of images makes an appearance at the same point. The birds, swallow and house-martin, have been related consistently to Gugolevo and Tselebeyevo respectively, and specifically to Katya and Matryona. They have also been associated with Dar'yal'sky's soul. House-martins are particularly strongly associated with the bell-tower of Tselebeyevo in the first chapter. On two important occasions the images of the two birds are juxtaposed. When Matryona comes to Gugolevo to sell flowers, Katya notices that what she took for a swallow is in fact a martin, at which Matryona rejoins: 'One of ours, from Tselebeyevo' (p.100). Later in the novel Dar'yal'sky has occasion to remark that a swallow he sees is the last swallow, and that they are flying away to the Cape of Good Hope, implying thereby that Katya's claim on his soul is lost, as her bird goes to seek good hope elsewhere (p.226). His next visit to the same place is the occasion he becomes caught in the spider's web; the bird he sees then is a house-martin, and he feels he has lost his soul.

Kudeyarov's soul is also associated with a bird, in his case a cockerel. His thoughts pursue Dar'yal'sky like a fiery cockerel (p.238), and when a cockerel inexplicably appears at the place where Dar'yal'sky and Matryona meet, they are unaccountably afraid (p.242). The table in Kudeyarov's hut is covered on special occasions with a red tablecloth bearing a design of red cockerels (p.246). The meaning of this image is extended by implied reference to the expression *pustit' krasnogo petukha*, meaning literally 'to let the red cockerel out', which is used to denote an act of arson. Towards the end of the novel the barn belonging to the shopkeeper, Ivan Stepanov, who has been following Dar'yal'sky and Matryona and denouncing the 'doves', is burnt down. Arson is mentioned, but Ivan Stepanov tries to scotch the rumour (p.295). Since the criminal propensities of the 'doves' are now entirely in the open, it seems clear that the fire was meant as a warning, which the shopkeeper has received and understood.

Eventually Dar'yal'sky realizes that Matryona's power over him is given to her by Kudeyarov and he comes to the conclusion that what he sees before him is not Russia, but 'the dark abyss of the East' (p.260). It is, of course, Dar'yal'sky's conscious mind that reaches this conviction. Its workings are rendered largely through direct intervention from the narrator. Dar'yal'sky is not heard expressing his ideas, since for the most part they belong to the past, and in any case he has no one to listen to him. In general, however, his conscious, Western aspect is subordinate to that which lies below consciousness and coherent expression. This is an area of experience for which there exist no ready-made formulations. It is well exemplified by the appeal of Matryona and the sense, intimated in the description of her as 'a dear sister, not yet wholly forgotten in the dreams of life', that the region of the mind in which this appeal evokes a response is linked, perhaps, to a life before birth. This is the inner experience which plays such an important role in Bely's theory, and which he sought to embody in the *Symphonies*. As in the *Symphonies* it is expressed in *The Silver Dove* through a complex system of symbolic imagery.

The imagery that performs this function is not separate from the complex of road–bush–East–Likhov–threat that has already been discussed. There is some justification, however, for treating it separately, since in the first chapter that series is presented independently, without reference to Dar'yal'sky's mind, while the workings of his mind are rendered by a second series. The connections between them are drawn only gradually.

When he is first introduced in the second section of Chapter 1, Dar'yal'sky is in a disturbed frame of mind. The happiness he has been enjoying of late at Gugolevo no longer seems real to him. In that section and the following three the various images are introduced separately, along with descriptions of the various inhabitants of Tselebeyevo, including Kudeyarov and Matryona.

Dar'yal'sky first clearly sees Matryona, described simply as 'a pock-marked peasant-woman' (*ryabaya baba*), in church, and feels a threat from her importunate gaze (p. 10). Later it is learnt that while most people in the village regard Dar'yal'sky merely as an eccentric there are some who understand him (p. 15). Later still it is learnt that Kudeyarov and Matryona are members of the 'doves', and that they are looking for a man, whom Matryona seems to have found (p. 30). Dar'yal'sky's confusion is described as he walks through the village. As he stands at the pond he cannot tell whether what he sees is water or sky (p. 8); beside the pond he glimpses a peasant-woman, and is inexplicably perturbed. These various strands are brought together in the sixth section of the first chapter. At the end of a party at the priest's house his wife plays her favourite waltz, 'Irretrievable Times', and all the people present begin to reflect on their past. Dar'yal'sky finds that his irretrievable time is only the previous day; a single glance from Matryona has altered everything (p. 34). As he leaves the priest's house the things he notices are combined in such a way as to bring all the separate images together:

along behind Dar'yal'sky were borne vibrant sounds; they broke up the pond into thousands of splashes; flashes-splashes, like silver doves – in the water, or in the sky? – skipped past, when the breeze touched the pond with a ripple and the green air rushed by. In front a puff of smoke rose from the sloping hollow: a red headdress flashed past there, a kerchief flashed past with white apples on it; they flashed past and were hidden in the sloping hollow, by Mitriy Mironovich, the carpenter's hut. Dar'yal'sky shuddered. (pp. 34–5)

The juxtaposition of air and water, expressing the confusion and ambivalence of Dar'yal'sky, is repeated; the ripples on the water are described as 'silver doves' (the reference to the title is perhaps a little too obvious, though the simile is apt); the word *ryab'* (ripple) refers back to *ryabaya baba* (the pock-marked peasant-woman); the red headdress and the kerchief with white apples on it were the only features Dar'yal'sky noticed of the peasant-woman he first glimpsed, and it thus becomes evident, when the woman wearing them is seen going to Kudeyarov's hut, that she was Matryona. Thus Dar'yal'sky's state of mind is linked through the chain of images with Matryona and Kudeyarov and all the associations that they are in the process of acquiring.

A straightforward narration of the novel's plot would leave the impression that the hero is an entirely passive character who simply allows things to happen to him. An examination of the way in which his subsconscious mind is revealed through the imagery leads, however, to a less simple conclusion. Dar'yal'sky succumbs to the temptation of the 'doves' not merely because he is unable to resist it, but because he has within him that which predisposes him to succumb; in one sense he brings his fate upon himself.

This state of affairs is intimated by the fact that some important images are introduced in relation to Dar'yal'sky's thoughts or observations before the outer phenomena to which they will refer have appeared. The spider, later to be associated with Kudeyarov, appears as a thing noticed by the hero long before he is enmeshed (p.8). The expression *razvody kakiye-to* first occurs in the same passage, as Dar'yal'sky, in confusion, tries to recall Katya's image, before the carpenter has ever been mentioned. The predisposition to yield to the 'doves' that is implied here is expressed at a conscious level in the narrator's remarks about his past life in chapter three.

Chapter three offers a particularly clear example of Dar'yal'sky's subconscious motivation. It describes the events leading up to his departure from Gugolevo. The objective motivation is clear: the Baroness, overwrought by an accumulation of unpleasant events, first the complaints of the peasants, then the malicious visit of Yeropegin, loses her temper with the final visitor, the foolish but apparently innocuous Chukholka, and shows him the door. Dar'yal'sky, attempting somewhat violently to intercede on his behalf, receives a slap in the face for his pains. His reaction is described in a way that shows his duality:

Like a whirlwind it passed through his mind that now, this minute, he would consider himself insulted and would leave Gugolevo forever, and would have to spend the night in Tselebeyevo; and while he was thinking this, he was already feeling insulted, and saw that his presence here was impossible... (pp.131–2)

But there is no objective reason why this quarrel should not be healed almost immediately; the Baroness regrets her action almost as soon as it is performed, and Dar'yal'sky fully understands this. Even after his departure Katya and the Baroness remain convinced that they have only to write to his friend Schmidt and the quarrel will be settled. The reason why it is not healed lies in the secondary line of motivation. The events leading up to the quarrel have quite a different significance for Dar'yal'sky.

Chapter 3 begins with his return, late at night, from Tselebeyevo to Gugolevo. His thoughts of Katya as a guide through life that he is losing are paralleled as he loses his way in the forest (p.76). He then recollects how once, as a student, he had a hallucination of a face like Matryona's, inviting him to cast propriety to the winds (p.77). But he seems to find protection in Gugolevo, when he finally makes his way back there. The events of the following day, however, destroy his protection and expose him once more to the chaos that he has borne inside him and which now has a concrete objective equivalent in Matryona. The illusoriness of his sanctuary is exposed in a passage from the narrator, where it is explained that a feeling of ease, following a period of turmoil, is only a sign that it is too late to escape. Immediately after this passage, which ends: *budet pozdno* (it will be too late), both the Baroness and Katya mention that it is late. They are referring to Dar'yal'sky's hour of rising, but the juxtaposition of their remarks with the previous passage gives their words another meaning (pp.94–5). It is too late for Dar'yal'sky to escape. The first visitor to Gugolevo is Matryona, who comes on the pretext of selling flowers. She is followed by the other emanations of chaos, the other visitors, one of whom tells Dar'yal'sky about the existence of the sect of the 'doves'.

'Here it is', thought Dar'yal'sky; – 'the disintegration has set in. . . ' He was replying to a thought of his own: hardly had the chaos subsided that raged the previous day in his soul, hardly had victory been attained in him over the destructive feeling that knocked him off his path, and the devils left his soul – when already they began again to swarm about him, taking on absurd, but completely real forms; and truly – was not this troika, and the general himself, born from the misty filth that had settled over the neighbourhood: the troika was the sediment from the mist, cast on to the estate by someone's vengeful hand. Lord alone knew from what places the troika had brought these people; was it not in order that the secret monstrousness of lascivious longings should again encircle him in a surrounding throng?

As though in answer to his thought, someone's steps were heard from the terrace. . . (p.117)

The new arrival is Chukholka. His advent is objectively motivated by nothing more than his untimely desire to visit a friend. But his presence is invariably an evil omen to Dar'yal'sky, and in this case is the final link in the chain of causes that results in Dar'yal'sky's departure from Gugolevo and surrender to the 'doves'.

Dar'yal'sky's realization that he has lost the struggle against the chaos within and around him is rendered in a passage that combines several recurrent images. Escaping from the conversation of Chukholka he goes to the lake and looks at the reflection of

Gugolevo. An inverted bird takes off from the house-top and disappears in the depths. Dar'yal'sky associates it with his soul:

'. . .my soul is a martin, cutting through the depths. Where is it flying to, my soul? It is answering a call; how should it fail to fly, when the abyss is calling it?' (p.122)

He comes to the realization that his soul is no more present in Gugolevo than Gugolevo is really present in the water of the lake. A single ripple (*ryab'*, referring again to Matryona as *ryabaya baba*) is enough to remove the illusion entirely.

Dar'yal'sky's death also shows a dual motivation. The external events leading up to it are clear enough. It is evident even before Matryona and Dar'yal'sky come together that Kudeyarov is likely to be jealous of the man Matryona will find; it has to be someone else, he tells Abram, because he is himself too old (p.30). When he returns from Likhov he is perturbed to find that they have come together without waiting for his blessing (p.167). He has promised his followers that their redeemer will be born, and the fact that Matryona does not become pregnant both undermines his own position and seems to confirm his suspicion that their union was insufficiently spiritual. He also resents Matryona's attachment to Dar'yal'sky. All this, combined with the fear of betrayal by Dar'yal'sky once his disaffection is noticed, builds up into a motive for murder.

Dar'yal'sky suspects a plot against him. The secondary line of motivation is to be found in the reasons why he nonetheless fails to escape. It is clear that one part of him intends to escape. He spends his last night in Tselebeyevo at Schmidt's house, instead of returning to Kudeyarov's. He changes back from the clothes he has been wearing into clothes that correspond to his real social status, and on his last meeting with Kudeyarov adopts for the first time the manner of master (*barin*) (p.288). On the way to Likhov he resists the efforts of Sukhorukov to wrest his stick from him. Once arrived he makes his way straight to the station, intending to catch the Moscow train. Although he has missed the train he now believes himself safe.

But there is a parallel with the situation in Chapter 3, when he temporarily thought himself safe on returning to Gugolevo. When he leaves the station to find somewhere to sleep (there is no train to Moscow until the following day), everything has changed:

The day had been azure when he entered the station; the day was. . .–but no: when he came to leave it, there was no day; but it seemed to him that there was no night either; there was just a dark void; and there was no darkness even: there was nothing... (p.307)

The one hotel in town is full. As he walks on he meets, as though by chance, Sukhorukov, who suggests he could spend the night at Yeropegin's house. Dar'yal'sky knows nothing of that house's connection with Sukhorukov and the 'doves', and accepts the suggestion. Throughout the journey to Likhov and his walk around its streets he has been followed, mostly without his knowledge, by a 'dark figure', the final embodiment of the threat carried by the bush. This figure now shows him the way to Yeropegin's house. As he follows this 'resident of Likhov' (*likhovskiy meshchanin*) through the streets he seems to experience a timeless void. His guide is shortly identified as the devil (p.309), which should come as no surprise, since 'belonging to the devil' is an obvious reading of the town's name.

If the earlier mention of 'someone's vengeful hand' and other references to Dar'yal'sky's 'invisible enemies' (e.g. p.120) were not sufficient, it is now abundantly clear that Dar'yal'sky is involved in a struggle with a real occult force, which stands behind the ostensible motivation of the novel's events in the relationship of a real cause to an apparent one. It operates upon him through that area of the mind which is rendered by imagery; Dar'yal'sky is vulnerable to it because of the particular sensitivity that sets him off from all the other characters. As his friend Schmidt explains to Katya: '...only great and powerful souls are subject to such temptation; only giants fall as Peter has fallen...' (p.174). By joining the 'doves' he has inadvertently put himself into the devil's power. The final sealing of the pact, it seems, was made just after the scene in which he found himself caught in the radiant web. He wished to himself that he might perish if he should every betray the 'doves', and the narrator intimated that he was thereby inviting death.

Death itself has more than one aspect for Dar'yal'sky. In one straightforward sense he fears it and seeks to avoid it. Yet when he is locked in his room at Yeropegin's house and knows that the 'doves' are outside waiting to come in, it is his cry to be let out that actually provokes them to come in:

By this cry and his invitation *to perform on him what they intended* he was himself writing, as it were, under his completed life: 'death'.

Then the lock clicked, and *they* appeared; up to that moment *they* had still been wondering whether *they* should cross the fateful threshold: for *they* too were people; but now *they* appeared. (p.319)

There are other intimations that in some sense he connives at his own death. He sits musing over his own fate in the tea-shop, before his final journey to Likhov, but after he has told Matryona he believes Kudeyarov intends to kill him. The narrator's comment is:

he who is doomed to pain and crucifixion, which can no longer in any way be avoided, tries yet to bless that crucifixion... (p.278)

The idea of his death as a crucifixion, a redeeming sacrifice, is echoed at the very end, when the murder weapon in one of the assassins' hands – the last thing Dar'yal'sky sees – is compared to a raised crucifix. It follows, of course, from the parody of the Last Supper in the 'doves'' rites.

With the exception of one voice, which is identifiable as Sukhorukov's, because it boasts of using Dar'yal'sky's own stick that he refused to yield on the journey, the 'doves' kill Dar'yal'sky without malice, as though performing a ritual for which they are not personally responsible. The maid, Annushka-Golubyatnya, who plays a leading part in showing him to his room and locking him in there, appears to him not as his murderess, but as a 'dear sister', through whom he comes to full understanding, relief, and peace with himself (p.317). He sits down and writes a letter to Katya, to whom he still hopes to return, in which he explains to her everything which until now has been incomprehensible to him; although the reader is not told what the letter says, he is invited to believe that Dar'yal'sky found the right words (p.317). At this moment of enlightenment Dar'yal'sky recalls his last evening in Tselebeyevo, described in the section 'What the dusk told him' (pp.295–6). That scene seemed also to speak of enlightenment and a return to innocence:

on such nights one must weep and be proud of one's obedient sobbing, which yields itself up to the fields: these are sacred tears, crime is washed away in them, and in them the soul stands naked before itself.
And Peter's soul was bathed in tears...

His recollection is expressed in a repetition of the same imagery:

Peter's soul was bathed in tears: he was already in oblivion: and it seemed to him that Likhov was left far behind his back, and he was walking across an empty field, crushing the bitter-scented, heady grasses, gazing at the yellowish pearls that were passing with the dusk beyond the fields: on his breast was the touch of invisible fingers, on his lips the kiss of gentle,

trembling lips; on and on he went across the empty field towards the wordless songs that quietly sounded to him; and all the while the same immemorially familiar, long forgotten sisterly voice could be heard: 'Come to me – come, come!' 'I can hear, I am returning...'
 And he returned from oblivion... (pp.317–8)

On the first occasion his trance was interrupted by a song and a fire-alarm. Now on the second it is broken by the return of Annushka-Golubyatnya, who, on the pretext of seeing if he needs anything, has come back for the key to lock him in. This action seems to peel yet another layer of misconception from Dar'yal'sky's mind: 'Thereupon he understood everything.' The ambiguity of his moments of clarity is compounded by the fact that both the expression 'dear sister' and the word *zarya* (meaning either 'dusk' or 'dawn') have been used in relation to Matryona. It is possible that his ultimate enlightenment is no more than a further snare and delusion. In view, however, of the letter to Katya, and the tone of the passages concerning his revelation, which are quite lacking in irony, it seems more appropriate to take it at face value. When he realizes he is to be killed, Dar'yal'sky wonders:

'What for?'
But a guileless voice answered him meekly:
'What about Katya?' (p.319)

The word *nelukavyy* (guileless) is the negative of an adjective frequently used substantivally to denote the devil. The voice that Dar'yal'sky hears is thus specifically distinguished from the source of all error, and may be taken as indicating truthfully that he is to die for his treatment of Katya. This in turn, however, seems to raise more problems than it solves, for the question of retribution in this sense has not previously appeared. In particular it does not help to elucidate the nature of Dar'yal'sky's ultimate insight, and the reader is left only with the knowledge that there was such an insight, which he could not have had without his descent to the 'doves', and the price of which is his death.

 Most critics, in interpreting *The Silver Dove*, have laid considerable emphasis upon the character of Schmidt.[35] He has no function in the plot, which does indeed point to a particular importance in his commentary (while also raising unanswerable questions about his proper integration into the novel). He appears to have the answer to Dar'yal'sky's problems:

he must conquer himself in himself, and abandon the individual creation of life; he must reassess his attitude to the world; and the ghosts, which have taken on flesh and blood for him, will vanish... (p.174)

Mochul'sky points to the significant part played in Bely's later novels by the theme of 'worldwide provocation', first expressed in Kudeyarov and the 'doves', and also the great importance as a counterbalance to it of occult knowledge and initiation such as Schmidt appears to possess.[36]

They are perfectly correct observations. Nevertheless, the character of Schmidt does not solve the conflict of *The Silver Dove*, since the hero fails to take his advice. Apparently alone among the novel's critics, Vera Stanevich concentrates upon the actual outcome of the action, and asserts that the theme of return is the lyrical theme of the novel, as it was of the *Symphonies*.[37] This is an important comment for two reasons. In the first place it does justice to the way in which Dar'yal'sky's death is depicted: as a return to a homeland of the soul, as it were, which was illusorily realized in the 'doves'. Dar'yal'sky's return to Schmidt on his last night in Tselebeyevo and his hope of return to Katya also belong to this theme. Secondly it is true that the novel's ending is lyrical in character. The whole novel is lyrical in the sense that everything is filtered through the experience of the single central hero; but the significance of the conflict he embodied extended to embrace a complex comment on Russian culture and history. That conflict is not resolved, and in the last chapter the cultural and historical perspective gives way to a more privately lyrical theme of the individual hero's fate. The intimations of redemptive sacrifice are not clear enough to be built into a consistent interpretation; they seem to express a hope, but no more.

The legacy of the *Symphonies* is clearly seen in the way imagery is used in *The Silver Dove* to render the subconscious workings of the hero's mind. Although the inherent optimism in the idea of anamnesis is replaced in the novel by an ominous occultism, the techniques expressing them are essentially the same. The other most significant way in which the technique of the *Symphonies* continues to influence Bely's novels lies in the division of the chapters into shorter sections of varying length, each of which has its own unifying devices. In *The Silver Dove* this practice of subdivision is not allowed to interrupt significantly the flow of the narrative, as the sections are relatively long and the transitions between them not particularly abrupt. In *Petersburg* they will become shorter and the transitions sharper, restoring much of the kaleidoscopic effect of the *Symphonies*. What unites these sections is the repetition within them – often with minor variations – of mainly descriptive leitmotifs, which serve to establish a general atmosphere that is further sustained by other imagery. This is precisely how 'mood' or 'key' was established in the *Symphonies*. Examples could be taken from most sections of the novel, for instance:

a bird of the swamp lets its voice be heard, and then hides away for a long time... (pp.239, 241)

or:

lamp-black, smoke, fumes, din, peasants... (pp.278, 286)

Landscape and natural description are further important ingredients in the creation of the novel's atmosphere. The elements come to possess a malevolent, animate quality that is not in evidence in any of Bely's earlier prose, but is familiar from his second book of poetry, *Ashes*, published in the same year as the novel.[38] The forest, for instance, in which Dar'yal'sky will lose his way both literally and metaphorically in Chapter 3, is first introduced with a note of foreboding on the second page of the novel:

the whispering forest pours drowsiness over you; and there is no way out of it... (p.4)

The evocation of the overpowering heat of Whit Sunday, on which the action, and Dar'yal'sky's fall begin, or the rain, mist and mud of Whit Monday, on which Kudeyarov and Abram trudge to their formless rites in Likhov, have a part to play here. They establish the tone of the respective chapters: the oppressive threat of Chapter 1, and the contrast of formlessness and form in Chapter 2. The novel's action extends from the height of summer to a cold September with overnight frost; it is significant how often the summer days are described as anticipating autumn (pp.202, 205, 233, 245). Such anticipation of the action through symbolic description complements the anticipation that is created through the imagery rendering Dar'yal'sky's state of mind.

In turning back from the experimental form of the *Symphonies* to older traditions of prose, Bely turned first and foremost towards Gogol'. His stylistic debt to Gogol' in *The Silver Dove* has been noted by practically every critic who has commented upon the novel,[39] and is seen in a number of ways. The narrative device of breaking off in a quasi-conversational manner to introduce a correction is one example:

two years ago – no, come now: when did Konovalov's pigsty burn down? There – it's three years since the pigsty burned down... Well, then, it's three years since Fyokla Matveyevna went over to the faith of the dove... (pp.52–3)

or:

And that's all that happened in those days that's worth remembering – but what's this? I haven't said a word about the most important adventure of all. I do beg your pardon, I quite forgot. That's about the bicycle, of course... (p.150)

The substitution of rumour for authoritative narration is used in a manner reminiscent of such passages from Gogol' as the ending of 'The Greatcoat'. It provides an opportunity of linking phenomena and events that have no causal connection in the plot, but are understood as having some common relationship to the underlying occult forces:

in the village there wandered a rumour about a slap in the face, about rebellion, Cossacks and pillars of crimson... (p.158)

The greater part of chapter four, during which Dar'yal'sky is wandering about the district with no apparent aim, is narrated in the form of rumour. The apostrophe to Russia and its broad expanses (p.229) is reminiscent of Gogol''s lyrical digressions in *Dead Souls*. The universal uncertainty about the true identity of General Chizhikov (pp.109–11) recalls the chapters of that novel in which the townspeople vie with each other in fatuous explanations of Chichikov's provenance – and the similarity of their names is hardly accidental. The introduction of the deaf-and-dumb Sidor, reputed to be the worst gossip in the district (p.14), is a typically Gogolian oxymoron. Beyond these specific points the general atmosphere of Bely's Russian countryside is clearly indebted to Gogol''s Ukrainian stories.[40]

At the same time that he was working on this novel, Bely was preparing an essay for the centenary of Gogol''s birth, in which he interpreted Gogol''s life and fate in terms which, as T.R.Beyer has pointed out, bear a very close resemblance to the fate of Dar'yal'sky. It is clear that the stylistic indebtedness to Gogol' was by no means fortuitious. To claim, as Beyer does, that Dar'yal'sky can therefore be understood as 'a fictional interpretation of Gogol''s moral quest'[41] is probably too restrictive. Bely's general preoccupation with the fate of the artist is evident from several other essays, and it is perhaps truer to say that Gogol' served as a particular example of the general destiny that Dar'yal'sky's story embodies.

D.S.Mirsky asserts of *The Silver Dove*, acknowledging its debt to Gogol', that 'it is always on Gogol''s highest level, which is seldom the case with Gogol' himself'.[42] Such praise is perhaps more than Bely's first novel deserves. There are a number of sentences in the novel where word-order and syntax are so contorted that the sense does not easily yield itself up.[43] For the most part, however, the stylization is remarkably well controlled and sustained.

The function of rhythm in *The Silver Dove* is somewhat similar to its function in the *Symphonies*, except that as the paragraphs lengthen the reader's attention is not so immediately drawn to it.[44] The resemblance to Gogolian 'skaz', however, the colloquial narrative tone, suggests that the text be read aloud; and if that is done it soon becomes apparent that it is dotted with motifs of a distinctly rhythmic character.[45] Even in passages that do not display a regular metre it can happen that the rhythm is nonetheless a dominant impression on reading, particularly when it is combined with concentrated effects of alliteration, assonance and rhyme.[46] The passages concerned with the rites of the 'doves' are especially rich in such cumulative effects.

James Rice has pointed out that the novel rests, in one sense, upon a pun between the words *golub'* (dove) and *glubina* (depth), and that a reference is implied to the apocryphal folk-song about the *Golubinnaya kniga*, which might be translated as 'The Dove-Deep Book'. The adjective is known nowhere else and carries connotations of both roots:

This song tells of an enormous tome containing all answers to all vital questions, of the origins of the earth, the protocol of ranks among all animals, vegetables, minerals, and social classes, and the reasons for man's unhappiness. And by way of conclusion the song relates an epic contest between Truth and Falsehood of the Russian land.[47]

The play between these two words can indeed be seen to underlie much of the novel's central imagery. Such a formulation as *golu-*

boy vozdukh (the dove-blue air) carries, in this context, reference both to depth and to the 'doves'. A more complex example can be seen in the image *rasstrigayushchiy glubinu strizh* (a martin, cutting through the depths), with which Dar'yal'sky compares his soul. Not only is there a further pun between *strizh* and the root of *rasstrigayushchiy*, but *rasstrigayushchiy* also carries a connotation of removing sanctity, as it is the word used for the unfrocking of a monk. The visual image of the bird in the sky reflected in the lake then turns into a symbol connoting the removal of sanctity from the depths of Dar'yal'sky's soul, which depths are phonetically associated with the 'doves'. When the word *glubina* is then replaced in the following sentence by the word *bezdna* (abyss), the ambiguity of Dar'yal'sky's soul – sinking when he thought it was soaring – comes to full realization.

Puns of this kind, which provide links at the phonetic level between semantically distant words, form a further strand in the system of interlocking imagery that creates the novel's deeper level of meaning. The device itself could well have been learnt from Gogol', who frequently enough makes play with phonetic similarities. But the consistent incorporation of the pun into the novel's texture is Bely's own peculiar hallmark. Word associations by synonym, such as exist between *glubina* and *bezdna*, function as a direct message to the reader's consciousness that a particular idea is ambiguous. Transitions through interconnected imagery, such as were discussed above, serve to convey mental activities of the hero that exist below the level of consciousness. But a pun like *glubina/golub'* pushes the unconscious connections beyond individual psychology into the very language itself, the vehicle of the common culture, and hints at the mythic nature of language that Bely seeks to demonstrate in 'The Magic of Words'.

The Silver Dove stands at the end of the decade that belongs peculiarly to the second generation of Russian Symbolists, and sums up what was perhaps their most characteristic contribution to Russian culture: their vision of the religious regeneration of culture through, and transcending, art. The novel embodies in its hero a real attempt to achieve this (as opposed to its mere scholastic discussion) and culminates in that hero's sacrificial death. The conclusion is inescapable that the attempt in this form has led at best to heroic failure. The failure of the movement's religious impulse, in the sense that it had given way to a more narrowly aesthetic concern, was the main substance of its reappraisal by Ivanov and Blok in the following year.[48] Bely's novel is clearly concerned with a similar reappraisal, and the terms of it are expressed by Schmidt in his call for patient and disciplined esoteric studies. As an artistic monument to the second generation of Russian Symbolists *The Silver Dove* has no rivals.

The 'symphonic' form was based upon a more or less literal understanding of the notion that art, as it tended more and more towards music, could further the kind of communication between men that would lead to the transformation of culture. The underlying 'mystical' experience that it is designed to convey is supposed to be imparted by the work to each individual reader. The communication is lyrical in nature, and the question is not faced of how such individual readers are then to recognize each other and realize themselves as a community. That is the central problem that *The Silver Dove* poses. In order to depict collective experience, interaction between individuals, Bely needed a plot and so turned to the novel. The fact that the creation of a religious community becomes the central thematic problem of the novel shows the distance Bely has moved from his original naive understanding of the 'theurgic' nature of art. That distance is also essential for the formal success of the novel, which requires a much more stable and distanced narrative standpoint than the arbitrary fluctuations of the *Symphonies*. *The Silver Dove* might be taken to exemplify the argument of Blok and Ivanov, that the loss of the Symbolists' religious attitude to art made possible a greater aesthetic achievement.

In the long term neither the idea that art has an active role to play in the renewal of culture, nor the idea that art must be transcended in order for that renewal to take place, will entirely disappear from Bely's work. The active function of art comes to be embodied more and more in the nature of language itself, rather than solely in the structural properties of the work; *The Silver Dove* shows the beginning of this development. It is certainly no purely aesthetic impulse that guides Bely's innovations in the novels that follow. The theme of the repudiation of art in the name of higher values is one to which Bely will return, not only in critical essays on Tolstoy and Dostoyevsky,[49] but also in his uneasy amalgam of fiction and autobiography, *Notes of an Eccentric*.

4

Petersburg

Bely's second novel, *Petersburg*, has a more complex history than any of his other works. It was originally planned, under the title *The Wayfarers* (*Putniki*), as a continuation of *The Silver Dove* and the second part of the prospective trilogy. In the course of composition, however, it grew into a separate work with a different setting and different characters.[1] Bely envisaged several possible titles for this new novel: *The Admiralty Spire, Evil Shadows, The Lacquered Carriage, The Red Domino*;[2] its definitive title was the idea of Vyacheslav Ivanov, whom Bely called the 'godfather' of his novel.[3]

The novel exists in two principal versions. The first was published in three numbers of the almanac *Sirin* in 1913 and 1914, and in book form in 1916 with the pagination unchanged; the second, considerably shortened, edition was published in Berlin in 1922. There are, however, a number of other versions, either extant in part or in full, or reported as having existed. The first of these dates from 1911 and was to have been published in the periodical *Russian Thought*, but was rejected by the editor, P.B. Struve.[4] This version was consulted by Ivanov-Razumnik, but is apparently no longer extant.[5] A separate edition was then planned with the publisher K.F. Nekrasov, of Yaroslavl', of which nine printer's sheets (the first chapter and approximately half of the second) were printed before the rights were transferred by agreement to *Sirin*.[6] These nine sheets have been known to scholars from a copy preserved in the Central Archive of Literature and Art in Moscow;[7] they were further revised for publication in *Sirin*. Between the two principal versions there were two further modified versions, one, dating from 1914, for a German translation which appeared in 1919,[8] the other, the date of which is not known for certain, but is evidently prior to the Berlin edition, for a proposed second edition to be published in Russia.[9] A further edition was published in 1928, which is based on the Berlin edition, but differs from it in the deletion of a certain amount of religious imagery. This was re-published in 1935 and again in 1978, and has also been reprinted in the West. The *Sirin* edition re-appeared in the West in 1967, and very recently has been re-published in full in the Soviet Union, with the previously unpub-lished 'Nekrasov' text included as an appendix.[10]

Bely also adapted *Petersburg* for the stage. Two dramatized versions of the novel are preserved in the Central Archive, the shorter of which (the one Bely considered less successful) was per-formed in the Moscow Arts Subsidiary Theatre on 14 November 1925, but never repeated.[11] According to Bugayeva and Petrovsky there also exists the manuscript of a third dramatized version, and a film version was at one time planned.[12] None of the dramatized versions have ever been published.

The novel has been translated into English (twice), German (twice), Czech (twice), French, Spanish, Italian, Serbo-Croatian, Polish, Swedish, Finnish, Rumanian and Dutch.

The plot of *Petersburg* is considerably more complex than that of *The Silver Dove*. A far larger number of characters take a positive part in the action, so that there is not the same qualitative distinc-tion that there was in the earlier novel between a single major hero and a host of minor characters that merely form the background.

The novel's action takes place during a few days of October 1905. Both the Russo-Japanese War and the 1905 revolution are present as part of the background. The central hero, Nikolay Apollonovich Ableukhov, is the son of a high-ranking Petersburg bureaucrat, senator Apollon Apollonovich Ableukhov, with whom his relationship is outwardly cool and distanced, but inwardly explosive, an insoluble confusion of love and hatred. He is in love with Sof'ya Petrovna Likhutina, the wife of an upright but ineffectual army officer. She has rejected his advances, but he nevertheless continues to pursue her. In a moment of extreme depression, occasioned both by his disappointment in love and by a philosophical nihilism engendered by his study of neo-Kantian philosophy, he has evidently made a rash promise to 'the party' that, should they require it, he will assassinate his own father.

Apollon Apollonovich has a similarly ambiguous attitude towards his son, reflecting, when he is on his own, that his son is a scoundrel, but behaving in Nikolay Apollonovich's company as though there were nothing the matter. The relationship between them has been strained for two and a half years, since the senator's wife, Anna Petrovna, eloped to Spain with an Italian lover.

Nikolay Apollonovich's contact with 'the party' (which is never more closely identified) is through an ostensible fellow-student, a terrorist, the Elusive (*Neulovimyy*), who lives under the name of Aleksandr Ivanovich Dudkin. The action of the novel is set in motion by a visit Dudkin pays to Nikolay Apollonovich to ask him to store, on the party's behalf, a small package that he brings with him. Relieved that the party's request is so trivial, Nikolay Apollonovich agrees, but Dudkin does not reveal the package's contents.

A letter addressed to Nikolay Apollonovich with instructions on what he is to do with the package falls into the hands of Sof'ya Petrovna, who is requested by a mutual acquaintance to pass it on to the addressee. She has lately been pursued and frightened by Nikolay Apollonovich, dressed in a red domino, and she vindictively opens the letter. She realizes that its receipt will be a serious blow to him, and in her desire to see this blow fall rejects her husband's insistent request that she should not go to the masked ball, where she knows she will meet Nikolay.

At the ball both Sof'ya Petrovna and Nikolay Apollonovich are masked; his mask is the red domino with which she is acquainted, but hers is unfamiliar to him, so that he does not know from whose hands he receives the letter. Apollon Apollonovich is also present, but does not recognize his son behind the mask; nevertheless he takes the red colour of the domino to be a personal affront to his function as a preserver of the machinery of state. It is whispered to him that the red domino is his son and that he is suspected of being in contact with the party. On reading the letter, which informs him that the package is a bomb which he is to use to fulfil his promise, Nikolay Apollonovich removes his mask and rushes from the room. When his father leaves the ball some time later he is approached by one Morkovin, alias Voronkov, a police agent, who intimates to him that an attempt on his life is being planned.

Meanwhile Likhutin, in despair at his wife's inattention to him, attempts to hang himself, but succeeds only in bringing down the ceiling plaster. Sof'ya Petrovna returns home in great agitation, realizes what has happened there, and is reconciled with her husband. She tells him the contents of the letter she has delivered to Nikolay Apollonovich.

Nikolay Apollonovich is also followed by Morkovin who reveals himself to him as a double agent, working for the secret police on behalf of the party. With this double authority to invoke, he has Nikolay completely in his power: if he declines to carry out the assassination, Morkovin will see to it that he is arrested. He offers him three ways out of his predicament: murder, suicide or arrest.

Apollon Apollonovich, on his way home, reflects on his loneliness, and recalls the failure of his marriage, which until now he has kept from his mind. He and his son meet as they both arrive home in the small hours, but conversation between them is prevented by an access of hatred on Apollon Apollonovich's part. Next morning, when it seems they are ready to talk, their explanations are forestalled by the news that Anna Petrovna has returned, and is staying in a hotel in the city. Back in his own room, Nikolay Apollonovich half inadvertently winds up the clockwork mechanism of the bomb. Nothing can now prevent it from exploding in twenty-four hours' time, and the anticipation of the explosion, as this period elapses, dominates the rest of the novel.

Dudkin receives a visit from Nikolay Apollonovich, who has woken up to the full horror of the situation and requests Dudkin's help. Dudkin is convinced that the party would not make so cruel a demand of him and assures Nikolay that there must be some mistake. He promises to go and see Lippanchenko, the agent from whom he receives his instructions, to clarify the matter, and advises Nikolay Apollonovich to go and throw the bomb in the river. Lippanchenko, however, tells Dudkin that there is no mistake, that Nikolay Apollonovich is a traitor to the party and must be destroyed along with his father. He gives Dudkin to understand that only at the price of abandoning all efforts to help Nikolay Apollonovich will he be clear of suspicion himself. Afraid for his own safety, Dudkin is at first willing to believe Lippanchenko, but on his return home he undergoes a series of visions, or occult visitations, which persuade him that he must destroy Lippanchenko. He buys a pair of scissors, returns at night to Lippanchenko's *dacha*, murders him by disembowelling, and goes mad.

Nikolay Apollonovich, on his way home to retrieve and dispose of the bomb, is waylaid by an excited and incoherent Likhutin, who takes him to his own apartment. Nikolay expects reproaches, indeed even fears violence, because of his treatment of Sof'ya Petrovna. It transpires, however, that Likhutin, informed by his wife of the assassination plot, is trying to prevent the catastrophe and has even been to the Ableukhov house in his quest for Nikolay Apollonovich. Nikolay Apollonovich denies that there is any such plot, and the two fail to communicate with each other.

Apollon Apollonovich appears now to be a broken man. He has realized that because of his son's behaviour he must decline a new post that was being offered to him, and now, instead of going to the office he stays at home dusting his books. His deputy, after a number of vain telephone calls, comes to visit him with an urgent paper requiring his signature. There is unrest throughout the country. Ableukhov perversely refuses to sign, and within a few hours the news is spread of his retirement. Obsessed with the idea of finding out precisely what his son is doing he goes to his room and finds the bomb, not recognizing it because of the sardine tin in which it is concealed. He carries it off to his study in order to examine it at leisure, but almost immediately forgets about it. He goes to the hotel where his wife is staying, is reconciled with her, and brings her back home.

Nikolay Apollonovich returns home to find the bomb missing. He bursts into tears on meeting his mother and the family seems to be peacefully reunited. But the bomb is nowhere to be found. He recollects that Likhutin had called in his absence and persuades himself that he must have taken it. But he is not sure and spends the night in suspense, knowing that it must shortly explode. It duly explodes in Apollon Apollonovich's study, injuring no one.

Apollon Apollonovich retires to the country and writes his memoirs. Nikolay Apollonovich goes abroad with his mother, who returns the following summer. He does not return to Russia until his parents are dead, but spends his time studying Egyptian archaeology and the philosopher Skovoroda.

The novel is thus a suspense story, but one which culminates in a double anti-climax. When, despite all efforts to remove it, the bomb does explode as originally intended, no one is hurt. Since, however, by that time the senator has in any case retired, even a successful assassination would be politically meaningless. Even the failure of the original plan is robbed of its meaning as a failure.

Suspense is engendered not only by the presence of the bomb with its clockwork mechanism activated. It is created further by the characters' ignorance about the motives, intentions, indeed often the identity of other characters. For the most part the reader shares that ignorance; where he is better informed, as in the question of the whereabouts of the bomb in the last chapter, that serves to heighten his anxiety on the characters' behalf. His ignorance is studiedly fostered by the narrator, who drops hints but withholds details. There are long spaces of anticipation, for instance, between the first mention of Nikolay Apollonovich's promise and the revelation of its nature, or between the intimation that there is a letter on the way to him and the disclosure of its contents.

The suspense is, however, so pointedly and self-consciously established by the narrator that the effect is one of self-parody. The reader's anxious anticipation is not thereby cancelled, but his involvement in the fates of the characters is modified by the narrator's irony. The same is true of the climactic moments in the emotional lives of the characters. The scene of reconciliation between the Likhutins, for instance, is to some extent moving, yet the reader is simultaneously aware both of a distinct absurdity in the characters and their situation, and of a tendency to sentimentality and cliché in the writing, which, without being overtly ironic in tone, serves nonetheless to deflate the psychological value of the episode. There is no character in *Petersburg* who can make the same claim on the reader's sympathy that Dar'yal'sky made in *The Silver Dove*. The reader is restrained from making a naive response to the characters or the action. While in the structure of its plot *Petersburg* invokes the general tradition of the nineteenth-century novel, it also consistently subverts it. In the demands it makes of its readers it is much further from the traditional realistic novel than was *The Silver Dove*.

Despite its separate development a clear link with the first novel remains in the function performed by the notions of East and West. In *The Silver Dove* they were separately and somewhat schematically embodied in the various locations and the characters who inhabited them. This state of affairs meant that the two ideas were seen quite unambiguously as opposites. It also created a necessary limitation on all characters except the hero, which was one reason why he stood out, in his possibility of movement, as qualitatively quite distinct. In *Petersburg* the one city is the only location of the action and embodies both polarities, so that the relationship between the ideas of East and West can become much more complex and ambiguous. The symbolic significance of

Gugolevo and Likhov was conveyed only by the behaviour of their inhabitants and the intervention of the narrator, while that of Petersburg is established in large measure by development of the already existent literary myth, and is thus achieved with much less visible contrivance.

The quasi-geographical opposition of Gugolevo and Likhov has a corollary in *Petersburg* in the opposition that is set up between the mainland part of the city and the islands. The characters particularly associated with one or the other location are also specifically linked with particular and opposite political attitudes. Apollon Apollonovich, the principal representative of political reaction, belongs to the mainland, and the strict geometry of its streets and squares provides the principle by which he organizes his public, and as far as possible his private, life. He thinks of the rectilinear prospects as iron bands restraining the entire earth. He designates the drawers and shelves in his dressing-room by compass directions and letters. Above all he fears the islands and their inhabitants, and dreams of pinning them down with the iron of the bridge (I, 20).[13] Those islands (whose actual street plan is scarcely less rectilinear than that of the mainland) are seen from the mainland as a threatening vision on the horizon, or from closer to as a maze of overcrowded tenements; their main emissary is Dudkin, bearer of the revolutionary bomb. Nikolay Apollonovich, the central character with links to both extremes, is frequently to be observed on the bridge that joins them.

The Ableukhovs themselves are likewise divided between '*logika*' and '*psikhika*' (logic and psyche). There is a discontinuity in each of them between an autonomous cerebral life and a disordered emotional life. The opposite pole from Apollon Apollonovich's bureaucratic geometry is expressed in the involuntary upsurges of his heart disease, or the incomprehensible 'second space' that he glimpses on the borders of sleep. Most of all, however, it is perceptible in his relations with his wife and son. Of Nikolay Apollonovich the narrator says:

Soon we shall prove to the reader beyond doubt that Nikolay Apollonovich's soul, too, is split into two independent dimensions; a god-like ice and simply a frog-like slime. (I, 90)

The image of ice immediately links him with his father, who in his youth nearly froze to death in the wide open spaces of Russia, and has suffered from agoraphobia and rigidity ever since. Nikolay Apollonovich's passion for abstraction takes the form of the study of neo-Kantian philosophy. But this philosophical background is no less responsible for his other aspect. Speaking of his own experience in the years 1904–8, Bely wrote of the 'disastrous consequences of an over-estimation of neo-Kantian literature; the philosophy of Cohen, Natorp, Lask has an effect on one's feeling of the world, and produces in one a split into *hardness* and *sensuality*'.[14] This clearly is the experience reproduced in Nikolay Apollonovich. His emotional life consists in his unhealthy passion for Sof'ya Petrovna; she had once glimpsed his god-like attributes and fallen in love with them, but that love turned to disgust when she noticed his other aspect, the sensuality of his 'frog-like slime'. It is this that ensures the failure of the advances he makes to her, and thus provides part of the motivation for his promise to the party. The other part of his motivation comes from the 'hardness' derived directly from his philosophical studies, a cultural nihilism from which he 'condemns the world to fire and the sword' (I, 103).

Nikolay Apollonovich is well aware of the split in his own personality, and would remove it:

in his study Nikolay Apollonovich performed acts of terrorism upon himself – number one upon number two, the socialist upon the aristocrat and the corpse upon the lover; in his study Nikolay Apollonovich cursed his frail being, and inasmuch as he was the image and likeness of his father, he cursed his father. (II, 8)

His hatred for this 'frail being' (*brennoye sushchestvo*), the flesh by which he is bound to his father, is expressed in his feeling of revulsion at the thought of his father exercising his conjugal rights. His attitude to himself is given an alternative motivation in a description of his conception:

between two smiles of different kinds: between smiles of lust and of obedience; was it surprising that Nikolay Apollonovich became thereafter a combination of revulsion, fear and lust? (III, 186)

It is in this unwanted 'frail being' that such love as there is between them is to be found:

It was clear that his godlikeness was bound to hate his father; but maybe his frail being loved his father nonetheless? (II, 8)

Sometimes when they are together this love is allowed a fleeting appearance, as, for instance, when they dine:

And a semblance of friendship usually arose between them towards the dessert: they were sometimes sorry to break off their dinner-time conversation, as though they were each afraid of the other; as though each of them, alone, were sternly signing a death-warrant for the other. (II, 26)

Apollon Apollonovich, on his own in his study, comes to the conclusion that his son is a scoundrel (I, 65), but this decision, being abstract, is not brought with him into the dining-room (II, 22). Nevertheless he performs, in reaching this conclusion, a theoretical act of terrorism upon his son. Nikolay Apollonovich comes to precisely the same conclusion about his father, and plans a real act of terrorism upon him.

Thus Nikolay Apollonovich rebels against his father because he hates his own resemblance to him, but the rebellion is itself determined by the features they share. Each aspect of Nikolay Apollonovich's motivation is attributable back to the fundamental split between reason and feeling. Both Ableukhovs are typical examples of what Bely, in his theoretical essays, diagnosed as the crisis of European culture, and the symptoms they reveal match exactly the duality of the city itself.

As if to emphasize their similarity to the city, both father and son are spoken of as centres from which forces radiate (I, 55, 63). The city of Petersburg is introduced in the prologue as two concentric circles with a dot in the middle: this is its representation on the map and, so the narrator tells us, the proof of its existence. From this mathematical point with no dimensions it radiates printed matter, specifically in the form of government circulars. The mathematical point that has no dimensions is of course an abstraction. Dostoyevsky's underground man had already spoken of the misfortune of living in Petersburg, 'the most abstract and intentional city on the entire globe'. Apollon Apollonovich, the bureaucrat, is 'the soul of circulars' (III, 143). But just as the forces of abstraction radiate out from the centre, so the forces of chaos and destruction stream in from the periphery. The periphery begins at the islands and extends to the battlefields of Manchuria (I, 107). It is not by chance that the workers who surge across the bridge are clad in Manchurian hats. And it is by the same route that Dudkin arrives with the bomb.

The city and the principal protagonists are linked in a yet more fundamental way. Nikolay Apollonovich turns out to be the progeny of his father in more than the straightforward biological sense.

Much of the first chapter, which carries the subtitle, 'In which is told of a certain worthy personage, his cerebral play and ephemerality of being', is devoted to the way in which Apollon Apollonovich's mind gives rise to phenomena in the outside world. We are told that he was 'in a certain sense like Zeus':

The cerebral play of the wearer of bejewelled insignia was distinguished by strange, very strange, exceedingly strange qualities: his cranium became the womb of mental images, which were forthwith embodied in this spectral world. (I, 40)

In particular his cerebral play produces the stranger with the bundle, whose zig-zag gesture casts terror into him – and who will be identified anon as Dudkin on his way to deliver the bomb – and also the senator's own house and his son. Evidently if his son is his product in this sense too, then the notion of paternity can be extended to cover all such relations of cerebral genesis, and Dudkin is his son no less than Nikolay Apollonovich. We then enter a complex system of interchangeable paternal, filial and sibling relationships. Dudkin must be a kind of brother to Nikolay Apollonovich; indeed he appears at times to be his double, or alter ego.[15] But then Dudkin has his own quasi-paternal mentor in Lippanchenko, the father of the conspiracy, arch-terrorist and *agent provocateur*. His murder of Lippanchenko is an enactment of the parricide that fails to come about in the main plot.[16] Through Dudkin's agency it is Lippanchenko who issues all the instructions about the bomb to Nikolay Apollonovich, so that he stands in a similar relationship of cerebral paternity to him. There also results an initially unsuspected relationship between Apollon Apollonovich and Lippanchenko, who are both parents of the same offspring. There is a further sibling in the double agent Morkovin, alias Voronkov, who claims in an interview with Nikolay Apollonovich that he is the product of an illicit relationship of his father's; that biological affiliation is then discarded as a joke, but only to be replaced by the assertion that they are spiritual brothers.

But behind all these particular relationships between the individual characters of the novel lies the original paternity of Peter the Great to his offspring, the city. The city founded by autocratic decree is well suited to express the idea of a reality that owes its origin to human thought. The theme of the city's foundation parallels that of the senator's cerebral play in the first chapter. Peter the Great, in his capacity as founder of the city, appears as the Flying Dutchman, who emerged from the mists of the Baltic Sea 'to raise here as an illusion his misty lands and give the name of islands to a wave of scurrying clouds . . . ' (I, 19–20). In so doing he 'lit the hellish lights of drinking-houses for two hundred years', and the people of Russia succumbed to their temptation:

Long years the Christian people caroused here with the ghost: a hybrid race arose from the islands – neither men nor shadows – settling on the borders of two worlds that were alien to one another. (I, 20)

No doubt it is to this manner of foundation that the city streets owe their strange quality:

The streets of Petersburg possess the most indubitable quality: they turn passers-by into shadows; but shadows the streets of Petersburg turn into people. (I, 43)

In his hypostasis as the Flying Dutchman Peter appears on one other occasion: in the scene between Nikolay Apollonovich and Morkovin. Morkovin leads Nikolay, after the ball, over the bridge to Vasil'yevsky Island, into a drinking-house. Its walls are decorated with scenes whose description recalls the arrival of the Flying Dutchman as given in Chapter 1 (II, 158). The scene is replete with references to that version of the city's foundation: the drinking-house they are in is a 'hellish drinking-house'; the people in it are 'a hybrid race carousing'. A sailor, sitting at an adjacent table, appears (for no stated reason) to be a Dutchman, and his companion is gigantic, and apparently made of stone. This prepares the transition to Peter's other hypostasis, for he, like all his works, appears in two conflicting guises. On the way to this place Nikolay Apollonovich and Morkovin had crossed the Senate Square, and the statue of the Bronze Horseman had been concealed by mist (II, 154). On the way back home after the interview the statue confronts Nikolay Apollonovich with the words: 'I destroy beyond redemption' (which had been heard in a different context in the drinking-house). This transition from Flying Dutchman to Bronze Horseman clearly establishes their identity. The double image embodies the complexity of the traditional literary myth of Petersburg: the elegant imperial metropolis, mainly associated with Pushkin, and the hallucinatory, mist-wrapped city of Gogol' and Dostoyevsky.

E. Starikova has pointed out how the Bronze Horseman is connected with both revolution and reaction, while remaining, as it was for Pushkin, 'a symbol of the terrible might of the Russian state, which both defeats its enemies and destroys its children'.[17] This indeed summarizes its role in the novel, and shows its connection with the pattern of parental conflicts. The Bronze Horseman is one of the fathers, along with Apollon Apollonovich and Lippanchenko. The whole system of relations is summarized in the myth of Saturn – the father who devours his children and the child who devours his father.[18] The statue's principal victim is Dudkin, who is cast as a second Yevgeny (III, 102). It is a visit from the Bronze Horseman that gives Dudkin the strength to commit the murder of Lippanchenko. The statue's hooves are heard ringing through the streets, as in Pushkin's poem, and once in Dudkin's room its molten metal is poured into his veins. Lippanchenko is destroyed, but Dudkin meets the same fate. He goes mad like Yevgeny, and, as Yevgeny was found during the flood astride a lion on Senate Square, parodying the pose of the statue, so Dudkin is found astride the body of his victim.

The faculty of 'cerebral play' is not restricted to Peter the Great and his latter-day minions. Dudkin, himself the first product of the senator's 'idle thought', proceeds to have idle thoughts of his own, which behave in precisely the same way:

And one such fleeting thought of the stranger's was the thought that he, the stranger, existed in fact; this thought ran back from the Nevsky into the senator's brain, and there established an awareness to the effect that the very existence of the stranger in that head was an illusory existence.

Thus the circle was closed. (I, 41)

But as a second source of such ephemerality, besides the city and its spectral founder, there stands behind the novel as a whole the self-conscious narrator, who cannot forbear to press the point that it is all in turn the product of his own cerebral play (I, 72). The first appearance of Apollon Apollonovich himself is accompanied by the ironical question from the narrator: 'What was the social standing of the character who has arisen here out of nonexistence?' (I, 9). The fact that Dudkin is the narrator's product (since the senator, who creates him, is the narrator's product) is implied in the fact that he appears in the novel before the senator is seen to notice (or evoke) him, and also in a couple of ironical comments, where he is spoken of as 'my stranger', and said to 'follow immediately behind the senator in our humble story' (I, 22, 43). The whole relationship is explained at the end of the first chapter:

Cerebral play is only a mask; beneath this mask takes place the invasion of the brain by forces unknown to us; and even though Apollon Apollonovich is fabricated from our brain, he will still be able to frighten with another startling existence that attacks at night. Apollon Apollonovich is endowed with the attributes of this existence; and with the attributes of this existence all his cerebral play is endowed too.

Once his brain has broken out in the mysterious stranger, that stranger exists – exists in fact: he will not disappear from the Petersburg prospects, so long as the senator exists with such thoughts, because thought, too, exists. So let our stranger be a real stranger! (I, 73)

Cerebral play, then, may be in the service of external, occult forces. The occult, which made only a fleeting appearance in *The Silver Dove* in the 'invisible enemies' of Dar'yal'sky and his mysterious adventures in the last chapter, is much more manifest in Bely's second novel. Not only are there several scenes in which the characters, particularly Dudkin, are confronted by occult visitors, but it is thus suggested that the entire system of relationships in the novel is governed by baneful powers. The duality of all the novel's central images does not contradict this fact; it does not provide beneficent opposites to the forces of negation. That duality is itself a symptom of the malady. That is why on closer examination all the apparent alternatives on which the novel is based are reducible to identity. East and West, revolution and reaction, father and son – these are not opposites, but warring embodiments of a single principle: Mongolism.

The first thing learnt about the Ableukhov family is that they are descended from a Russified Mongol Ab-Lai (I, 7).[19] The deeper link between them becomes explicit in the section describing the senator's 'second space'. He has a vision of a Mongol with the face of Nikolay Apollonovich, who asserts that there are no longer any paragraphs or rules (II, 55). The possibility is still given here of interpreting Mongolism as a destructive force to which Apollon Apollonovich is opposed, but that possibility is removed when the son later has a similar experience:

Nikolay Apollonovich rushed up to his guest – Turanian to Turanian (subordinate to master) with a pile of exercise books in his hand:
'Paragraph one: Kant (proof that Kant, too, was a Turanian).
'Paragraph two: the value, understood as nobody and nothing.
'Paragraph three: social relations built upon value.
'Paragraph four: the destruction of the Aryan world by the system of values.

'Conclusion: the age-old Mongol business.'
But the Turanian replied:
'The exercise has not been understood: instead of Kant should be the Prospect.
'Instead of value – numbering: by houses, floors and rooms for all time.
'Instead of a new order: the circulation of the citizens of the Prospect – even and in straight lines.
'Not the destruction of Europe – its stagnation ...
'That is the Mongol business ... ' (II, 205–6)

The Turanian then takes on the features of Apollon Apollonovich, and Nikolay Apollonovich realizes that he and his father, for all their apparent difference, are in the service of the same force.

The principle of the reduction of apparent opposites to identity is one that can be seen in operation throughout the novel. Since it affects all the characters and the political attitudes they stand for, it comes into play even in the plot. Not only is the outcome an anticlimax in the sense already discussed, but even if the assassination were to take place as planned it would only constitute the victory of one aspect of Mongolism over another – a revolution that perpetuates the evils of the regime it overthrows. The novel has all the appearance of a charmed circle.

The techniques by which this state of affairs is established in *Petersburg* extend beyond the plot and the characters to the most apparently insignificant details of imagery and description.[20] Some of the most pervasive imagery is derived direct from the idea of Mongolism. It is carried in the references to the Russo-Japanese War and the Manchurian hats worn by the islanders. It is associated with the colour yellow, which is used particularly to describe the Ableukhov house and the clothes of Lippanchenko. Although he is ostensibly a Ukrainian, Lippanchenko is said to look like a mixture of Semite and Mongol. In reply to Dudkin's question as to whether he is a Mongol, he declares that all Russians have Mongol blood in their veins. Dudkin suffers a particular recurrent nightmare, in the course of which the yellow patch of damp on the wallpaper in his room and the woodlice that abound there are transformed into threatening oriental faces. Sof'ya Petrovna likes to dress up in Japanese costume, and has a picture of Mount Fujiyama in her room. Mongolism is further associated with a series of tactile images referring to things variously slimy, particularly fish. The woodlice on Dudkin's wall belong to this series. The greasy salmon Lippanchenko is eating when first seen is another example, and is clearly akin to the sardines that Nikolay Apollonovich will not touch because he once ate too many, and the sardine tin in which the bomb is housed. Dudkin, for good measure, keeps his soap in a sardine tin, where it slides about in its own slime. Nikolay Apollonovich's 'frog-like slime' belongs here too; and the same word (*slyakot'*) is used for the human pulp, imagined in the event of the assassination's success.

The same feature can be seen in passages which on the surface tell of the past history or the motivation of the characters. Dudkin's occult visitation is given an alternative motivation through his confessed over-use of alcohol and tobacco. The question does not really arise, however, of whether the reader is required to believe in the occult or can dismiss the event as a hallucination. In Pushkin's *Bronze Horseman* we can assume that the peregrinations of the statue take place only in the sick mind of the hero. In Ivan Karamazov's interview with the devil, the other obvious literary precedent of this scene in *Petersburg*, such an interpretation is also available, though perhaps less obligatory. The lack of psychological realism in the parts of *Petersburg* that do not relate to the Ableukhov family drama makes this question idle in the case of Dudkin. The alternative motivation itself, although a certain psychological verisimilitude does emerge from it, serves principally the function of establishing further links in the imagery. It was, after all, the Flying Dutchman who set the inhabitants of the islands drinking, and Dudkin is merely following his precept under the guidance of Lippanchenko. When he explains his own attitudes to Nikolay Apollonovich he speaks of himself as a pianist for whom the masses are the keyboard; and he makes a point of stressing the word '*p'yanist*', which contains the word *p'yan*, meaning 'drunken'. Apollon Apollonovich attributes the red colour of the noses of middle-aged Russians to their immoderate consumption of the same commodities; and the colour red is associated with Nikolay Apollonovich through his red domino, and ultimately with both revolution and perverse sensuality.

In other instances, too, the apparently realistic motivation of the characters' actions is reduced on closer inspection to a system of imagery that points elsewhere. Dudkin's past history includes a period of exile in the Yakutsk region, as a result of which he came to acknowledge only one 'category' (a reference to Nikolay Apollonovich's preoccupation with Kant) – the 'category of ice'.

This serves to link him with the Ableukhovs. It is that symbolic association that matters, while any notion of the actual past history of the characters is of no consequence.

But what most claims attention about these all-encompassing patterns of imagery is their circularity. The further one pursues their ramifications, the more evident it is that one is eventually brought back by all routes to the same starting-point: the charmed circle which is the enclosed cranium of Apollon Apollonovich, his house, the city itself, the history of Russia. Or perhaps it is the novel, its author's mind, from which there is no escape. All choices are in the end the same, and the public on the streets, like the readers of the book, continue to 'circulate', just as Apollon Apollonovich would wish.

An essentially similar function is performed by the many literary references in *Petersburg*. With a few obvious exceptions like the Flying Dutchman – Wagner's ghost-ship that knows no haven, used to evoke Peter's nautical studies in Holland, or the echoes of *Anna Karenina* in the family relations of the Ableukhovs, they are taken from the traditional theme of Petersburg in nineteenth-century Russian literature, from Pushkin, Gogol' and Dostoyevsky.

No discussion of the novel can avoid mentioning the role played by the Bronze Horseman and the way in which Dudkin's fate parallels that of Pushkin's Yevgeny. The image of the statue gives rise not only to Dudkin's parody of it, in imitation of Yevgeny's, but also to other images related to Nikolay Apollonovich's childhood. Apollon Apollonovich recalls dandling him as a baby to the accompaniment of a ditty of his own invention:

Durachok, prostachok,	(Little fool, simpleton,
Kolen'ka tantsuyet,	Kolen'ka is dancing,
On nadel kolpachok,	Dunce's cap upon his head,
Na kone gartsuyet.	On a horse he's prancing.)

Later Nikolay Apollonovich recalls his nurse's and his father's recitation to him of Goethe's 'Erlkönig', in which the father, clutching his sick son on horseback, fails to save him (III, 118). The word *vsadnik* (horseman), established as a reference to the statue, occurs also in the context of 'the iron horsemen of Genghis Khan', an unambiguous image of Mongolism (III, 165–6). When the Bronze Horseman visits Dudkin he is spoken of as *Mednyy*, or *Metallicheskiy gost'* (Bronze or Metallic Guest), a reference to the title of Pushkin's 'little tragedy' *Kamennyy gost'* (*The Stone Guest*), his version of the

Don Juan legend, in which the statue visits the hero as a figure of retribution. The description of the city's inhabitants as 'neither men nor shadows' sounds as a faint echo of Pushkin's lines describing Yevgeny after he has lost his mind:

Ni to, ni syo, ni zhitel' sveta,
Ni prizrak myortvyy ...

(Neither one thing nor another, not an inhabitant of the world, nor yet a dead ghost ...)

The place where the murder of Lippanchenko occurs, the only occasion in the whole novel when the action moves outside the city, is a country *dacha* by the sea, where a sailing boat, mentioned for no otherwise apparent reason, bobs in the background, and is reminiscent in a general sense of the place where at the end of *The Bronze Horseman* Yevgeny's body is found beside the washed-up ruin of his fiancée's house.

'The Queen of Spades' appears not in Pushkin's own version, but in the operatic version by Tchaikovsky. Sof'ya Petrovna has cast herself in the role of Liza, and expects from Nikolay Apollonovich the passionate behaviour of the operatic Hermann.[21] His failure to meet her expectations in this respect is one of the reasons for her vindictiveness towards him later. The scene at the masked ball, in which she hands over to him the note with instructions about the bomb, is clearly a parody of Act 2 Scene 1 of Tchaikovsky's opera, in which Hermann, similarly at a masked ball, reads a note from Liza and later is given by her, masked, the key to her room.

References to Gogol' are somewhat less in evidence, but the insistent references to noses among the features to be observed on Nevsky Prospekt, and the consistent use of metonymy, the naming of articles of clothing, in particular various kinds of hat, to stand for the people wearing them, both provide covert reference to Gogol''s Petersburg tales. Bely himself pointed out how Apollon Apollonovich resembles simultaneously Akaky Akakievich and the 'important personage' from Gogol''s 'Greatcoat'.[22]

The allusions to Dostoyevsky reveal a complexity equal to that of the echoes of Pushkin. The themes of revolution and parricide are presented in such a way as to carry general reminiscences of *The Devils* and *The Brothers Karamazov*. But there are further echoes of specific scenes and situations. The scene between Nikolay Apollonovich and Morkovin is set in a drinking house that resembles the location of Raskol'nikov's first meeting with Marmeladov. Their conversation begins, however, in the manner of Smerdyakov's obsequious talk to Ivan Karamazov; and Morkovin, claiming to be an illegitimate brother of Nikolay, clearly thereby declares his own affinity to the Karamazov bastard. But the tone of the discussion soon changes, as Morkovin shows his double identity, and suddenly resembles the interrogation of Raskol'nikov by Porfiry Petrovich. Apollon Apollonovich, as he leaves the ball, goes out of his way to rescue a young girl who is being molested by a man; he does that which Raskol'nikov, on reflection, decided not to do. Nikolay Apollonovich in his 'god-like ice' bears a clear resemblance to Nikolay Stavrogin.[23]

Once the reader has become aware of the novel's tendency to such prolific allusiveness he begins to see similarities where it is no longer possible to be certain that they were deliberately planted by the author. The occasion when Nikolay Apollonovich winds up the clockwork mechanism of the bomb partly because he fears he will be unable to do so might carry an echo of Raskol'nikov, who sets out to commit his murder just when he has despaired of summoning the courage. It does not matter in the end whether such a parallel is intended or not, for the whole principle behind this network of literary allusions is, as E. Starikova has put it, one of 'maximum generalization'.[24] The effect is not to establish a specific set of comparisons of one thing with another, but through the gradual merging and fading of references to suggest an infinite comparability of anything with anything else. In this way the system of literary allusions performs exactly the same function as the system of interchangeable characters subsumed by the single myth or the general network of images that refer back upon themselves. No object or episode stands on its own in phenomenological clarity, but can always be related to, and in the end replaced by, another. The reader acquires a constant sense of *déjà-vu*, a sense that everything that happens has happened countless times before and is stored in the receding corridors of memory. The world of the novel seems to be hermetically sealed.

It would take an apocalypse to destroy the charmed circle that Bely has constructed here. And the novel contains numerous references to that idea. The Bronze Horseman himself is associated with a notion of Russia's destiny as a 'leap over history', a great battle with the Mongols in the course of which Petersburg itself will disappear (I, 140–1). The murder of Lippanchenko is spoken of in anticipation in very similar terms:

under the blow of the metal that splits stones Lippanchenko will fly apart, the attic will collapse and Petersburg will be destroyed; the caryatid will be destroyed under the blow of the metal; and the bare head of Ableukhov, from the blow to Lippanchenko, will collapse into two pieces. (III, 102)

Both Dudkin and Nikolay Apollonovich are forced to realize that nothing can change until the apocalypse comes. Dudkin, in his interview with the Bronze Horseman, comes to the realization that 'everything past, together with all that was to come, was only a spectral transition through ordeals until the Archangel's trump' (III, 102). When Nikolay Apollonovich has understood his full responsibility for the assassination plan he experiences a desire to return to childhood, to a state of innocence, but realizes 'there can be no answers yet; the answer will come later – in an hour, in a year, in five years, or maybe even more – in a hundred years or a thousand; but the answer will come' (III, 122). D. Burkhart has pointed out a number of images in the novel which may be traced back to the Book of Revelation: fire, smoke, ash, dust, the eagle, the lion, the panther, the horse.[25]

Within the novel's action there seems to be no event possessing an apocalyptic standing. Dudkin's murder of Lippanchenko might perhaps be read as some provisional victory over Mongolism; indeed his madness has been interpreted as evidence of his accession to a higher truth.[26] In his *Third Symphony* Bely did use the idea of madness with such a connotation, but it does not seem an appropriate reading here. Dudkin is too clearly identified as a victim, and there is nothing in the text to support the idea that his madness is to be interpreted positively. Indeed the murder by one of the sons, at the instigation of one of the fathers, of another of the fathers, seems to possess the same senseless circularity as the rest of the novel. The apocalyptic event, promised from this murder, fails to take place.

But what of the bomb? Its connection with the forces of chaos is clear in the viscous sardine tin it inhabits and its route of arrival across the bridge from the islands. But that by no means exhausts its associations. In the course of the novel Nikolay Apollonovich becomes more and more closely associated with the bomb, until in one scene he actually identifies himself with it. This takes place in a dream, after which he wakes up to find his head resting on the sardine tin that contains the bomb. Recalling this occasion later, he decides that the plan to kill his father was thought not by his head, but by the bomb. Now chronologically the plan to assassinate the senator took shape before the bomb was delivered to Nikolay Apollonovich. If the bomb is responsible for the plan it must have existed in Nikolay Apollonovich's head before it was seen to exist in external reality. In this way it can be seen to conform to the same pattern of genesis as the city itself. A further ambiguity enters, however, through the series of images relating to expansion, a series that necessarily culminates in the bomb, which is thought of as liable to produce 'a rapid expansion of gases'. The idea of expansion is contained in Apollon Apollonovich's cardiac complaint, known as 'expansion of the heart', and also in a childhood fantasy of Nikolay Apollonovich's, in which he swallowed a rubber ball called Pepp Peppovich Pepp, which expanded inside him. There is a phonetic association between the word for ball, or sphere (*shar*) and those denoting expansion (*shirit'sya, rasshireniye*). In *Glossolalia* Bely used these words for examples of the way in which the combination of *sh* and *r* rendered the sensation of the etheric body (the next stage of spiritual evolution).[27] The image of explosion was always one of Bely's favourite ways of expressing the idea of an apocalyptic transformation, and the identification of the self that undergoes spiritual transformation with a bomb recurs later, too, in *Notes of an Eccentric*. The imagery of expansion and explosion in *Petersburg* appears to stand in a relation of parodic quasi-identity to that of radiation from a centre. That notion is expressed through the words denoting 'circulation' – *tsirkulyar, tsirkulyatsiya, tsirkulirovat'* – though here too an ambiguity is introduced when the phrase '*tsirkuliruyet brauning*' (there circulates a revolver) is smuggled in (I, 20).

It is not to be expected that any major image in this novel should have a single and unambiguous meaning. The relation of the bomb to the forces of destruction cannot be overlooked. But there is sufficient evidence that the image also contains, through its other associations, something of the idea of a real spiritual transformation, indicating the potentiality in the Ableukhovs, particularly in Nikolay Apollonovich, for an act of self-transcendence such as the theory of Symbolism discusses. This then induces the reader to look for a sense in which the explosion at the end might signify, or might in other circumstances have signified, the performance of such an act. In a comment written three or four years after completing the novel, Bely wrote that its subject was the failure, through lack of courage, of Nikolay Apollonovich to blow up the yellow house of Ahriman, as he knew he should.[28] Ahriman, in theosophical or anthroposophical parlance, is the evil spirit devoted to the maintenance of the status quo, who prevents human spiritual evolution. The yellow house is, of course, the house of the Ableukhovs, identified in the novel with Apollon Apollonovich's head. This suggests that had the assassination taken place Nikolay Apollonovich would have achieved the desired transformation. But that is to ignore the Mongol associations of the bomb, and to overlook the vividly gruesome way in which the possibility of successful assassination is projected in the novel. There does not seem to be any conceivable alternative outcome of the plot in which a successful explosion could indeed be interpreted as the achievement on Nikolay Apollonovich's part of the apocalyptic spiritual transformation which is the only possible positive resolution to the problem. Nevertheless it is worth mentioning in passing that Bely did pursue this reading of the image, and in the dramatized versions of the novel on which he worked in the 1920s produced an ending in which the explosion is identified with the revolution in a positive sense, and the last words are given to Nikolay Apollonovich, who exclaims: 'I said we were all bombs, and look – we're exploding!'[29]

The failure of Nikolay Apollonovich accounts for his appearance as a parody of Christ.[30] The idea of crucifixion is associated fleetingly with Dudkin, where he says of himself: 'my favourite pose during insomnia, you know, is to stand by the wall and spreadeagle myself, spread out my arms on either side' (I, 130). But in the case of Nikolay Apollonovich the theme is developed in such a way as to make his last encounter with Likhutin a parody of Golgotha. Apollon Apollonovich has a vision of his son crucified (III, 205–6). Likhutin sees him in an aureole, and in reply to his apology for reading the letter Nikolay Apollonovich says: 'You knew not what you did' (III, 202). Ada Steinberg has shown a number of other details in this scene which reinforce the parallel with Christ. The identification is dependent on Nikolay Apollonovich's refusal to admit his responsibility for the assassination plan, and the falseness of the role is quickly shown. He expects to hear a voice say to him: 'You have suffered for my sake: I am standing over you'; but no such voice is heard, and the narrator continues: 'Why was there no voice of reconciliation: "You have suffered for my sake"? Because he had suffered for no one's sake: he had suffered for himself' (III, 202–3).

The Christ-parody of Nikolay Apollonovich has its double in the episodic figure of the 'white domino', matching the 'red domino' of Nikolay. This figure, also spoken of as 'someone tall and sad', is glimpsed at crucial moments by several of the characters. Sof'ya Petrovna is the first to see him. As she prepares to leave the ball the white domino appears. At first she thinks it is her husband, come to take her home, but realizes her mistake when the figure says to her: 'You all deny me: I keep watch over you all. You deny me, and then you call me . . . ' (II, 108). Dudkin sees him after his penultimate visit to Lippanchenko, before his occult visitation. To him the figure says nothing, although Dudkin has a burning desire to speak to him. He is addressed by someone else as Misha (III, 71). Nikolay Apollonovich sees him on two occasions, once when he is leaving the ball, on which occasion the figure is identified as a police officer (II, 120), and once in the later scene of his wish to return to childhood. He seeks reassurance from the white domino, but realizes there can be no answers yet.

Although this enigmatic figure does not satisfy the demands that the characters are disposed to make of him, they all experience him as a kind of guardian. This is ironically sustained by the identification of him as a police officer, and more seriously supported by the use of the name Misha. The archangel Michael was supposed by the anthroposophists to be the guardian angel of Russia. He appears here as the frail harbinger of a redemption that is not seen to come about.[31]

The explosion of the bomb is not the very end of the novel. It is followed by a short epilogue describing very briefly the lives of the Ableukhovs thereafter. Already in the eighth chapter a change in emphasis can be seen, away from the political and cosmic theme of revolution and Mongolism, towards the private and domestic theme of the reunion of the Ableukhov family. It has been noted that the motif of reconciliation and reunion runs throughout the novel, affecting also the relations between Sof'ya Petrovna and Likhutin, and between Lippanchenko and his mistress Zoya Fleysh.[32] As with the Ableukhovs, whose reunion is in one sense no more than an ironic hiatus before the inevitable explosion, these reconciliations are partial and imperfect. The disruption of inter-personal relations was one of the symptoms of cultural crisis that Bely diagnosed, and there is a clear coherence between this theme and the larger issues that the novel treats. It is nevertheless true that the last chapter is much closer in tone to the conventional nineteenth-century domestic novel than is any earlier part of *Petersburg*.[33] It was noticed that a similar shift takes place in the final chapter of *The Silver Dove*, as the hero appears to exchange his wide symbolic connotations for a narrower personal destiny. If the theme of 'return' underlay that ending, as V. Stanevich suggested, than the same can be said of the ending of *Petersburg*, as the reconciliation of the Ableukhov family means for Nikolay something of a return to childhood and innocence.

The epilogue takes up none of the themes that have run through the rest of the novel, and depicts no characters other than the three Ableukhovs. None of them is in Petersburg, and the city is not even mentioned. Apollon Apollonovich, writing his memoirs in the country, still follows his son's activities. Nikolay Apollonovich is in Egypt, where he has come to the conclusion that 'all culture is like this mouldering head [the Sphinx]: everything is dead; nothing is left' (III, 275). He also visits Nazareth. He has given up Kant for Skovoroda, and has written a monograph on the Egyptian Book of the Dead (Daufsekhruti).

These references come as new material and cannot be explained from the text of the novel alone. The epilogue acquires a certain opaqueness as a result. But inasmuch as the epilogue asserts the cancellation of all previous culture, it would be inappropriate for it to take up the themes derived from that culture. The references can be elucidated from other sources and the esoteric meaning of the epilogue largely revealed. Bely's notes on his own visit to Egypt in 1911 show how he felt he had discovered in the pyramids and the Sphinx emblems of the abstract and alien culture in which he found he was himself living.[34] The Book of the Dead was placed in the graves of the deceased to help them in the life to come; this idea of death and re-birth is the clearest statement of the epilogue's main theme. The mention of Nazareth suggests a truer affinity with Christ than was present in the earlier parody. It has been shown that Skovoroda, the eighteenth-century Ukrainian religious philosopher, was regarded by Bely, and by many of his contemporaries, as an important precursor of the spiritual revival to which his own efforts were directed.[35] It has also been suggested that the epilogue indicates, through the experience of Apollon Apollonovich, who has forgotten ordinary words – the language of the former abstract culture – but remembers exactly the name Daufsekhruti, the possibility of a renewed attitude to language, a re-birth of the magical language spoken of in 'The Magic of Words'.[36]

It seems clear, then, that the epilogue intimates a replacement of the 'eternal recurrence' of the novel's eight chapters by a return of a different kind, a retrieval of the innocence of man's childhood and the commencement of a new culture. It can be no more than an intimation, and the obscurity of the references is inevitable. The epilogue stands in a relation to the rest of the novel very similar to that of the epilogue of *Crime and Punishment*; the conversion of Nikolay Apollonovich, like that of Rodion Raskol'nikov, is the beginning of a lengthy process of regeneration, which must be a separate story; 'our present story is ended'. There is little in *Petersburg* that can strictly be called anthroposophical. The occult references in the novel belong to the general Hermetic tradition which is not original to Steiner and with which Bely was well familiar before 1912. His deepening commitment to anthroposophy was taking shape at the same time as the writing of the novel, and by the end of 1913 both were complete. *Petersburg* is the full and final statement of the theme of the crisis of European culture on which Bely had been working since the beginning of his career. It is in the novel that follows, where Bely adopts the vantage point of one who is himself commencing that lengthy process of regeneration, and returns to childhood for his material, that the distinctive, constructive qualities of anthroposophy make themselves felt, and the task of creating a new culture is approached.[37]

Stylistically *Petersburg* represents a considerable advance on *The Silver Dove* and marks the establishment of the prose style with which Bely exercised his greatest influence on writers of the next decade. There are traces, particularly in the *Sirin* edition, of the Gogolian 'skaz' that was typical of *The Silver Dove*, but the style of *Petersburg* is in general far less derivative. The most significant advance lies in the way in which the language of the novel is made to participate in the creative process enacted in the minds of the characters and the narrator. At one level this involves the attribution of particular qualities to particular sounds. Within the text it is seen most clearly in the use as a leitmotif of the sound *-uuu-*, which is spoken of as 'the song of the year 1905' (I, 108; I, 139; II, 17), and in the declaration that the sound *y* possesses a Mongol character. In this latter case one of the words particularly chosen to demonstrate the fact is the word *ryba* (fish), which belongs in the Mongol series also by virtue of its sliminess. Such identification of sound and meaning is evidently a step towards the kind of theory Bely later enunciated in *Glossolalia*, and it is not surprising to find further such identifications there, and elsewhere in Bely's later work, that suggest other similar parallels in the novel. In *Gogol''s Craftsmanship* Bely mentions the preponderance in the novel of *pl, bl,* and *kl* combinations, associating them with the sense of pressure and impending explosion. These combinations are present not only in the names of the Ableukhovs and Lippanchenko, but also in the leitmotif '*lak, losk i blesk*' (lacquer, gleam, brilliance) of the Ableukhov house, and in the name Pepp Peppovich Pepp, associated with Nikolay Apollonovich and the bomb. There thus arises a kind of phonetic leitmotif, linking together all the main strands of imagery and plot. Bely also notes the presence of the sounds *s* and *r*; *r* is associated with explosion, and *s*, along with *sh*, with the expansion of gases – either in the stomachs of the characters (from over-indulgence in sardines) or in the bomb.[38] Writing in the Soviet Union in the 1930s Bely naturally excluded from *Gogol''s Craftsmanship* any assertions about the occult nature of sounds, such as he makes about the combination of *sh* and *r* in *Glossolalia*. Other descriptions in *Glossolalia* come close to those in *Gogol''s Craftsmanship*: *s* is said to connote light, *r* is the sound of energy, while *k* is associated with suffocation, death and murder, and *p* with 'dried-up form and the old age of animals' (Apollon Apollonovich in his less explosive aspects, perhaps).[39]

These descriptions clearly indicate ways in which the images of the novel develop out of each other through phonetic association. Helene Hartmann-Flyer has shown how the words '*sardinnitsa uzhasnogo soderzhaniya*' (sardine-tin of horrible content), used as a euphemism for the bomb, are gradually introduced partially, individually and separately in other contexts, before being ultimately composed into that formulation as Nikolay comes to the full realization of his plight.[40] A similar device on a smaller scale can be seen in a section of Chapter I where chance snatches of conversation on the street are distorted and re-assembled to produce words denoting that a bomb is to be thrown at Senator Ableukhov (I, 30ff.). The device of allowing meanings unintended by the speakers to appear between the lines of conversation had already been used by Bely in *The Silver Dove*, and indeed in his earlier stories too.[41] But the much more consistent and systematic use of related devices in *Petersburg* creates a sense that events flow inadvertently from the minds of all the participants, and even from the environment of the city itself. The language performs its own 'cerebral play', regardless of anyone's conscious intentions.

As regards the rhythmic character of his prose *Petersburg* likewise first establishes the principles by which Bely's mature style is to be recognized. The prose of this novel shows an easily perceptible tendency towards the rhythmic regularity of verse. As has been noted by critics, the rhythm and euphony are important as organizing principles in this novel where the action refuses to satisfy traditional expectations of linearity.[42]

Differences in the rhythmic character of the two main editions of *Petersburg* have been singled out as a way of distinguishing between the two texts. Ivanov-Razumnik argued that while the *Sirin* edition was fundamentally anapaestic, the Berlin edition was typically amphibrachic.[43] The analytical methods he used have since been rightly called into question; he disregarded word boundaries and punctuation to an unacceptable extent. In fact, his determination of anapaestic or amphibrachic character depends solely upon the position of the first stress in the passage under analysis, whether it is preceded by one or by two unstressed syllables. He also considered that the later edition showed a purer rhythmic outline. In this latter point G. Janecek, his chief critic, concurs, asserting that while the change from anapaest to amphibrach cannot be sustained, the second edition shows an intensification of the ternary character. The statistical evidence for this consists in a rise from 48% to 52% in the number of instances (in a given sample) where the interstress intervals are two syllables. Janecek's statistics also show an increase of 5% in words beginning with a single unstressed syllable before the stress, and a decrease of 3% in words with two unstressed syllables before the first stress.[44] Assuming the same proportions to operate in words at the beginning of what Ivanov-Razumnik took to be rhythmic units, this fact would correspond with his distinction of anapaest and amphibrach. This suggests that both critics are observing the same phenomena, though calling them by different names.

Both also argue that the character of the novel is significantly altered by this change in the rhythm of its prose. Ivanov-Razumnik developed at some length the viewpoint that it denotes no less than a reversal of Bely's attitude to the revolution: that whereas the earlier edition saw the prospect of revolution as destructive, the later one, completed when it had already taken place, demonstrated an affirmative attitude towards it.[45] J. Holthusen has responded that however much the rhythm may have changed the action and the imagery of the novel are the same in both editions, and could therefore not possibly support Ivanov-Razumnik's argument.[46] To this it may be added that Bely's attitude to the revolution had itself changed by 1922 from the enthusiasm of 1917, when he had been close to Ivanov-Razumnik, and that since he was now abroad Ivanov-Razumnik could presumably not know about that further change.[47]

Janecek argues more circumspectly that the Berlin edition removes a certain ponderousness, and that this change is appropriate, since heavy style 'runs counter to the tension and rapid forward motion of the plot'.[48] This conclusion matches that of Bugayeva and Petrovsky, who, without mentioning rhythm, declared that the general condensation of the later edition, affecting mainly epithets, definitions and parallelisms, led to an overall acceleration of the text.[49] It is, however, far from obvious that such a change of tempo is required from the point of view of the plot, which, although it engenders a great deal of tension, does so precisely at the expense of not moving forward rapidly. The novel abounds in devices of delay, retardation and misdirection, and it is just as plausible to argue that this aspect of the novel is better served by the ponderousness and sometimes laborious narratorial intervention of the *Sirin* edition.

It is instructive that the same conclusion about the acceleration of the later text can be reached without even mentioning rhythm. The features adduced by Bugayeva and Petrovsky are probably more immediately apparent to the reader comparing the editions, and contribute more to his perception of their differences. The reduction of epithets and definitions has a marked effect upon the narrative voice, which must be perceived as the source of the judgements they contain. The narrative voice loses definition in the Berlin edition; even dialogues lose their precision, with uncertainty creeping in about which character speaks which words. The impression is in places akin to that of Blok's poem *The Twelve*, where separate voices are used in separate sections without any organizing narrator. The consequence is that an even greater organizing function is borne by the phonetic properties of the language, the rhythm and euphony. Perhaps the difference between the two editions lies not so much in the change of rhythm as in the greater functional importance of rhythm in the later version. This change is in keeping with the development of Bely's prose in the years after the completion of *Petersburg*, in that it accentuates certain features of his style that first became manifest in that novel, while reducing other features that linked it to *The Silver Dove*.

The idea of shortening the text of *Petersburg* came to Bely within months of the completion of the *Sirin* edition. A letter to Ivanov-Razumnik of 2 July 1914 tells how the publisher of the planned German translation insisted on accommodating the text in one volume, and that in the process of re-writing that was thus forced upon him, Bely came to the conclusion that the novel gained from it, and that he would reduce it by some 150 pages for a new Russian edition.[50] Nevertheless the final Berlin edition is essentially the work of Bely's period in Berlin. This was a period of his life when he was greatly concerned to interpret, or re-interpret his past experience. It is the time during which he wrote an extensive quantity of memoirs and also revised his poetry for a new edition, designed to reveal with greater clarity his spiritual development.[51] It is generally agreed that the revisions of his poems in this edition are not improvements, and subsequent editions have reverted to the original texts of the first editions.[52] The generally valid textological argument that the canonical text is the last lifetime edition produced under the author's aegis is not held as valid in the case of Bely's poetry.[53] In the case of *Petersburg* the motives for revising the text cannot be reduced to such an attempt to re-interpret the author's own past, yet neither can such an attempt be entirely excluded as a motive. Reference to the general textological rule is not therefore sufficient as a reason for giving preference to the later edition as the canonical text of the novel.[54] A decision on this question has ultimately to be made on aesthetic criteria.

The Berlin edition in its final form comes chronologically after

Kotik Letayev, *The Baptized Chinaman* and *Notes of an Eccentric*. Bely's novelistic technique, as will be seen, underwent more than one change during this period. It is only in the more regular rhythm that the Berlin edition approximates to the styles of the later novels; their narrative manners and linguistic inventiveness are not reflected in the revised *Petersburg*. This is inevitable, since the revisions consist entirely in excisions. It means, though, that the greater importance that falls to the novel's acoustic properties does not receive the support that is given to it in other late novels by other structural devices. To speak of the Berlin edition of *Petersburg* as parallel to *Kotik Letayev* in demonstrating Bely's 'definitive resolution of the problem of how to handle rhythm in poetic prose'[55] is insufficient, as it disregards the considerable differences between the prose of the two novels in all respects other than rhythm. If all the characteristics of the prose are taken into account it is difficult to place the Berlin edition anywhere in Bely's development. His prose developed from the *Sirin* edition of *Petersburg* to *Kotik Letayev* and onwards from there; there are no positive qualities in the Berlin text that are not present in the *Sirin* text, and no developments that are not better exemplified in *Kotik Letayev*.

The strongest argument against the revised text, in either the Berlin version or that of 1928, is that the alterations Bely made were both inconsistent and damaging. It was first pointed out by Ivanov-Razumnik that the evident haste with which the revision was done had led to inconsistencies and on occasion complete distortion of the meaning.[56] Dolgopolov has added to this a detailed demonstration of the way in which many highly effective passages in the *Sirin* edition have quite lost their force in the truncated form in which they appear in the revision.[57] The inability of the revised text to stand entirely on its own is shown by the fact that the recent translators into English and French, both preferring in general the later edition, have been constrained on occasions to resort to the original text in order to restore the meaning. The more this issue is examined, the more it becomes apparent that it is the *Sirin* edition of *Petersburg* that must be regarded as the canonical text of the novel.

5

Kotik Letayev

The idea of writing a trilogy of novels remained with Bely after the completion of *Petersburg*. There is a sense in which *The Silver Dove* and *Petersburg* can be regarded as thesis and antithesis, the former novel concentrating on 'the dark abyss of the East', and the latter upon the most traditional symbol of Russia's westernization. Yet already in *Petersburg* these opposites were seen to be ultimately indistinguishable from each other, and the same line of thought is pursued in much of Bely's theoretical writing.[1] That does not, however, mean that they are synthesized. Such a synthesis was the dream of Sergey Musatov, and of Dar'yal'sky himself, and, expressed in somewhat different terminology, was the main burden of Bely's ideas about Symbolism.[2] Clearly it is because of their separateness that they are identical in their destructive qualities and the culture built upon them is consigned to extinction. They will be synthesized only by a new cultural beginning, and that is what Bely believed he had found in anthroposophy.

The self-conscious narrator of *Petersburg* had created a situation in which it was impossible to tell whether the narrated action was supposed to be taking place in some replica of the real world or solely in the mind of the novel's author.[3] That state of affairs may rightly be regarded as part of the ironic nature of that novel, but it corresponds also, and more fundamentally, to an element in Bely's perception that was confirmed and systematized by his introduction to anthroposophy. The identity of the inner and the outer worlds means that the content of the self and the content of the outer world are the same, and thus that the examination of the self is the surest route to knowledge of the world. Just as cultural products are seen as the external expression of human psychic conditions, so the individual soul, properly searched, reveals itself as the locus of all cultural forces and values. This is the burden of practically all that Bely wrote between the completion of *Petersburg* in the late autumn of 1913 and his departure from Russia to Berlin almost exactly eight years later.[4]

It is to that proper search of the self that Bely's next novels are devoted. Crucial to its understanding is the anthroposophical doctrine of recapitulation. The adult who is initiated into anthroposophy learns to recapitulate his own childhood, understanding it as the recapitulation of the psychic history of the race. That history itself consists of innumerable recapitulations, so that the child and the adult whose consciousness provides the focus are merely the two most recent stages in a process that stretches back infinitely. It stretches forward nearly infinitely too, but is understood as a positive evolutionary process, and the present transition, the ascent to the new stage represented by the initiated adult, is regarded as the essential step that generates the new culture. The charmed circle of *Petersburg*, with its endless iterations of an eternally unresolved conflict, now turns into a soaring spiral.

It appears to have been Bely's intention to describe, as the third part of the trilogy, one complete cycle of this spiral. He envisaged a massive, multi-volume work which would carry the overall title *Epopee – My Life*. The three works *Kotik Letayev*, *The Baptized Chinaman* and *Notes of an Eccentric* were all to be parts of it, although Bely's accounts of their precise relationship are not entirely consistent. *Kotik Letayev* and *The Baptized Chinaman* are thematically contiguous, the former depicting the author's life up to the age of four, the latter at the age of five. In a plan, dating from 1925, for an unrealized edition of his collected works, Bely indicated that they were both parts of the uncompleted *Epopee*, and that they should be designated *Kotik Letayev, Parts One and Two*.[5] The first edition of *Kotik Letayev* bears the subtitle *First Part of the Novel, My Life;*[6] and in a letter to Sologub of 1915 *My Life* is stated to be the third party of the trilogy *East or West*.[7] The proposed relationship of *Notes of an Eccentric* to the two parts of *Kotik Letayev* is explained in a prefatory note to the first published version of *The Baptized Chinaman*. It was to be the beginning of a series of volumes comprising the introduction to the *Epopee* proper. In this note, however, no mention is made of *Kotik Letayev; The Baptized Chinaman* is designated as the first chapter of the novel *The Crime of Nikolay Letayev*, which is the first volume of the *Epopee*.[8] In a similar note to *Notes of an Eccentric* Bely speaks of it as the first volume of a work which will appear in

a number of volumes.[9] Some two thirds of the work published in
1922 as *Notes of an Eccentric* appeared in 1919 under the title
Return to the Homeland, which was stated to be the first part of
Notes of an Eccentric, itself designated as the first volume of *Ego,
an Epopee*.[10]

While *Kotik Letayev* and *The Baptized Chinaman* recount the
author's childhood, *Notes of an Eccentric* is concerned with the
experiences of the adult during and after the period of mystical
insight and initiation which made the re-interpretation of his childhood possible. Although there is no documentary evidence for
this, it appears likely that the entire *Epopee* would have consisted
of an introduction describing the initiation, followed by a series of
autobiographical novels proceeding all the way from early childhood back to the initiation period. However, it is of no great
consequence whether that supposition is true or not, since the
three works as they stand differ from each other in too many ways
for the further pursuit of their unrealized affinities to be fruitful.

Bely's third novel, *Kotik Letayev*, was written in Switzerland in
1915 and 1916.[11] It has for subject-matter the author's recollections of his earliest childhood, his awakening self-awareness and
perception of the external world. It does not allow precedence to
the normal adult interpretation of the child's experience. Bely's
child has access to valuable states of being from which the ordinary
adult is excluded, and it is to the retrieval of these states that the
novel is devoted. It is necessarily the novel's imagery that provides
the vehicle for this process. Frequent reference is also made to
objective facts such as the child's illness or growth, or the true
identity of characters to whom the child attributes mythical identi-
ties, but the adult viewpoint expressed in these does not cancel the
child's understanding. If the adults of the novel see the child's
condition as caused by these objective facts, the viewpoint of the
narrator is that both are reflections of profounder events. The
external occurrences themselves stand in no particular causal connection to each other, and cannot be thought of as constituting a
plot. *Kotik Letayev* does not have a plot in the conventional
meaning of a series of events in the real world linked by material
causes.

The need to retrieve the child's condition is, of course, also an
adult's insight, but that of an adult who has transcended the view

of material causation represented by the novel's adult characters. The novel is introduced by the narrator, who describes in the prologue the narrative standpoint, or perhaps vantage point, from which it is written. The narrator is at a half-way stage in life: thirty-five years old and standing on a mountain from which he can survey the route by which he has ascended, as well as glimpsing less clearly the path by which he has yet to descend. The mountain ascent expresses a real experience of the author's,[12] which he felt to have, and which acquires in the text, a symbolic import. The path traversed consists of conceptions of the world that he has now rejected (*bylyye smysly*); but from the summit to which that path has brought him, he can see again the child of thirty-two years previously, and it is his new-found understanding of the child that will guide him on the path down. He is himself a child in a new sense: just beginning to develop occult awareness. This identity of adult narrator and child hero over a gap of time that has led them apart but together again creates the complex narrative attitude of the novel; the voices alternate between that of the narrator immersed in the child's recollected experience, that of the narrator standing aside and commenting on that experience, and those of other adults expressing the views of adult common sense, views of which hero and narrator conspire to disabuse the reader. It is only in relation to these last voices that there is any trace of irony. Author and narrator in *Kotik Letayev* are essentially identical, and there is no place for the ironical use that Bely made of his narrator in the earlier novels.

The past that the narrator surveys consists of rigid, petrified concepts; the new vision to which he looks forward is expressed in the image of a rainbow in the dancing drops of a waterfall (p.13). This image is borrowed from the first scene of *Faust, Part Two*, where Faust turns away blinded from the rising sun, but catches its reflection in just such a vision of a rainbow. Faust's concluding line: 'Am farb'gen Abglanz haben wir das Leben', is one of Bely's favourite quotations from Goethe; he uses it to express the idea of the non-static, metaphoric thinking, with which the anthroposophist would replace conceptual thought.[13] The concept corresponds to one of the drops of water, which on its own cannot create a rainbow. Such a relation of concept to truth is also expressed in the laborious arithmetic of *On the Meaning of Cognition*. This flexibility, then, this plurality of possible interpretation, is something that narrator and hero, adult anthroposophist and untutored child, have in common.

The novel follows the child's development roughly from the age of three to the age of five. The child at the end of the novel no longer possesses as fully as at the beginning the features that the narrator sought to retrieve. The child's development, clearly, must be towards that state of ordinary adulthood that the narrator has transcended. Yet that was the only path to the mountain-top of the present. The process of development involves both gain and loss, and is evidently thought of as necessary. But what the novel is concerned with is not so much the process itself as the panorama that emerges from the superimposition of the two perspectives. In re-immersing himself in his childhood experience the narrator adds a further facet to it; and the child at the end of the novel anticipates, in the image of crucifixion, the condition that is the narrator's in the epilogue, the very condition that has led to the writing of the novel but also looks beyond it. The temporal gap between hero and narrator is removed by this two-way reflection and the notion of development in one-dimensional time is absorbed, without being cancelled, into a pattern that suggests spiral evolution.

The narrator is recapitulating his childhood, while the child recapitulates earlier stages of evolution. This double recapitulation is expressed in the recurrent motif 'memory of memory'. Clearly what the child is remembering are things which took place long before his birth, and this fact is accounted for by the other crucial anthroposophical tenet embodied in the work. The spiritual essence of the human being, the ego, which resides in an eternal world of the spirit between its successive incarnations, does not enter the body immediately upon birth, but some time between the second and third year, when the physical body is first able to receive it. Once descended, this ego swiftly loses contact with the spiritual world it came from. The earliest recollections of Kotik Letayev, however, are of the very period of the ego's descent, before it was finally imprisoned in the physical body. Kotik thus has access, if only faintly, to spiritual states prior to incarnation and is aware of having recapitulated pre-cultural stages of evolution. The descended ego – the child in whom consciousness has awakened – then begins to recapitulate the cultural process by which man subjugates the chaos of the external world. The first chapter of the novel brings the child up to the beginnings of culture, while the rest takes him on through later stages culminating in an anticipation of crucifixion, which to the anthroposophist is the central event of cosmic evolution.

An examination of the structure of the first chapter can demonstrate the way in which the plurality of possible interpretations is realized in the novel, and provide a paradigm for the reading of the rest. The necessary first function of the imagery is, of course, to induce in the reader something akin to the remembered experience of the hero; there is no point in reproducing many details of it here, since they could not conceivably replace the experience of reading the novel. A certain amount of the imagery is very obscure and probably in the end only fully accessible to a trained anthroposophist; but enough can be fathomed by the ordinary attentive reader to make an analysis of this kind fruitful.[14]

The first three sections are concerned with the descent of consciousness into the body; consciousness is regarded as prior, in that until the two are united it is consciousness, and not the body, that does the remembering. The earliest state of consciousness, then, is an awareness of itself with no differentiation into I and non-I. The body is experienced as an absence, a vacuum, a sponge which sucks consciousness in. Thought can enter the body, uniting it with the universe, and creating the division of world and thought. This idea is expressed in a metaphor which becomes one of the dominant metaphors of the chapter. World and thought are portions of solidity emerging from the seas of myth. This world of cosmic images, with which 'the blood pulsates' (p.19), was a familiar home until the arrival of thought; thereafter those ancient seas receded, but they can return to flood the solid ground, and thought is the ark on which man sails away to a new world. There are two main anthroposophical ideas underlying this passage. The idea of spiral evolution, involving recapitulation, emerges in the parallels evoked here between the Biblical flood, the myth of Atlantis, and the emergence of solidity from fluidity which is the transition from the previous planetary condition (that of the moon) to the present one of the earth. Parallel evolutionary events, which might be thought of as existing on quite different time-scales, are superimposed on one another in just the same way as the narrator's and hero's perspectives in the novel's overall structure. At the same time Steiner's view of the nature of myth is utilized; he understood myths as expressions, in the era of human development just prior to the emergence of thought proper, of the actions of spiritual forces experienced in the individual soul. In the evolution of the individual this corresponds to the period immediately prior to the descent of consciousness. The realities that the myths express can be retrieved through occult initiation.[15] It is thus doubly appropriate that myths should be used to express the newly initiated narrator's recollection of this stage of his childhood. At the same time the idea that just beneath the level of consciousness there lies an area of experience that can impose itself upon the unwilling conscious subject is one that runs throughout the novel, and provides that transparency of the real world which governs the experience of both child and adult.

The sea-metaphor is then transferred from the idea of myth to that of birth, while elements of actual myths continue to be used to describe the recollected sensations of this pre-conscious condition. Evidently the descended consciousness is thought of as being able to retain in memory something of the pre-conscious experience of other parts of the human body it has entered. The experience of the moment of emergence from the womb is rendered as a sensation of having one's legs bound, of resembling a serpent. The combination of this idea with that of emergence from the seas, which provides the title as well as the governing metaphor of the third section, serves also to evoke, if only dimly, some idea of a biological evolution which is also being recapitulated. Kotik's thoughts at this stage are said to be 'serpent-legged myths', and his experience to be an experience of the Titan. Steiner, discussing the myth of Prometheus, interprets the Titans as 'the force of will, proceeding as nature (Kronos) from the original universal spirit (Uranus)'.[16] Prometheus, it will be remembered, was the son of a Titan; Kronos was the youngest Titan, who dethroned his father Uranus, and was in turn dethroned by Zeus, with the help of Prometheus.[17] The Titan, that Kotik experiences here, is thus the part of man that belongs to base nature, as opposed to Zeus. The rest of the third section appears to be a version of the myth of Prometheus in terms similar to Steiner's rendition of it. The image of the serpent also gives rise to the image of the comet, a metaphor for thought, which descends into the sea of sensation – the body prior to its arrival.

What happens in these three sections, then, is that a single basic image, the emergence of something solid from an encasing sheath of fluidity, is made to render numerous different processes: various stages of cosmic development, the mythic stage of cultural development, the birth of the individual human body. Each may evoke any of the others, none has absolute priority over the others; when an adult voice is heard explaining the child's consequent anxiety as caused by 'growth', this simply adds a further material interpretation to the several spiritual ones already available. The plurality of possible understanding is created in such polymorphous images.

One of the images expressing the idea of emergence is the image of a soap-bubble emerging from a straw. The bubble expands and bursts. Expanded, it has a world within it; burst, it is a drop within the world. This alternation embodies the ancient mystical intuition of the identity of the sky within and the sky without, the idea that 'everything is within me, I am in everything' (p.26).[18] The process of emergence is paralleled by a process of encasement; the body emerges, while the ego becomes encased in the body. The ego's further explorations inside the body are then further paralleled with the child's experience within the space of his rooms and corridors. The visible, external world is interpreted as the sloughed-off corpse of a former life, cast aside as a snake discards its former skin. The ego descends from its real abode into this dead product of former lives, to re-work its forms and carry evolution further. The image of the body as enclosed space is developed into that of the interior of the skull as at once a temple, and the whole world beneath the vault of the sky (p.34). The identity of sky within and sky without is repeated here; at the same time a faint but recognizable reference is made to the time of writing, the time of the prologue, which is the time of the building of the Johannes-gebäude in Dornach;[19] and a further parallel is thus created between the processes of the time of action, the child's perspective, and the time of narration, which also seeks to establish them as comparable, but different stages in a similar evolution. There are further parallels with the period of cave-dwellers and the interior of Egyptian pyramids. The parallel which is most fully developed in later sections of the chapter is that of the child's growing perception of space and the gradually increasing rigidity with which this external world replaces the impermanence of the soap-bubble.

Three sections are devoted to a particular episode, Kotik's encounter with the Lion, which is his first distinct image (p.42).

The objective facts are clearly rendered: not far from his home there was a circle of sand with benches round, where nannies used to take children to play, and it was there that Kotik met the Lion. When he told friends about it twenty years later, one who had grown up in the same part of the city told him it was merely a St Bernard with the name Lev, whose descendants were still to be seen in the district. A further twelve years later (that is to say, at the time of writing) the Lion, however, appeared again and threatened the narrator with destruction. The rational explanation is not accepted as final, and the child's experience, which was often recollected in later life, is re-instated as valid in its own terms. The yellow circle of sand is an island of light, or of dry land, that the sun has dropped into the darkness; it is a place of refuge for nannies and children. It thus partakes in the chapter's central image of an area of solidity, or security, emerging from chaos; even its circular shape relates it to this complex. The appearance of the Lion, which seems to tower over the child, obscures the sun and re-establishes chaos on the island sanctuary. Its later appearances reinforce the apocalyptic connotations of this event. Twenty years later the narrator is reading *Also sprach Zarathustra* and recalls the words in the closing section of Nietzsche's book, as Zarathustra hears the Lion approach: 'The sign is nigh' ('Das Zeichen kommt', translated as '*Blizko znamen'ye*', p.47). The apocalyptic significance of the later encounter, though imprecise, is unmistakeable. It is thus established that the child's first distinct image, as the external world takes on form for him, already anticipates the dissolution of the rigid forms that are not yet fixed, and that the original episode in childhood already pre-figured its recollection and re-interpretation as presented in the novel.

The process of the ego's descent into the child's body is guided by an unnamed Mentor-figure, who disappears with a promise to return (p.50). This same figure also appears as the priest in the temple of the skull, who after conducting the service returns to the homeland (p.37). A figure that stands in the same relation to the hero reappears a number of times in the novel; on one occasion it is identified as Vladimir Solov'yov (p.262), but that is hardly a conclusive identification. On its appearance in the prologue (pp.11–12) or in Chapter 1 it might well be thought to have some connection with Rudolf Steiner. Clearly what lies behind this fluid image is a spiritual entity that is finally ineffable, but may be reflected, or hypostasized, in real figures, and that stands in a relation to the individual ego as its universal spiritual ground (an anthroposophical development of Bely's earlier notion of the supra-individual ego), and acts as protector and guarantor of the ego's spiritual evolution. It serves, of course, a structural function in the novel of linking all the instances of its appearance and reinforcing the non-sequential interpretation of the events.

The references to Ancient Egypt and to Greek mythology in the earlier parts of the chapter are succeeded towards the end by references to pre-Socratic philosophy. In particular the child's sense that he can live safely within a limited sphere, surrounded by chaos, is likened to Anaximander's notion of the Boundless that surrounds the cosmos (p.56). The sensation of the fluidity and warmth of the surrounding world is reminiscent of Heraclitus (p.60), while the non-distinction of sense and thought (expressed in the combination *mysle-chuvstviya*, p.60) reflects the lack of division between matter and spirit that typified pre-Socratic thought. Thus if the task of the human spirit at each successive stage of evolution is, as Steiner maintains, to recapitulate all previous stages of evolution as a preparation for further progress, then by the end of Chapter 1 Kotik has recapitulated evolution up to the beginnings of pre-Socratic philosophy.

Each chapter of the novel is similarly constructed around a series of polyvalent images. Events are related in the child's consciousness to structures of images that are open to a variety of interpretations in the mind of the adult anthroposophist. The first chapter, since it describes a state of affairs before the external world has taken on fixed form, and recapitulates spiritual and cultural states for which there is no lucid verbal formulation, necessarily contains the most fluid imagery. Once this pre-historic period is past, the cultural references in the images become more recognizable, particularly inasmuch as they offer a parallel between the child's development and the story of Christ. The novel as a whole is held together not merely by this interpretative superstructure, but also by complex interrelationships between the images of the separate chapters. Through such connections the child's increasingly dim recollection, in later chapters, of the experiences of earlier chapters is established; and similarly faint anticipations of later experiences are established in the earlier ones. Specifically, the ego's recollection of its pre-corporeal condition becomes increasingly faint after the first chapter, while the anticipation of crucifixion and redemption grows in clarity as the novel progresses. Both the gain and the loss that are inherent in the child's development are thus incorporated into the imagery.

In the second chapter, for instance, the imagery of tubular shapes from which other shapes emerge is carried over into a set of variations on the theme of crawling through pipes. In the section '*Roy – stroy*' (Swarm – form), which describes the first creation of solid forms out of chaos, Kotik has a sensation of creating a kind of hole or tube within this 'swarm' by a kind of centrifugal action. The sense of being in a tube gives meaning to the expression used by adults of one Yezheshekhinsky, who has gone bankrupt: '*v trubu vyletel*' (literally: 'he has flown up the chimney'). He understands the chimney-sweep as one who perhaps rescues people from such a plight, and may have rescued Kotik himself. The notion that the chimney-sweep may have legs like a serpent's tail recalls, but only dimly, the sensations associated in Chapter 1 with Kotik's birth. The idea that Kotik had been pulled out to safety by the chimney-sweep had already been mentioned, without development, in Chapter 1 (p.58).

It is also in Chapter 2 that the first association of Kotik with Christ is made. Lying in bed he screws up his eyes in such a way that the shapes in the wood-grain of the wardrobe door come to appear like human figures bending over him. By rubbing his eyes he can also create the impression of a star falling down to his bed, which is also associated with the red icon-lamp in the corner, at which his nanny is praying. Through the combination of these images the child Kotik comes to resemble the Christ-child in a traditional picture of the Adoration of the Magi. At the same time the section contains a reference to the narrator's experience as an adult at the pyramid of Cheops, which re-instates the mystery of the child's experience, and indicates the theme of re-birth in the narrator's time-scale, of which the child's assimilation to the Christ-child is then an anticipation (pp.77–81)

The following section, 'The Church' (pp.81–84), combines the impressions of the bent backs of the praying congregation with those of the Magi. It also creates more distant and less distinct associations with both the image of skull as temple in Chapter 1, and the image of the head as censer, which arises in Chapter 6 through a pun on *dukhi* ('spirits' or 'scent'). The scent of the incense is associated with things spiritual: since it is with his head he thinks of things spiritual, his head is the censer (p.267).

The internal ramifications of the imagery in *Kotik Letayev* are of such inexhaustible complexity that to attempt more than this sketch of the way they operate would necessarily be self-defeating. Bely succeeds in evoking the experience of the child in such a way that it is both intrinsically coherent, in that each new experience and image builds upon, expands and re-interprets the stock already available, and extrinsically susceptible to that multiplicity of spiritual readings which is the essence of an anthroposophical interpretation.

The first three of the novel's six chapters, by the end of which the child has reached the age of four, are principally concerned with the movement away from the fluidity of the earliest sections, the increasing rigidity of the world as the child perceives it. The mythic stage of the first chapter is succeeded by the pre-Socratic stage of the second; there are forms established within the chaos, but they are not stable. This theme is expressed by such verbal devices as the antinomy of *roy – stroy* and various puns on the word *stroy* that denote law and discipline.[20] Puns are also made from the word *obraz* ('image', 'form') and its negative *bezobraziye* ('lack of form', but also 'ugliness', 'ugly behaviour') and *bezobraznik* ('miscreant'); a young man guilty of ugly behaviour threatens the whole tenuously established cosmos. In the third chapter the child's reflection on his birth, on the basis of stories told by his mother, replaces his own mythopoeic recollection of it. The notion of rhythm acquires a great importance as the form of Kotik's self-awareness. He first becomes conscious of language at this stage, but words, like his world, are still not static, and have not become concepts. The child still retains an understanding of what, in the introduction to *Glossolalia*, Bely calls 'the gesture of lost content':[21] 'an unknown word is made meaningful in the recollection of its gesture...' (p.115). This rhythmic perception of the world also has an important visual aspect in the imagery of flashes and spiralling lights which gives the third chapter its title and provides a system of puns on the word *blesk* ('flash', 'brilliance'), the surname derived from it, Bleshchensky, and the word *svet* ('light', or 'high society'), which will reappear in the sixth chapter.

In the second half of the novel, Chapters 4 to 6, the emphasis is upon the growing conflict between Kotik's parents, which was already intimated in Chapter 3. They are associated with different attitudes to the world. The father's rationalism is in conflict with the mother's anti-intellectual attachment to the brilliance of high society. The rationalism comes into evidence in Kotik's experience in Chapter 4. It is here that he begins to form his own cosmogony. In so doing he turns words into concepts, which he regards as a means of protection against the Titan. As a consequence the objective world becomes autonomous: 'the effects of my thought upon objects, the metamorphosis of objects through my thinking about them – all this is now at an end' (p.150). This externalization, objectification, of a world originally created in the human mind is a further form of the process expressed in Chapter 1 in the image of rooms and corridors as the sloughed-off skins of former lives. It also recalls the basic epistemology of Bely's earlier articles, and particularly the petrified world of *Petersburg*, where that process had reached a culmination.

In the fifth chapter the idea of sin is introduced. The parental conflict centres upon Kotik himself, who, in his mother's opinion, is being 'prematurely developed' by his father's attempts to educate him. 'I am a sinner; I sin with mother against father; I sin with father against mother...' (p.209). The route of return to the child's previous world is now through music. In this chapter his awareness of time extends to a sense of the future as well as the past, and the theme of expectation begins to appear.

The notion of sin leads to the story of the Fall, which occupies a central place in the sixth chapter. Guilt is expressed also in sexuality, of which Kotik was dimly aware in Chapter 4, and which now appears both as a more distinct element in Kotik's own experience, and as the implied basis of stories about other characters. Kotik's nanny is banished because of his mother's jealousy. Poliksena Borisovna Bleshchenskaya suffers similarly for a matrimonial indiscretion. The serpent of Chapter 1 reappears as the tempter and is linked by a pun with Bleshchenskaya's boa (boa-constrictor). The world of spiralling lights and high society, recalled from Chapter 3, is discredited by Bleshchenskaya's fate, and Kotik's father tries to persuade his mother that the life of the Bleshchenskys had no content. The theme of Fall and exile gives way to the theme of crucifixion. The identification of Kotik with the Christ-child in the Adoration scene is recalled from Chapter 1, and associated with Vladimir Solov'yov as an embodiment of the

Mentor-figure. The image of the head as censer, faintly intimated in Chapter 1, plays a central role in this process of the final entry of the spirit. The process that began in Chapter 1 is completed in Chapter 6. Kotik anticipates that he will be crucified by the women, who have been prominent in the exile from paradise; but he will also fail to satisfy the professors, like his father, who expect from him what he cannot give.

The idea of crucifixion is to be understood in anthroposophical terms as the most essential stage of initiation. The initiate re-enacts the crucifixion,[22] and it is this re-enactment that the child anticipates at the end of the novel. This is what the adult narrator has been through in order to be able to retrieve the child's experience. The conflict between the child's parents is a conflict between two principles, two attitudes to the world, which are closely similar to the system of dualities Bely originally outlined in his theory of Symbolism, and which he wrote about more extensively later under the shorthand titles East and West. Kotik's father is associated with analytical thought, on which the child embarks in the second half of the novel. His mother is linked with rhythm and music, through which he is able to regain access to the 'memory of memory', at the expense of which his analytical thought is developed. The crucifixion motif indicates the impending synthesis of these two forces, each of which is incomplete and uncreative on its own. The person of the adult narrator stands as the guarantor of this synthesis, since he is seen to have regained the intuitive understanding the child loses, without losing the analytical capacity the child gains.

In the development of his language towards the stasis of concepts, the child re-enacts something of the history of language as Bely had outlined it (in Potebnya's terms) in 'The Magic of Words'. But the adult narrator has progressed to the stage of writing 'The Magic of Words' and devising a linguistic style to re-instate the immediacy of pre-conceptual language. One very astute critic of *Kotik Letayev* has argued that 'the action of the novel consists of the child's acquisition of language' to articulate the pre-natal experience he recollects, but that as he learns speech, so he unlearns recollection.[23] The unlearning of recollection corresponds to the change in the child's perception of language that takes place between Chapter 3 and Chapter 4, as his words begin to turn into concepts. The language of the novel is not, of course, the child's language, but that of the narrator recalling the child's experience. There is, however, no recollection without language; without the language invented by the narrator his recollection of the child's recollection ('memory of memory') could not be articulated. It is in the novel's language that the two consciousnesses are fused. The child's acquisition and awareness of language – as subject-matter – is ultimately indistinguishable from the adult's exploitation of language as style.

The child's awareness of language is particularly marked by a tendency to understand metaphor literally, to interpret unfamiliar words in terms of distant, no longer active etymologies, and to invest words with non-abstract, often animate meanings.

It is said of Valerian Valerianovich Bleshchensky that he is 'burning up with drink' (*sgorayet ot p'yanstva*). Kotik is astonished when Bleshchensky then appears at his parents' apartment bearing no traces of incineration. He preserves the literal understanding of the metaphor by identifying Bleshchensky with a wooden dummy bearing some resemblance to him that he has seen in a barber's shop window. He invents a myth to the effect that Bleshchenskys are expendable and replaceable, and are sold as fuel (pp. 117–18).

Kotik's understanding of words through inactive etymology is illustrated by his derivation of *postupok* ('an act') from *stupat'* ('to step') (p.88). This is an exploitation of the 'inner form' of the word, as Bely had explained Potebnya's theory in 1910.[24] The word *postupok* used by his father evidently referred to a particular act, but Kotik had either not heard or not understood the conversation that would tell what act that was, and makes it intelligible to himself as a particularly heavy and noisy tread – which he can then relate to his own experience of making inopportune noises.

The most abstract of things, his father's mathematical symbols, can be animated by Kotik's naive ingenuity. He combines the xs (*iksiki*) and the interjections his father makes on reading them through: *tak-s*, turning to *taks* and then *taksiki*, which means 'dachshunds' and thus becomes virtually a pun. And so the mathematical symbols are imagined as turning into the dogs he meets on his walks (p.97).

A further instance of the child's retention of the link between 'gesture' and 'meaning' is his encounter with the character Mrktich Avetovich. Kotik knows that Mrktich Avetovich has been quarrelling with his father, and has been told that the reason is the difference of their convictions (p.163). He, however, makes friends with Mrktich Avetovich, and takes this to mean that their convictions coincide. The child has not yet finally made the division between subject and object that leads to abstraction and the possession of what the adult world calls convictions (*ubezhdeniya*); his friendship with Mrktich Avetovich springs from the latter's attempt to convince him (*ubezhdat'*) that he has no reason to be afraid of the sounds of the countryside in the evening. Their relationship is below the level of abstraction, on the level of that which Bely had earlier called 'the motives underlying convictions'; and it is at that level that Kotik understands the word.

These examples of Kotik's perception of language might be multiplied almost at will. They all show the child using language to tame the chaos around him and render it comprehensible and harmless. The natural end-product of the process is the creation of myth, as Bely had argued in 'The Magic of Words', although a fully-fledged myth is not, of course, created in every instance. The style of the novel as a whole represents the extension of the same principle to include everything that the child is not aware of as a specifically linguistic problem.

The use of a regular ternary rhythm has a general motivation in the idea that the child's self-awareness, the form of his thought, is a rhythmic dance. This conception of rhythm is evidently associated with the anthroposophical notion of etheric forces, whose pulsation through a body is the definition of life, but which are lost to uninitiated consciousness. It can be traced further back in Bely's own thinking to the quasi-Kantian idea of time, expressed in rhythm, as the form of inner experience.[25] It is particularly appropriate in *Kotik Letayev* inasmuch as the rhythm of the utterance has to be thought of as expressing the inner experience of the speaker, the author-narrator, and in this novel there is no division between that and the mind of the child-hero. The theoretical justification of such rhythm in a third-person novel such as *Petersburg* is a more complicated issue.

The rhythmic character of the prose in *Kotik Letayev* is very similar to that of *Petersburg*. G. Janecek has demonstrated that while there is a clear preponderance of two-syllable intervals between the stressed syllables, the actual percentage of such intervals is only slightly over fifty. In Bely's later novels this figure will rise to eighty and the prose will acquire a rigidly rhythmic outline.

In *Kotik Letayev* the rhythmic tension of the prose is skilfully varied to allow distinction between a general background and particular foreground passages of precise rhythmic consistency. Sometimes such foregrounded passages are provided with rhyming end-words, producing what are essentially poems inserted into the text.[26]

The phonetic properties of the language are also very intricately incorporated into the novel's texture. On occasion they are employed for a purely onomatopoeic effect, as for instance in the description of a chicken (p.89). Such a usage has, of course, the effect of reproducing the immediacy of the child's first perception of a creature that he is unable to relate to any previously familiar word. Throughout the novel recurrent alliterative patterns are used to reinforce constant associations; the gentleness of Kotik's nanny, for example, is supported by alliteration on *m*, *l* and *kl*.[27] They extend further, however, establishing relations of similarity between images that might otherwise not appear as similar. Their use in this manner complements precisely the fluidity of the imagery and the associations created between things apparently unlike by the employment of puns.

Phonetic properties can also be used to create a kind of pseudo-etymology which renders the change in Kotik's perception. The antinomy of *roy* – *stroy* in Chapter 2, already mentioned, is reached by a gradation from *roy* ('swarm', where no order is perceived) to *sroyonnosti* (parts 'swarmed together' and thus distinguishable from other parts), and finally:

Sroyonnoye stalo mne stroyem (p.65).

The addition of *s* to *r*, and then the merging of *sr* (*sroyonnoye*, 'the swarmed-together') and *st* (*stalo*, 'became') to produce *str* (*stroyem*, 'form') imitate in sound the process described.[28]

The word *sroyonnosti* is a typical example of the way in which Bely coins new words in *Kotik Letayev*. A transitive verb *roit'* is posited where only the reflexive verb *roit'sya* exists in standard Russian. It is compounded with the prefix *s-* in a manner that is entirely normal. From the past participle passive of this compound verb a noun is derived with a suffix, *-nost'*, which normally connotes an abstract quality. By then using this neologistic noun in the plural, Bely gives it a sense of particularity rather than a general abstract meaning.[29] The manner of its formation corresponds to normal processes of word-formation in Russian, so that the word in its context is quite readily comprehensible. By the creation of possible, but previously non-established forms, the language's capacity for registering previously unregistered experiences is demonstrated. Words are coined to express that which is lost in the gaps between words that have become concepts, and a fluidity of perception is rendered. Similarly, by the blurring of established distinctions between categories such as abstract and concrete, the language of *Kotik Letayev* recreates a world where such distinctions do not hold.

Carol Anschuetz has provided a skilful and thorough examination of Bely's word-creation in both *Kotik Letayev* and *The Baptized Chinaman*.[30] She has shown numerous ways in which Bely disrupts the standard grammatical categories such as abstract and concrete, or relational and qualitative adjectives, or derives adjectival short forms or adverbial forms from adjectives which do not normally produce any. The overall result is everywhere the same: the removal of the conceptual distinctions built into the language, but by means which are fundamentally consistent with the nature of the language. A precisely similar effect is produced by neologisms which are compound adjectives or nouns; the noun *zheltolistiye*, for instance, presents as a single perception what would conventionally be divided into object and quality, *zholtyye list'ya* ('yellow leaves'). *Kotik Letayev* is the first of Bely's novels in which neologisms are a fundamental feature of his style.

The main reason why the neologisms of this novel present few problems of comprehension is that they are directly derived from, and sustained by the context in which they occur. The child's apprehension of the world is seen to provide their motivation, so that the text effectively explains words which in isolation might be difficult to understand. The same is true *a fortiori* of the myths derived from literally understood metaphors or revitalized etymologies. The density of Bely's text and the constant interaction of its several levels have been impressively demonstrated in recent research.[31]

The formal unity of *Kotik Letayev* is greater than that of *The Silver Dove* or *Petersburg*. It seems to be completed in one breath, as it were; framed as it is by a prologue and epilogue that vindicate the dual narrative standpoint, it shows none of that disconcerting tendency to change emphasis, to move away in the closing chapters from the epic to the lyrical that is present in both the earlier novels. This is achieved, of course, by the removal of the distinction between epic and lyrical; the world's history is enacted in the hero's mind, and the function of the hero, both child and adult, is not to act, but to understand. This is what justifies Bely's remark in a letter to Ivanov-Razumnik that *Kotik Letayev* was his 'fifth symphony';[32] it reverses the development towards plot and narrative that led him from the 'symphonic' form to the novel in the first place. But it goes far beyond anything achieved in the *Symphonies*, for in them too, even more than in the first two novels, the lyrical and narrative modes were at war. The dual first person viewpoint of *Kotik Letayev* imparts to that novel a lyrical consistency that the 'symphonic' form as used earlier could not attain, and the linguistic innovations give it a brilliantly appropriate texture. Instead of relying on a spurious analogy with music, which operates only in specific limited ways, Bely is now exploiting the real properties of language at all levels, semantic, phonetic and rhythmic, to produce a text of remarkable density and consistency. The internalized cosmic panorama of *Kotik Letayev* is magnificently achieved by these means.

The linguistic innovations of *Kotik Letayev* can be seen as developing not only from the theories Bely expounded in 'The Magic of Words' and his review of Potebnya, but also from his practice in the earlier novels. It was particularly clear in *Petersburg* that the language had, as it were, a life of its own, performing feats of association that did not correspond to the intentions of any of the characters. It functioned there as part of that hostile reality to which Russian history and all modern European culture was reduced. In *Kotik Letayev*, however, it has changed into what Bely's theory claimed it to be: a creative force for the regeneration of culture. Structurally this change is likewise made possible by the particular narrative standpoint of *Kotik Letayev*, while philosophically it is due to the great hopes Bely invested in anthroposophy.

The anthroposophical inspiration of *Kotik Letayev* has caused embarrassment to critics, who have been reluctant to regard sympathetic knowledge of this arcane doctrine as a fair price to pay for the appreciation of the novel. Many other doctrines are echoed in it, from Platonic anamnesis to Haeckel's biogenetic law to the effect that ontogeny recapitulates phylogeny; as G. Janecek has put it, many passages have 'a whole gamut of referential possibilities';[33] but it is undoubtedly the omnivorous Steiner through whose prism they are all filtered. Reconciliation of all possible interpretations of experience is precisely what anthroposophy and *Kotik Letayev* are about. When Bely wrote in a preface for a projected second edition in 1928 that the novel was concerned with a 'palaeontology of consciousness', such as science was beginning to acknowledge,[34] he was not denying its anthroposophical import, but merely emphasizing one aspect of it that might cause no offence among opponents of anthroposophy. When P. Hart or S. Cioran find resemblances to the child psychology of Piaget or to theories of Jung's – systems of which Bely obviously had no knowledge – they are doing very much the same.[35] P. Hart tries to solve the problem of anthroposophy by separating off as 'superstructure' the adult narrator's commentary and relegating it to a historical view of Bely's works. The 'basic psychological structure of the childhood experience' can then, he believes, stand on its own.[36] But in terms of the structure of Bely's novel this is a very substantial piece of surgery indeed, removing the entire motivation for recalling that childhood experience. The problem of anthroposophy is not solved by seeking other sources or other parallels for Bely's ideas.

Shklovsky argued that a writer's philosophy is merely a working hypothesis with which he approaches the creative task, and that in the process of the creation of *Kotik Letayev* 'the device devoured the anthroposophy'.[37] Carol Anschuetz has contended that the novel is founded upon the linguistic theory that all forms of explanation, be they scientific or mythological, are based upon metaphor, and that that theory, though confirmed by Steiner, is originally derived from Potebnya.[38] It is indeed important, in assessing the role of anthroposophy in *Kotik Letayev*, to remember that the genesis of the novel's style lies in theories Bely was expounding some time before he turned to anthroposophy. There is no way in which Steiner's theories alone could have brought him to create the style of *Kotik Letayev*. Nevertheless it is not obviously true that the finished work possesses the degree of autonomy from the parent doctrine that Shklovsky asserts. Just as the style could not have developed as it did without Potebnya, so the overall conception of the novel, the general interpretation of experience to which all its metaphors point, could not have developed without Steiner. There is undoubtedly a level at which the novel can be appreciated without any prior knowledge of anthroposophy; the willing reader can be drawn into its world by the sheer force of the style. But if he then wishes to know what world this is he has entered, he will need anthroposophy to instruct him. Unless, that is, anthroposophy is actually *true* and the reader finds all the explanation pre-existing in his own mind. And since in fact the processes of reading novels and learning about philosophies do not take place in separate compartments of the mind, it is not in the end even theoretically possible to sever the umbilical cord connecting philosophy and style.

It is a truism that all literary works presuppose knowledge that they do not themselves impart. A reader of *Petersburg* who lacked all knowledge of Russian history would undoubtedly find that novel at least as incomprehensible as a reader of *Kotik Letayev* without knowledge of anthroposophy. But since there is not likely to be any such reader, that is knowledge which it seems entirely reasonable to presuppose. It does not seem so reasonable to presuppose knowledge of anthroposophy. That is not an aesthetic judgement. Aesthetically *Kotik Letayev* is in no way inferior to *Petersburg*; indeed there are grounds for regarding it as Bely's most perfectly achieved work in prose. If it is nevertheless a less important work than *Petersburg* that is because of its dependence on a doctrine to which most readers neither have nor desire access. The aesthetic success of *Kotik Letayev* is bought at a high price, though the reward of those who pay it is also great.

6
The Baptized Chinaman

The recollections of childhood that were begun in *Kotik Letayev* are continued in *The Baptized Chinaman*, which Bely wrote in 1920 and 1921. In the autumn of 1920 he drafted four chapters of a novel that was to be called *The Crime of Nikolay Letayev*. All but the first were subsequently lost.[1] That first chapter, however, revised in the spring of 1921, was published later the same year under the full title *The Crime of Nikolay Letayev* (*Epopee, Volume one*), *Chapter one, The Baptized Chinaman*.[2] In 1927 it appeared in book form under the original chapter title, with no mention of the intended volume title, and was designated as a novel. The original volume title could not be used because the extant portion does not take the action as far as the 'crime' which was to be its focus. That part of the story evidently was never written.[3]

In a short preface to its first publication Bely described *The Baptized Chinaman* as 'half biographical, half historical'.[4] He was referring in particular to the fact that there appear on its pages a number of real historical figures, mainly Moscow university professors who were his father's colleagues. In this respect it antici-pates the first volume of the memoirs Bely wrote at the end of the 1920s, *On the Watershed of Two Centuries*,[5] in which the environment of his childhood is described with a wealth of detail. A more immediate connection is with some articles written within a year or two of the novel, in which he recalled the Moscow of these early years and described the changes that its appearance had under-gone in the meantime.[6] The 'biographical' and 'historical' lines run for the most part parallel in Bely's work of the post-revolutionary period. The attempt to discover and express the meaning of his own spiritual biography starts with *Kotik Letayev* and proceeds through such works as *First Encounter*,[7] the Berlin edition of his collected poetry,[8] *Notes of an Eccentric*, and the unpublished *History of the Development of the Spiritual Soul*. The attempt to depict the world of his childhood and the Moscow intelligentsia of the first decade of the twentieth century appears only after the revolution, when it is clear that that world has passed, and it is in *The Baptized Chinaman* that it is first found. It is also present in *First Encounter*, but receives its greatest impulse from the death of Blok in August 1921. His *Reminiscences of Blok* were first written that autumn, re-written in Berlin, and later re-written at least two more times.[9] Finally they merged with the recollections of childhood and developed into the three volumes of memoirs that he produced at the end of his life. Apart from *First Encounter*, however, *The Baptized Chinaman* is the only work of Bely's in which the parallel lines of history and biography – in the sense in which Bely uses the words here – can really be said to meet.

This fact immediately distinguishes *The Baptized Chinaman* from *Kotik Letayev*, where the historical played no part. Nevertheless it is closely related to its predecessor by the presence of the biographical line and the similar function that it performs. The conflict between Kotik's parents, which had assumed increasing importance in the later chapters of *Kotik Letayev*, is once again the novel's central theme. Objectively the child plays a passive role, being pulled in opposite directions by his father and mother, because of their conflicting views on his development. On the esoteric plane, however, his role is a positive one, since he synthesizes in himself, in the growth of his ego, the conflicting spiritual forces that his parents represent. The novel's biographical line, its inner action, embodies a dialectical process in much the same way as *Kotik Letayev*.

The dual narrative standpoint of *Kotik Letayev*, which made possible that novel's peculiar incorporation of temporal processes into non-temporal panoramas, was motivated by the parallel between the adult narrator on the threshold of occult knowledge and the child who still retained traces of anamnesis. But it was also noted that the child at the end of the novel was already developing beyond the stage at which this parallel could hold. The child in *The Baptized Chinaman* is already five; the kind of pre-corporeal recollection that is so important in the early chapters of *Kotik Letayev* makes very little appearance in *The Baptized Chinaman*. The parallel is no longer operative, and there is no place in the later novel for the dual narrative viewpoint of the earlier one. The narrator, indeed, does not acquire in *The Baptized Chinaman* the degree of specific identification given in *Kotik Letayev*. There is

essentially only one narrative voice here, that of a narrator recalling the child's experience and identified above all by his language.
There are a few occasions, perhaps half a dozen in the entire
novel, when the narrator refers either to the time of writing or to
other events that have taken place between the time depicted and
the time of writing. He recalls, for instance, walking recently along
the now *Soviet* Nikitskaya Street and seeing something that had
frightened him there thirty-five years before (p.58); or he refers to
an occasion when fellow-students had asked him to identify the
strange eccentric professor who was his father (p.20). These passages are in keeping with the novel's 'historical' aspect, and serve to
focus the reader's attention upon the gap between time depicted
and time of writing. They carry a certain nostalgia and give the
empirical passage of time an irreversible quality that was not
present in *Kotik Letayev*. The voice that speaks here, however, is
not essential to the rendering of the child's spiritual development,
and nothing is made of the contrast between the two. The result of
this is that there is less emphasis upon the peculiarly infantile
nature of the child's experience. This may appear paradoxical; but
the emphasis upon the child's experience in *Kotik Letayev* was
achieved by the contrast between it and other viewpoints; it is
logical that in the absence of the contrast its childish nature comes
less to the fore. A. Veksler commented that *The Baptized Chinaman* possessed a more directly epic character than *Kotik
Letayev*;[10] the basic singularity of narrative viewpoint and the
acceptance of the passing of time provide a basis for this assertion.

The Baptized Chinaman has no more of a plot, in any conventional sense, than *Kotik Letayev*. The parental conflict develops through a series of quarrels of increasing violence, but each of
them is caused by the basic situation of conflict and only arbitrarily
provoked by specific events. They do, however, provide a distinct
development in the external action, such as was not evident in
Kotik Letayev. The minor characters are as episodic and anecdotal
as in the earlier novel, and only the peripheral members of the
family appear in more than one scene. Most of the others have
their principal function in the 'historical' aspect of the novel, as a
part of the background against which the child's development, the
inner action, is set.

It is clear that the external world of space and time enjoys a
relative autonomy in *The Baptized Chinaman*; experience is not as

totally internalized as was the case in *Kotik Letayev*. This is itself in keeping with the stage of development that Kotik has reached. The opposition of self and world, towards which he developed in *Kotik Letayev*, is given as his starting-point here. His task now is to assimilate and order the external world, to assert the control of reason over chaos. Kotik perceives the elements and the seasons; these eventually add up to an awareness of the passing of time, and the way in which the child comes to terms with time provides the central thread of his inner development. Time is not only the medium in which all change in the external world takes place; it is also the form of inner experience. Similarly, the conflict between his parents is not simply external to Kotik; it is a conflict between principles that he also embodies, and is able at last to reconcile. Thus although the opposition of self and world is present in *The Baptized Chinaman*, it is not a total separation; it is clear that the basic substance of the two is the same, and that the order imposed by the creative mind corresponds to an order latent in nature itself.

The first two chapters consist principally in the introduction of Kotik's father, who is the Chinaman of the title. In the first he and his typical surroundings, his study, are described externally: his appearance is asymmetrical, there is a slant to his eyes and his misshapen jacket which seems oriental. He resembles a Chinese sage, and is also spoken of as a Scythian and as having Tatar eyes. The study is his territory, where he buries himself in mathematics. His attempts to instal a set of bookshelves in the drawing-room are repulsed by Kotik's mother, who, however, for her part successfully installs a wash-basin in the study. His father's excursions into the kitchen involve the dispensing of impractical advice about the most rational way of executing household chores. To the servants he appears as an eccentric. The mother plays only a minor role in this chapter, but she is seen opposing him through music, bright colours and exotic scents.

The second chapter is concerned with Professor Letayev's attitude to the world, and contains very little external description. His axiom is the clarity of reason, but in a static and dogmatic sense. He prefers water to champagne because of its simpler chemical composition, and believes that complex thoughts and feelings can be likened to mathematical formulae that have not been reduced to their simplest possible form. He holds that the world is 'the result of complex processes, but it is not a process: it is a result' (p.25). In his passion for abstraction he is ineffectual; his 'rational methods of living' do not work in practice, and although it is methods, results and conclusions that he loves, in his own life he reveals not methods (*sposoby*) but only the potentiality (*sposobnost'*) for inventing them. A visit by a professor from Kiev is described, during which Professor Letayev, having identified him as a liberal, argues violently against his views. Kotik's mother, having listened with pleasure to the 'champagne' of his conversation, but having been prevented from saying a word by her husband's loquacity, pursues him round the apartment complaining about 'certain people, who' (*nekotoryye, kotoryye*) do not put into practice their own doctrines about measure and proportion.

The third chapter is the first in which the child's perceptions are presented in their own right. It opens with a passage rendering his sense-impressions on waking in the morning. Visual impressions are paramount: a crow's footprints in the snow outside, the objects and colours in his room; but the auditory impression of his mother's piano-playing is also important, and tactile impressions are implicit in the visible texture of things. The whole is united by a certain sense of mood, expressed in rhyming motifs which always include the theme of time:

Vrashchayetsya vereten' dney – ten' teney ... (The axis of days revolves – shadow of shadows ...) (p.40)
Nasvistal, pobezhal produvnoy vetrogon – v nezhivoy nebosklon: svirepevshikh vremyon ... (A scoundrelly windrush whistles and runs – to the lifeless horizon of times that grow fierce ...) (p.41)

A. Veksler describes the experience of time in this chapter as purely psychological with no involvement of reason, time seen from within the temporal process.[11] There are a number of other rhyming motifs later in the chapter which serve to fix and intensify the child's impressions, visual:

Pomnyu – ona vsyo belela; krugom zhe blednelo; i bledno serelo, i sero temnelo – v uglakh ... (I recall – she turned whiter; around all turned paler, and palely turned greyer and greyly turned dark – in the nooks ...) (p.50)

or auditory:

.. uselis' v temneyshiye nishi beleyshiye kryshi; gryzunchiki myshi – igrayut vsyo tishe ... (Whitest roofs are ensconced in the darkest recesses; the gnawing mice grow quieter at their play ...) (p.51)

The effort to understand, which these impressions call forth, is expressed in another somewhat similar motif:

... ponimaniye – devochka v belen'kom plat'itse – plyashet; i tyomnyye nyani prikhodyat bormochushchim royem: uzhasno nevnyatno, no – strashno zanyatno! – (Understanding – a girl in a little white dress – is dancing; and dark nursemaids approach in a muttering swarm: it's terribly hard to grasp, but frightfully amusing!) (p.49)

What Kotik begins to understand – or perhaps rather to be aware of not understanding – is expressed in the chapter's title: '*Edakoye takoye svoyo*', which is derived from a remark of his mother's about a particular man (meaning 'He has a certain "Je ne sais quoi"') and comes to connote a secret essence concealed behind the surface of things. It covers in fact very disparate notions, but by a series of puns and other associative connections this quality of all things acquires a kind of continuous identity. It has *inter alia* a sexual connotation, and is associated with a sense of shame. It is also particularly attributed to Kotik's father, whose hidden essence is the most mysterious of all.

The third chapter introduces two new characters: Kotik's German nanny, Henrietta Martinovna, who is an insubstantial reflection of both his parents, by virtue of her unfounded claim to understand all the professor's mathematics, and her ceaseless preening of herself in the mother's mirror;[12] and Malinovskaya, the professorial widow, arbiter of decorum and universal busybody, whose arrival always brings increased quarrelling into the family. The fourth chapter is mainly devoted to the introduction of three further characters, Kotik's maternal grandmother, aunt and uncle (his mother's unmarried sister and brother). They exist in a certain economic dependence on Kotik's father, but more importantly they reflect the basic principles embodied in his parents. The grandmother is characterized by her armchair, worn through from constant use; the stasis of her life is expressed in the neologism *bytopis'*.[13] Aunt Dotya lives entirely in her sister's shadow:

My aunt talks exclusively about mother – in words belonging to mother and addressed to mother, transmitting to my bored mother facts from mother's own life. (pp.65–6)

Uncle Vasya is an ambivalent character who is sometimes to be found profitably employed binding the Professor's learned journals, but at other times disappears on extended bouts of drinking and womanizing. At the end of the fourth chapter the under-standing-motif leads into a passage about Kotik's mother playing the piano:

And as mother plays: –
        – it's off and away:
life's incidents take wing in the unsolidity of sounds. (p. 78)

The 'dance' of understanding is linked with the fluidity and dynamism of his mother's music (as opposed to the stasis of his father's abstraction). In the later chapters of *Kotik Letayev* music provided the one route of return to the world earlier recalled in anamnesis. Here it breaks down the stasis of the professor's world, and sets things in motion so that another constellation can even-tually emerge.[14]

The fifth and sixth chapters then concentrate upon Kotik's mother in much the same way as the first and second concentrated upon his father. The themes that were merely stated in connection with her in the earlier chapters receive their development here. Her world of music is beyond good and evil; she belongs in an exotic environment and is completely out of place in the pro-fessorial circles of Moscow. She had attracted the attention of Turgenev (a noted authority) by her beauty, and the novelist P.D. Boborykin had suggested she should go on the stage. She is hap-pier in Petersburg and tells Kotik stories about her childhood and the gaiety of life in the imperial capital. Kotik's father tries to counteract her influence by teaching him about the forces whose balance sustains the world; but the deleterious effect, in his mother's eyes, of this 'premature development' is expressed in a pun on the word *sila* (force). Kotik had a young cousin called Silantiy, whose name forms the diminutive Sila, who had been of weak health and had died at an early age. If Kotik were to understand the 'forces' he too, like Sila, would grow weak and die (p.84). Professor Letayev overhears his wife's stories about Petersburg and interrupts with a tirade on the virtues of Moscow, as the cultural and economic centre of the state; this is his attempt to re-assert the ordered world that Kotik's mother tends to dis-solve. She loses her temper and the first quarrel-scene ensues, as the father strides about the room striking at the air with his hand, a gesture that will later acquire symbolic significance. Peace is restored and both parents depart to their respective activities. The sixth chapter is more concerned with Kotik's reactions to his mother and awareness of the conflict between his parents. He understands that she is ill and that that is the reason for the 'animal' glance with which she sometimes looks at him. He is so afraid of her withdrawal from him that he seldom spends time with his father and is no longer able to behave naturally in his company. He fears being abandoned by both his parents and has dreams in which they are replaced by unfamiliar people. Kotik begins to feel that he understands his parents better than they understand themselves, so that in a sense he is parent to them. Psychologically this only serves to increase his alienation from them, but it also gives the first intimation of a future synthesis.

Already in Chapter 3 Kotik's first awareness of the passing of the seasons, 'the order of measured months' (p.52), had been noted. In the seventh chapter this awareness takes on a new form, as his father celebrates his name-day. This chapter is the occasion for the greatest concentration of real historical figures anywhere in the novel, and clearly anticipates both the *Moscow* novels and the memoirs in its satirical depiction of them. Kotik becomes aware that his father's name-day recurs every year, and that his father is ageing; as he sinks back in fatigue at the end of the day Kotik feels an acute sense of pity for him. The idea of recurrence, however, is made to extend beyond empirical limits: 'all this will repeat itself; it has been repeating itself since Adam; and it will be still when the dead arise . . . ' (p.127). This is the first intimation of the idea of re-incarnation, which will appear later as the answer to the empirical power of time.

The child's extended awareness of the outside world, his knowledge that there is more of Russia than the Moscow he sees through the window, introduces the eighth chapter. Kotik's father is teaching him the geography of Russia, but Kotik, aware that his mother is about to wake up in the next room and object to this tuition, listens only for the sound of her stirring and does not attend to the lesson. When she appears a further, more violent quarrel takes place between his parents, and his father leaves the house. The chapter is entitled '*Ahura-Mazda*'; this is the name of the Sun-God in ancient Persian mythology, and there are a number of mentions of other things, such as a carpet, with Persian connections. In the latter part of the chapter, which describes evening, night and the following morning, Kotik builds up an elaborate mythology of the struggle of light and darkness. His mother comes to his bedside to grieve over the size of his forehead, which indicates that he takes after his father. At night he is a prisoner and identifies himself with the night itself, imagining himself nailed up – by mothers – in a coffin. But his awareness of the process of time teaches him not only that everyone ages like his father, but also that day will triumph again, and that he will burst forth from the coffin like the infant day, screaming at the top of his voice. Kotik's waking from the dream of his imprisonment in the coffin coincides with morning and his parents' reconciliation; Kotik anticipates that his father will give his mother a present of a lamp-shade, – a humorous symbol of reconciliation between light and darkness. The victory of light is associated with his father, who appears as Zoroaster (prophet of Ahura-Mazda) and speaks of the eventual supremacy of the principle of light in Russian history. Kotik's dream therefore clearly links him with the principle of light represented by his father, and justifies his mother's grief. The idea of his sacrifice and resurrection is also evident here.

A further quarrel takes place in the ninth chapter, entitled 'Papa doshol do gvozdya'. (The title might be translated as 'Father reaches the end of his tether'; literally it means 'Father reaches the nail', and the nail then introduces a system of related images.) Kotik's mother is taunting his father: ostentatiously seeing to her toilet, leaving the study door open, even washing in there, so that Professor Letayev is exposed both to her multifarious perfumes and also to her verbal assault. She talks, as previously, about 'certain people, who' live in straitened circumstances instead of possessing the worldly goods and social trappings that she loves in Petersburg. The father announces that he will tolerate it for five more minutes. When that time has elapsed, he strikes upon the metal of the washbasin with a nail, creating a noise that drives the mother into hysterics and apparently has a similar effect upon the child. Kotik's father appears here, in his re-assertion of order, as 'the terrible law-giver of Sinai', the Old Testament God in his relation to Moses; but he is also a Scythian (as he was in Chapter 1), pursuing a Persian with his spear.

This mythic version of the quarrel then gives the substance of the short tenth chapter, in which the battle of Scythian and Persian takes place within Kotik himself. His body arises from the dust of the battle, as it increases in density; this swirling dust is also associated with the revolutions of time. In the light of this notion Kotik now interprets to himself an occasion when his father set light to the curtains and had to stamp out the flames, ending up cheerfully smothered in soot. This pillar of flame will burn up everything that is mere appearance, that hangs loosely, like curtains, over that which it conceals. The Scythian's spear will descend like a meteor into the child's forehead which will crack like a broken Christmas-tree decoration (this refers back to an episode in Chapter 8, p.141).

The same imagery is continued and developed in the bewilderingly complex eleventh chapter, which is the main climax of the novel. Its title, '*Pfukinstvo*', comes from the word *Pfuka*, a private neologism to name Kotik's personal bogey-man. Kotik is feverish and sees this figure as a nocturnal visitor; the description of him coincides with the description of the Scythian and with a later description of his father; it also recurs later as a description of what Kotik fears he will become (pp.155–6, 162, 182):

barefoot, thick-heeled, in ancient patched trousers that hang from his skin like a half-flayed pelt, hirsute and coarse; a green tummy, like a woman's, sticking out above the trousers, grins with its navel at the hirsute ribs, where feebly sag two half-womanly protrusions ... (p.159)

With its loose-hanging trousers and sagging protrusions it recalls the same qualities in the curtains. This bogey-man's function is to teach Kotik that things are not what they appear, that broken toys reveal stuffing and springs and that behind the landscape painting is only the wall. The notion of a concealed reality behind the appearance re-introduces the idea of *Edakoye takoye svoyo* from Chapter 3, with its associated ideas of sexuality and sin. Kotik is in quest of his own such underlying reality, and finds his guilt in his mother's overwrought nerves, caused by his own difficult birth. In this chapter Kotik experiences a nightmare in which he attempts to climb a high drainpipe and sits without holding on at the top, on a spike that is identified with mathematics. He sits there shouting at the top of his voice (like the day-child in Chapter 8) and then falls, like the Scythian's spear, into the skull of his infant self. His mother explains his distress as the result of 'premature development', while his father claims that he is atavistically re-living the experience of primitive man. Both explanations are right in their way: it is indeed the development of the mind that causes Kotik's state, and this is explicable in terms of his recapitulation and anticipation of past and future evolution, which allows the idea of re-incarnation to make another appearance:

I know that the drainpipe which can't be surmounted in a hundred thousand years is the spinal column; I crawled from worm to gorilla, to ... to ... the expansion of the sphere – the sphere of my head, on which I am trying to take a firm seat, and I fall afresh, into the antediluvian past ... (p. 168)

The pill which Kotik is given for his bronchitis is identified with the apple of the Fall; apples are in any case already associated with his father from Chapter 1, and it is his father who teaches him about the Bible stories. Kotik's notional guilt because of his birth and because of his development, which causes the dissension between his parents, is complemented by a voluntary misdemeanour when he steals a herring-tail from the kitchen. Others are blamed before he finally confesses, and in his remorse he imagines himself cast out, whereupon paradise would return for his parents.

The passing of autumn and winter has been continuously observed from Chapter 3 onwards. In Chapter 11 the March thaw begins, and Chapter 12 bears the title 'Spring'. Kotik's illness is over and the tensions of the previous chapter have passed. Kotik's mother begins to play the piano again, and the movement of the music and the spring thaw is contrasted with the stasis of the olive-green drawing-room, where everything is timeless (*bezvremenstvuyet*). Under the influence of the music Kotik does not recognize the things which distressed him before; but the music itself disappears the moment his mother closes the piano.

The thirteenth chapter concentrates upon his father, who is described both as the child saw him then and also as the adult son later came to understand him. In his disregard for established prejudices he is compared to Diogenes. Many people held a low opinion of him because of his modest manner and lack of social finesse; but he could stand up to anyone if need be, and an incident is related in which he gave one of the Tsar's ministers a piece of his mind. The concealed power implicit here is what becomes apparent to the child. His father's weekly winding of the clock turns him into the originator of time. He tells of a dream in which he described his theory of evolutionary monadology[15] to Christ, 'the Absolute, so to speak'. In the 'spheres' – by which is meant the spheres of power – Professor Letayev was respected but not liked. Kotik uses the idea of 'sphere' to build up a conception of his father, through his intrinsic power, creating 'spheres' or 'worlds', like soap-bubbles.

Thus gradually Kotik's father comes to resemble the Old Testament God. It is now suggested that Kotik made a covenant with him on Sinai, which he must fulfil if he is not to be destroyed like the Sodomites. His mother is leading him to the worship of false idols, which he must resist. She will persecute him for this, but far better he should be tortured by her than that he should break the covenant.

Chapter 14 bears the mysterious title '*Om*', and provides the mythological culmination of the novel. The visual image from which the chapter begins seems to evoke a view of sunlight gleaming through the branches of trees as they drip with melting snow. The torrent of light thus created is identified with 'the waterfall of the beard' of the Old Testament God; the flow of this beard is time. But one of the luminaries comprising the beard became estranged – the fallen angel – and so there arose the serpent, infinite time that has lost its beginning. Thus the original estrangement of creation from God is brought into relation with the theme of time; it is because of that estrangement that there exists time as a purposeless, endless continuum, and the reunification with God is dependent upon the conquest of time in this aspect.

Om is a mystical word that is said to have, in almost all ancient languages, the meaning of 'divine' or 'divinity'.[16] According to C.W. Leadbeater it is the way in which the word *Aum* is normally pronounced, and is used at the commencement of every good work or thought because it symbolizes divine creation. It is related to the idea, prevalent in Hindu Scriptures, that the world was created by sound. *Aum* is the most complete human word because 'it begins with the vowel A in the back of the mouth, continues with the vowel U sounded in the centre of the mouth, and closes with the consonant M, with which the lips are sealed. It thus runs through the whole gamut of human speech and so represents in man the entire creative word.'[17] It is used in this capacity to create a series of incantatory formulations which carry direct reminiscences of *Glossolalia*:

'Om-mir-mira-am-amo' –	'Neizrechonnyy mir, divnyy, – lyblyu!'
	(Ineffable world, miraculous, I love you!)
'Amma-amo-mam-mama' –	'O, kormilitsa, lyuba: ty – mater′ materii!'
	(O, nourisher, beloved: you are the mother of matter!)
'Ram-rama-bram-brama' –	'Geroy, posvyashchonnyy, – kak bog!'
	(Hero, initiated like a god!) (pp. 218–19)

The re-creation of the world through language is the task of human culture, the task for which Kotik is being prepared in this novel. The word *Aum* has a variety of esoteric connotations which are evidently of relevance here. Its three sounds symbolize the many kinds of Trinity that are to be found in esoteric teachings. Specifically it relates to the awareness of time. *Aum* is the name of the bird Kala Hamsa, 'the swan of time', where A is the bird's right wing, U its left wing, and M its tail; the bird's flight through space carries the implication of time. Consciousness exists in time, because it evolves, but the consciousness of the Logos *is* time. Thus the bird symbolizes the Logos in the sense of Wisdom, and the initiate who reaches the appropriate stage of awareness bestrides the bird and realizes that 'he is the Self'; that is to say, he becomes aware that his consciousness is one with that of the Logos, time itself. Thus the mystical word *Om*, or *Aum*, carries for those who can read it a dense symbolism in which the novel's essential themes of the consciousness of time and the creative power of language are fused together.

Kotik's father appears as a Patriarch, and Kotik dreams that in teaching him, his father is preparing him for his kingdom. This prepares the transition to the fifteenth and final chapter, in which Professor Letayev has finished lessons on the Old Testament and begun to teach Kotik the New Testament:

the God is abolished who had the beard; the Son of Man commences, who suffered before me; and thereby brought redemption; I too must bring redemption; who is not yet redeemed?
Why, Mummy! (p.225)

Since the beard of the Old Testament God has already been identified with time, the transition to the New Testament comes to denote a new view of time, the overcoming of its endless circularity. This is redemption, and Kotik's idea of redeeming his mother is directly related to it. He is to reconcile in himself the chaotic, musical force of his mother with the creative force of thought imbibed from his father: human culture, the redemption of nature, will emerge from the synthesis of the two.

The idea of redemption is immediately paralleled on the level of external action. The worst quarrel of all takes place, during which Kotik's mother strikes him; this is interpreted as her 'sacrifice' of him. He is taken away from the house by his father. Kotik antici-pates crucifixion, which is associated in his mind with an incident when he saw the servant nailing up a strip of beading in the drawing-room. This beading is in turn associated with the loose-hanging curtains and related images, which revealed the inner essence of things. Thus indirectly the internal relations of the imagery point to the self-identification with Christ through crucifixion as Kotik's realization of his own inner essence. When Kotik then returns home his mother appears to him as an angel: she has been redeemed by Kotik.

The novel's last words are: 'Father is the baptized Chinaman', which clearly refer to the conclusion of a process that the novel's inner action has been depicting, a fusion of Eastern and Western features. This ending of the final chapter contrasts with the ending of the penultimate chapter, where nature is spoken of as 'the ancient Chinaman' (p.223). The father has been very much identified in the earlier stages of the novel with the un-Christian East; now that East is fused with Christianity. Both the stasis of Professor Letayev's view of the world and the chaotic emotionalism of Kotik's mother may be regarded as in some sense Eastern in nature; while the power of thought in the father and the dynamism of music in the mother are positive forces that have to be activated to produce the desired result. Kotik is seen as redeeming both his parents or the forces they represent, by his inner development.

Khodasevich objected to the novel's title, arguing that it was merely a mechanical repetition of the last words, and made the father appear to be the central character, instead of the son.[18] The only answer to this objection is to assume that Kotik, as a result of his development, becomes identified with his father in the manner that is suggested by their assimilation to God the Father and God the Son, so that the question of priority does not arise. But that symbolic interpretation, consistent though it is with the way in which the inner action is presented, cannot be meaningfully translated into terms of the external action.

The child's mythopoeic interpretation of the world is to a large extent motivated by puns and metaphors revitalized by literal understanding, in the same way as in *Kotik Letayev*, though their use here is more sparing. A particular example of the pun is the exploitation of the word *shayka*, which through its alternative meanings of 'bathtub' and 'gang' is used to associate Professor Letayev's views on the politically dangerous outlook of a certain intellectual group, the Antonovich 'gang', with dissolution in a literal sense, as a bar of soap dissolves in the water of the bathtub (pp.34, 48–9). Since the idea of a bathtub involves the idea of nakedness, this combination of notions also leads into the complex of imagery around '*Edakoye takoye svoyo*', the concealed essence, particularly in its sexual connotation. An example of the revitalized metaphor is the child's understanding of the expression 'points of view' as denoting his father's eyes, which at certain moments of tension remind him of the sharp points he produces on his pencils (p.14). This resembles the way in which, in the earlier novel, Kotik translated the ideological conflict between his father and Mrktich Avetovich into terms of his own emotional apprehension of the two men. The development of such conceptions into fully-fledged myths occurs much less frequently than in *Kotik Letayev*. This is consistent with the fact that the child is himself developing beyond the mythic stage of awareness; his entire development is eventually subsumed under the one myth of his identification with Christ.

A feature of the style of *The Baptized Chinaman*, that could be seen developing through *Petersburg* and *Kotik Letayev*, is the prominence of direct and consistent associations between phonetic patterns and systems of imagery. The clearest example is the use of the sound '*r*'. It first appears in a position of emphasis in Kotik's mother's talk of 'certain people who' (behave in such-and-such a way) – *nekotoryye, kotoryye*; it thus comes to be specifically associated with Kotik's father. It then appears in the expression *raz-raz-raz-raz-raz*, which imitates his father's gesture in striking at the air with his hand, a gesture that will later be repeated when he subdues his wife by striking on the washbasin with the nail; so that the sound is more particularly associated with the father's assertion of his authority. The increasing revelation of this authority as the parental quarrels follow upon one another, which is paralleled by the anecdote about the professor's unexpectedly berating a government minister, is accompanied by an increasing emphasis upon the sound '*r*', whose culmination appears in the chapter *Om*:

Uznayu, chto tot Mech yest' –	(I learn that that Sword is –
Arkhangel; zovut Ra-	the Archangel; his name
failom yego:	is Raphael:
Rafail	Raphael
Zvuk	is the sound
raz-	of ex-
ry-	plo-
va! – (p.217)	sion! –)

A. Veksler, noticing the way in which alliterative patterns were built into the novel's imagery, made an ingenious attempt to explain them in terms of Bely's *Glossolalia* (which, although not published until 1922, was written in 1917, that is to say between the writing of *Kotik Letayev* and *The Baptized Chinaman*).[19] As was pointed out above, however, *Glossolalia* does not represent a statement of 'dogma' on Bely's part, so that the automatic transference to *The Baptized Chinaman* of meanings attributed to sounds in that work would not necessarily correspond to his own conception of their value. In any case their aesthetic function in *The Baptized Chinaman* cannot be described simply by reference to such an external source. In the event, Veksler makes a number of assertions about the character Bely attributes to sounds which are not substantiated by the text of *Glossolalia*.[20] Nevertheless, inasmuch as some alliterative patterns perform a function in relation to the novel's imagery which apparently does correspond to the function attributed to them in *Glossolalia*, it is helpful to cast a glance at that work.

The sound '*r*' is said to be the sound of energy,[21] which corresponds reasonably closely to the process of revealing hidden power which this sound accompanies in the novel. There are also a number of combinations in which '*r*' is one component: it is combined with '*z*' in *raz-raz-raz-raz-raz* and in the name Zoroaster. The combination '*raz*' seems to be best understood through the association of the Archangel Raphael with a notion of explosion (*razryv*), connoting a great spiritual transformation. The name Zoroaster (or Zarathustra) is discussed in *Glossolalia*, where its first syllable is interpreted by way of the Russian word for dawn (*zarya*, plural *zori*), while its other syllables are understood either in terms of the Latin root that gives the English 'astral' – then 'Zaroastr' is 'the star of morning' – or else in terms of the common beginning of the German words 'strecken' and 'strahlen'. In sum Zarathustra comes to be 'spread out over everything in rays from the spiritual light-heat of the soul'.[22] This cannot be said to elucidate anything very much in the novel, but given the importance of imagery of light in the climactic chapter '*Om*' it appears likely that an esoteric connection between sound and meaning is intended. The combination '*str*' is described elsewhere in *Glossolalia* as connoting 'the growth of solidity';[23] this is an apposite description of the way it functioned in the notion of *stroy* in *Kotik Letayev*; but it is not employed in this meaning in the later novel.

In view of the central role of Kotik's parents, *papa* and *mama*, one would expect the sounds '*p*' and '*m*' to perform a significant function. '*P*' is said to denote 'the solidifying of feelings', 'dried-up form and the old age of animals', and to correspond to the rhinocerous or elephant in the animal kingdom.[24] This unappealing description does perhaps bear a certain resemblance to the static non-sentient nature of the father, but it would be difficult to reach such conclusions from the text of *The Baptized Chinaman* alone. '*M*', in contrast, is supposed to be the sound of animal warmth, and to contain both sensuality and spirituality.[25] This comes much closer to the way in which the mother is perceived in the novel. '*M*' also occurs in certain combinations which deserve a mention, most significantly with '*r*'. This combination is used onomatopoeically to express a complex musical chord: *mrmlya* (pp.192–3), which it may not be far-fetched to see as related to the function in Kotik's development of the dynamism of music as associated with his mother. In *Glossolalia* the combination of '*m*' and '*r*' is said to give 'Maria';[26] although this name does not appear in the novel, the last mention of Kotik's mother includes a reference to her 'annunciation' (p.233), which is a logical corollary of Kotik's identification with Christ. '*M*' also occurs in the word '*Om*', which is discussed in *Glossolalia* without reference to the occult tradition to which it belongs. It is said to denote the soul's attitude to the body before birth, where '*o*' represents the soul, and '*m*' the flesh:

... within 'O' (the soul) there ripen 'm's: the tissues of flesh; rays from the periphery (from 'O'), penetrating into 'm' (the flesh), from something sentient in the embryo: in the big 'O' there is now a circle of 'm's (flesh); within the circle of 'm's there ripens the small 'o'; it is linked with the world-soul: with the big 'O' . . .[27]

This description of how the sound '*Om*' renders the awareness of the true relation between body and spirit adds a further facet to the symbolism contained in the sound. It is this realization that is then expressed in the combinations of '*m*', '*r*', '*b*' that summarize Kotik's ultimate attitude to the world.

Although affinities exist between the alliterative patterns of *The Baptized Chinaman* and *Glossolalia*, and it is very probable, particularly in view of the interest he was taking in eurhythmy at the time of writing,[28] that Bely intended them, not a great deal of real illumination emerges from a comparison of the two. It is more fruitful to look at Bely's other major work on language from this period, 'Aaron's Rod', in which he developed his arguments about the essentially metaphoric character of the sounds of language, and indicated how poetry could be interpreted in such terms. The meaning of a poem lies neither in its ideas, understood abstractly, nor in its acoustic form divorced from those ideas. It is the imagery, the 'nerve fibres' of the poem, that links sound and meaning, and in relation to which the sound of a poem must therefore be examined. As an example Bely cites the famous lines from Pushkin's *Bronze Horseman*:

> Shipen'ye penistykh bokalov
> I punsha plamen' goluboy . . .
> (The hissing of the foaming goblets
> And the blue flame of the punch . . .)

and argues that of the 43 sounds in these two lines 29 are meaningful and only 14 neutral. He analyses the sequence of sounds in six ways, showing four kinds of alliteration and two kinds of vowel gradation, relating each to the meaning of the lines.[29] It is illuminating to undertake a modest imitation of this examination in relation to a passage of Bely's prose in *The Baptized Chinaman*. Take the sentence:

teplo razlivannoye luzh ostyvayet okladami kholoda .. (p.187)
(the warm unbounded flow of puddles congeals in a casing of cold ..)

The visual image is of a puddle that has melted during the day and on which a crust of ice is once more forming in the evening. The most obvious alliteration is on '*l*', which occurs five times, once each in all but one of the sentence's six words. In the words describing the melted puddle it occurs either on its own or in the combinations '*pl*' and '*zl*'; after the verb '*ostyvayet*' (congeals), which lacks the '*l*', it recurs in words describing its frozen condition in combination with '*k*', '*kh*' and '*d*', none of which occurred in the earlier part. It is clear that Bely is imitating phonetically the process that the sentence describes. The idea is that this transmutes the process into language, makes it 'real', without having recourse to the established concepts and notions of common sense, which, by referring back to imprecise trains of thought, presumed to be shared, robs communication of all real meaning.

Sound patterns of this kind are of course easiest to demonstrate when the sentence containing them refers to a physical process with which the phonetic features can be compared, even if, as here, it is a visually perceived process that is being synaesthetically rendered in the sound. Where the meaning of the words is such that no sense impression would normally be associated with it, it is difficult to imagine in what terms the sound pattern could be described. This is where a work such as *Glossolalia* comes in. For the anthroposophist there is no rigid dividing line between the world perceptible to the five senses and the spirit-world accessible to super-sensory perception. There is therefore no reason why sounds should not have the kind of spiritual equivalence attributed to them in *Glossolalia* and exploited in certain chapters of *The Baptized Chinaman*. Since the meaning of phonetic elements is not restricted, but, in keeping with anthroposophical pluralism, must have both physical and spiritual implications simultaneously, it is possible that Bely saw here a way of providing a link between the novel's 'historical' aspect, the observation and recollection of external reality, and its 'biographical' aspect, the rendering of the child-hero's states of mind. However, where the larger structural elements of the novel do not succeed in linking its two aspects, it is scarcely possible to perceive such connections at the phonetic level.

In the letter to Ivanov-Razumnik in which Bely spoke of *Kotik Letayev* as his fifth symphony, he also noted that his development from *Kotik Letayev* to *The Baptized Chinaman* involved a shift from 'symphonism' to 'verbalism'.[30] The 'symphonism' of *Kotik Letayev* is founded upon metaphor; the 'memory of memory' that creates the plurality of meaning motivates and is sustained by all the individual tropes and devices. It has been shown that all the linguistic innovations in *Kotik Letayev* have an immediate contextual justification in the child's perception.[31] Ultimately, therefore, the novel's 'symphonism' is dependent upon the specific character of the dual narrative standpoint that establishes 'memory of memory' as the principle motivating the metaphors. 'Verbalism' evidently signifies the autonomy of the individual word. This characteristic of the latter novel was noted already by Shklovsky, who declared that 'what is made strange here is no longer the image, but the word'.[32] This is exactly what one would expect to follow from the preference Bely gives in 'Aaron's Rod' to metonymy and phonetics over metaphor. C. Anschuetz has demonstrated various ways in which linguistic innovations similar to those encountered in *Kotik Letayev* occur in *The Baptized Chinaman* without the contextual motivation that they possessed earlier.[33] She shows for instance how neologistic compound adjectives which in *Kotik Letayev* were used to complement an image may stand on their own in *The Baptized Chinaman* as merely incidental detail. She indicates that the animism engendered by some neologistic nouns is no longer associated with Kotik's metaphorical world-view, but serves to create grotesque for its own sake, and points out that Bely uses adverbs to express the outer, rather than the inner state of the agent, or – to express it differently – to attribute syntactically to an action what is in fact the property of a thing.[34] These changes are motivated equally by the change in narrative attitude between the two novels. With a child of a different age, who has lost the 'memory of memory', the fundamental justification of the metaphorical systems is lost and the subordinate devices cannot have the same contextual motivation. The singular narrative attitude and the more epic character of *The Baptized Chinaman* thus contribute to the creation of Bely's 'verbalism'.

Another difference between *Kotik Letayev* and *The Baptized Chinaman* lies in the rhythmic character of the prose. G. Janecek has shown that while there are passages in *Kotik Letayev* which display the regularity of verse metre, the rhythm of the prose as a whole has scarcely any greater regularity than that of *Petersburg*. In *The Baptized Chinaman* the ternary metre is consistent throughout.[35] It is natural therefore that where in the latter novel Bely needs to make particular passages or motifs stand out, as the passages of exact rhythm did against the general rhythmic background of *Kotik Letayev*, he must give them further characteristics of poetry. The rhyming motifs that carry the theme of Kotik's perception of time stand in such a relation to the rest of the text. As A. Veksler put it: 'It is completely clear that the assonances and rhymes represent the highest points of the general rhythmic tension, in just the same way as lyricism is naturally born from the tension of the epic'.[36] This suggestion that other features of the style grow organically out of the tension of the rhythm calls to mind Bely's own description of rhythm in 'Aaron's Rod' as the blood of the organism that is poetry, the deepest level of language.[37] Bely's novels from *The Baptized Chinaman* onwards employ rhythm in the manner of verse, rather than that of prose. It is perceived as a constant underlying pulse, as the inescapable basic organizing principle of the language. The rhythmic monotony of Bely's later novels has frequently been commented upon, but it has never been explained. It is not true to say, as Janecek does, that in these works the artist was listening too closely to the theoretician, for in his essays on the rhythm of prose it is precisely the flexibility of prose rhythm that Bely singles out for praise.[38] Perhaps it is possible to approach this problem by way of narrative standpoint.

In *The Silver Dove* and *Petersburg* Bely employed an ironically self-conscious narrator who established viewpoint by direct address to the reader, and to whom all the idiosyncrasies of style were readily attributable. In *Kotik Letayev*, despite the lack of irony, a fundamentally similar situation is created by the framing device of prologue and epilogue and the dual narrative standpoint of the rest of the novel. In *The Baptized Chinaman* the identity of the narrator is scarcely at all conveyed by such overt devices; instead it is inferred from the character of the language, somewhat in the manner of traditional *skaz*.[39] It was suggested above in the comparison of the two main editions of *Petersburg* that it was the reduction in the stylistic features referring to the narrator's evaluation and judgement that led, in the second edition, to a greater perceived role for the rhythm. It appears to be the case in *The Baptized Chinaman*, too, that the disappearance, as it were, of the narrator into the novel's language leads to the reinforcement of the rhythm. It has to be remembered that rhythm, to Bely, is not only the deepest level of the language, but also, by that same token, the expression of the inner experience of the artist. Rhythm appears thematically in *The Baptized Chinaman* as the form of Kotik's perception (related to the underlying theme of time), while the rhythm of the language is attributable, of course, not to the child but to the author. A parallel is thus established between the child's recapitulation of the creation of culture in the awareness of rhythm and the author's recapitulation of that recapitulation through the manipulation of the rhythm of language, which is also his own creation of a new culture. A relationship between author and child is then ultimately re-established that resembles very closely their relationship in *Kotik Letayev*, but it is given only implicitly, only by virtue of the novel's language. Whether or not Bely intended this wider autonomy of language to be indicated by his word 'verbalism' is impossible to say; but at all events it seems quite feasible to argue that it is part of the same process, and that the insistent rhythm of Bely's late novels has its origin here.

Bely was aware that in certain respects his attitude to language was akin to that of the Futurists. To Ivanov-Razumnik he wrote of *Glossolalia* as 'further left than Futurism', and presumably in so doing he had in mind the attempts of Khlebnikov to identify particular sounds with particular ideas. There is, however, no affinity with the theories of the other main protagonist of Futurism's metalogical language, Kruchonykh. Bely does not coin absolute neologisms. The nearest he comes is in a passage describing Kotik's father's disastrous attempt to play the piano:

. . . i ukhnuvshim gudom, i bukhnuvshim dudom bebanit babonom, babunit pumpyanom . . . (p.203)
(. . . with thumping crash and clumping bash he clangles a dunder and dongles a glump . . .)

The lexical words denoting sounds are juxtaposed in such a way that they verge on nonsense – their rhymes are more important than their semantic content – while the four neologisms retreat, as it were, into the imbecility of meaningless noise, functioning only by their alliteration, their vowel gradations, and the relics of meaning contained in the grammatical forms. Even that, of course, is more meaning than is contained in neologisms such as Kruchonykh's *dyr bul shchyl*.[40] Indeed the passage functions quite precisely and meaningfully in context, as the depiction of a striving for expression that has failed to find adequate form. In view of Bely's insistence on the unity of phonetic and semantic elements it is not surprising that he comes closest to Kruchonykh precisely at a point where it is a deficiency of meaning he is seeking to evoke. He had already done something similar in the inchoate chants of the 'doves' in his first novel – a phenomenon Kruchonykh saw as exemplary for the creation of metalogical language.[41]

For all that Bely wished *The Baptized Chinaman* to be regarded as a continuation of *Kotik Letayev*, and there are essential senses in which it is such a continuation, it is a very different kind of novel. *Kotik Letayev* had brought him to an extreme of internalization, beyond which there was nowhere to go in the same direction. It is tempting to think that even if the anthroposophical logic of depicting the world as seen by a five-year-old had not necessitated a more external viewpoint, Bely would have been compelled to seek one anyway. His attempt here to create a language that would express the perceiving subject's acquisition of cognition, that is to say, his creation of the real world, without reference to established concepts or the categories of common sense, follows from that need, and leads directly to the stylistic developments of his last novels.

Never again did Bely combine in one work what he speaks of as the 'historical' and 'biographical' aspects of this novel. True, the *Moscow* novels similarly contain descriptions of the intellectual circles in which Bely moved during the first decade of the twentieth century, but they are used as the background to a fictional plot, rather than a spiritual autobiography. As long as the anthroposophical aspect of the novel has, despite its fictionalized form, claims to literal veracity, it must retain that veracity wherever it intersects with the 'historical' plane. There is no problem in the passages that render the child's perception of a historically undefined external world of landscapes and seasons, and Bely's linguistic innovations function most successfully precisely in those places. Where historical characters are introduced, as in the description of Professor Letayev's name-day party, the viewpoint necessarily shifts somewhat from that of the child who could not know them adequately, to that of the recollecting adult; this raises problems of relevance, as the information available to the adult can hardly impinge upon the development of the child, which is the novel's main theme. But where at the end of the novel the child's development is supposed to have a reciprocal effect upon the external world in the shape of his 'redemption' of his parents, the reader is suddenly required to substitute a purely symbolic understanding of the parents for what has so far been a concrete historical one. The real people disappear at the point where the fusion of the two planes is needed as the justification of the novel's dual character. And if Carol Anschuetz is harsh when she describes the novel's ending as 'ecstatic idiocy',[42] it is certainly the case that its symbolic conclusion can only be thought of as objectively motivated by some abnormal state in the child, dream or delirium, that leaves the novel's 'historical' and 'biographical' halves as separate as ever. It would appear to be for this reason that these two strands in Bely's work are thereafter kept apart.

The Baptized Chinaman is the most esoteric of Bely's novels. Anthroposophy is required for its comprehension, and for the perception of its unity, in a more imperative way than is the case with *Kotik Letayev*. The significance of *Om*, for example, cannot be perceived without external assistance, and there are many other instances where the imagery makes implicit reference to anthroposophical interpretations of past cultural stages, whose meaning cannot be derived from the novel's text alone. *The Baptized Chinaman* was written at a time when the old culture of pre-revolutionary Russia seemed to have vanished, and Russia was cut off from the West by civil war and political barriers. Bely was deeply reliant upon the anthroposophical colony of Moscow, which he believed to be the nucleus from which a new universal culture would grow. It is understandable that he should write a book designed to be comprehensible above all to them – and Aleksandra Veksler's essay is evidence that it was understood. To a wider audience it is bound to remain substantially inaccessible, despite its author's belief that it could be read by anyone of literary culture.[43] In view of this inaccessibility, as well as of the impossibility of satisfactorily reconciling its two aspects, *The Baptized Chinaman* cannot be regarded as one of Bely's most successful works. Nevertheless it has, within its own esoteric terms, a delicate inner coherence that can be perceived without inordinate effort, and it contains many passages of great charm, whose verbal inventiveness can affect the reader no less directly than *Kotik Letayev*. Furthermore it embodies stylistic features that are a logical and consistent development beyond the technique of *Kotik Letayev*, and which form a direct link with the language and style of Bely's last novels.

7

Notes of an Eccentric

Notes of an Eccentric occupies an ambiguous position in Bely's work. He began writing it in 1918, but abandoned it incomplete before the end of the year, and did not resume work on it until he arrived in Berlin in December 1921.[1] *The Baptized Chinaman* was one of several works he completed in the meantime. Thematically it shows important links with both the novels of childhood, but in style and genre it is a maverick, possessing no real connection with anything else that Bely wrote, and it has to be admitted that in most respects the book is a failure.[2] There exists only one complete edition, published by Helikon, Moscow–Berlin 1922, although several extensive extracts were published elsewhere; in particular thirty-seven chapters, corresponding to the first thirty-nine of the Helikon edition's sixty-three, were published with some significant variations in the almanac *Notes of Dreamers* in 1919 and 1921.[3]

The present tense action of the book concerns a journey from Dornach, in Switzerland, by way of France, England, Norway and Sweden, to Russia. It is a journey that Bely himself undertook in the summer of 1916; he left Dornach, where he had been living and working in the anthroposophical colony, on 26 July and arrived in Petrograd on 23 August (old style).[4] The narrator, like Bely himself, has been summoned for military service, and believes he is kept under surveillance by allied counter-espionage agents. The journey is presented as a journey from sanctuary to exile, a return to his geographical homeland and a loss of his other homeland, 'the brotherhood of nations', that Dornach had represented. It is also a spiritual journey in which the narrator re-lives and re-interprets his past spiritual development, at the same time passing through its next stage. The particular stage that this journey is felt to represent is his crucifixion.

The journey is structured around the town of Bergen. When the narrator had visited Bergen three years before, it had been the occasion of an immense spiritual enlightenment, which is seen as the birth of the infant in the crib, the advent of Christ, that is to say, into the individual consciousness. When he passes through Bergen again, he experiences that occasion as the infant's death. This three-year period, which is the period of Dornach and sanctuary, is different from his life either before or after. But earlier events are related to it as anticipations, and the book as a whole represents the narrator's attempts to understand and come to terms with the entire course of his spiritual development that has led to this disastrous journey into chaos. The period between the two visits to Bergen contained a promise that has apparently not been fulfilled. The narrator describes an illness (1, 180–5) that arose from his inability to bear the intensity of his insights; it is since the time of that illness that he has been pursued by the 'dark-haired man in a bowler' – the principal counter-espionage agent with the occult task of preventing spiritual development. The narrator attributes his departure from Dornach to his failure to read the occult signs correctly; indeed he takes the fact of his departure from Dornach to indicate that the whole course of his development there has been erroneous. The names of the places he has visited, Christiania, Bergen and Dornach, are used as puns to denote stages of spiritual development; but the departure from Dornach then signifies the removal of the crown of thorns and the suggestion that it – and the role it connotes – was undeserved.

The wrongly read sign tore away from me my Nelly, who remained at the stage we had attained together, which was determined by the names of the places where we had been raised above the veil of illusion: Christiania, Bergen and Dornach, [which means for us: where we were initiated into the service of Christian principles; from there the *mountains* arose for us: and in the *mountains* there awaited the *crown of thorns*.

My Nelly deserved it; but I received it undeservedly:] 'Dornach' was torn out. (1, 157–8)[5]

The book's scheme is based upon a series of dualities. On the one side stands the sanctuary of Dornach, the constructive labour of building the Johannesgebäude, the study of anthroposophy, the close friendship of an international community, and the presence and comfort of the narrator's wife, Nelly. On the other is the chaos and destruction of the First World War, whose gunfire in Alsace can be heard from Dornach, the narrator's phantasmagorical journey, and the literary life of Russia in which the narrator's literary pseudonym, Leonid Ledyanoy, takes the place of the real man. The terms of this duality are, however, complicated by the identification of events within the individual consciousness and events in the external world. The development of the Ego within the narrator's ego (of Christ, or the Christ-impulse, as Steiner calls it, within the individual consciousness) is the prototype of the outbreak of war. The two are essentially the same event, and in this context the narrator frequently speaks of himself as a 'bomb'. (The parallel with the central image of *Petersburg* extends to the retention of a similar ambiguity.) Now while the World War and the narrator's spiritual development have in common the fact that they both overturn and disrupt a state of affairs that existed before them, they are otherwise opposed to each other in the scheme of the book. It is difficult to determine whether it is the erroneous character of the development in Dornach that gives rise to the war (just as the narrator's inability to withstand his insights gives rise to the counter-espionage agents), or whether spiritual development necessarily engenders simultaneously forces that oppose it. It is these forces, at all events, that are felt to 'crucify' the narrator on his second arrival at Bergen.

But the status of that crucifixion also remains open to considerable doubt. In the first place it follows upon the *removal* of the crown of thorns that was associated with Dornach. As the narrator then subsequently returns to Russia he is once again recognized as the famous writer Leonid Ledyanoy. He accepts this substitution of pseudonym for spiritual man as his fate, and as he does so the counter-espionage agents cease to torment him. It is difficult to see this return to the *status quo ante* as the consequence of a spiritual event correctly identified with crucifixion; rather it appears that from this vantage-point the idea of crucifixion at Bergen, real though it seemed at the time, is now to be regarded as another false reading of the ciphers. Certainly no resurrection is forthcoming, although that had appeared to be the destination towards which the book was moving.

There is one underlying reason for the failure of *Notes of an Eccentric*: its ambiguity of genre. Is it autobiography or is it a work of fiction? The narrator is adamant that he is not writing a novel. He proposes to abandon his literary skill and write 'like a cobbler', on the grounds that the artifice of literary form conceals the truth of experience. A novel, he says, is always a game of hide-and-seek with the reader, concealing the event of inner importance that gave rise to it. This book, in contrast, is designed precisely to reveal that event, and aesthetic virtues must therefore be sacrificed.

On the other hand the narrator who makes this declaration is himself clearly fictionalized. He is known by the fictitious pseudonym Leonid Ledyanoy, while the authorial name under which the book is published is the real pseudonym Andrey Bely. The possibility is thus opened that *Notes of an Eccentric* is to be understood as a fictional work attributed to a fictional narrator who believes he is not writing fiction. The theme of truth to experience would then become part of the fictional subject-matter. But such an understanding of the work would require the constant support of an ironic distance between author and narrator. There is no reason in principle why a novel should not be written along these lines, but in *Notes of an Eccentric* the necessary ironic distance is simply not there, so that a consistent fictional reading of the text is precluded.

Kotik Letayev and *The Baptized Chinaman* differ from *Notes of an Eccentric* in that although they are based upon autobiographical material, they never propose to be anything other than fiction. Bely makes the distinction in a preface to the first publication of *The Baptized Chinaman*, where he explains that the *Epopee* itself (of which this is part) is accessible to anyone with sufficient artistic sensitivity, while the 'preface' (i.e. *Notes of an Eccentric*) is for an elite.[6] Fiction, then, is public, while the non-fictional account of experience given in *Notes of an Eccentric* is esoteric.[7] Through this distinction between private esoteric truth and public artistic fiction Bely seeks to solve the problem of genre by identifying two different classes of readers to whom the work is addressed in two different ways – in two different genres. It is a perennial problem in the literary discussion of esoteric works that they demand to be approached in a frame of mind that precludes criticism; the literary critic is not supposed to be able to make valid judgements about them. In this case, however, the critic is still left with his option to read the work as fiction, and the strictures already indicated remain valid. No problems are solved by this equivocation.

The most helpful definition of the genre of *Notes of an Eccentric* is one that occurs in the text itself, where it is spoken of as 'a diary in story form' (I, 68). This, too, of course, is equivocal, in implying that it may be viewed either as truth or as fiction. But by defining the kind of truth in question as that of a diary it points to an essential feature of the book. The difference between an autobiographical account of experience and a diary is that the former would be expected to be written from one consistent viewpoint outside (i.e. after) its material, while in the latter the attitude to the material of experience may vary from occasion to occasion. The diary form also potentially absolves the author from final responsibility for the views expressed; if he can change his mind during composition, so can he afterwards. This, indeed, appears to be what happened with *Notes of an Eccentric*. Bely's attitude to it fluctuated continuously during the period of composition and publication. His uncertainty as to whether his experience of the summer of 1916 has been correctly interpreted is evident in the text itself:

And the description of the journey is not a description of what happened; it is a description of how I read it; and how I lost my way.

In this sense my descriptions are those of a blinded traveller.

The light blinded me.

Now I have become blind: I can see nothing. (I, 158)

But beyond that he is increasingly uncertain as to whether he has an audience for the esoteric aspect of the book. The book is about his separation, his exclusion from his fellow anthroposophists, and in particular from his wife, Asya Turgeneva, who figures in the book as Nelly. If he is indeed as completely excluded as he sometimes fears, then that audience is lost to him. He must then address the book to his other audience, and correspondingly treat it as fiction. There are no misgivings about the availability of that other audience; he has turned, by the end of the book, back into the literary pseudonym, the publicly acclaimed author of fiction. His only doubts, as expressed in the preface to *The Baptized Chinaman*, hinge upon whether this text is accessible to that audience. But if that is to be the audience, then the work is fiction.

Thus the generic ambiguity of *Notes of an Eccentric* is directly attributable to real uncertainties in the life of its author. It is possible to trace a parallel between the tendency of the text at different periods of composition towards truth or fiction and what is known about Bely's relations with Asya Turgeneva and the anthroposophists in Switzerland.[8] As his relations with them cool, so he becomes increasingly adamant that *Notes of an Eccentric* is fiction. This process culminates in the prefaces and the first afterword written in 1922 after completion of the main text. In the preface to the Helikon edition, dated 2 January 1922, he claims that the narrator, Leonid Ledyanoy, is purely fictitious and not to be confused with the author, Andrey Bely. In the first, undated afterword, entitled 'Afterword to Leonid Ledyanoy's manuscript, written by someone's hand', an interview with Leonid Ledyanoy is described, in which he himself denies any autobiographical truth to the book.

In a final 'Afterword', however, dated September 1922, Bely cancels these appeals to fiction, and adopts a different means of distancing himself from the text. He admits now that there is not a line of the book that does not correspond to his own experience, but claims to have recovered entirely from the illness that the book records and to hate the record of it. He finds the book thoroughly bad as regards style, structure and plot; and in making this aesthetic judgement about it, while continuing to assert its validity as a true record of experience, he cancels the notion that bad writing serves the interests of sincerity and removes in principle the stark opposition between truth and fiction which underlay the book's aesthetic failure. But it must be observed that this is only possible because the book's 'truth' is seen from this standpoint to reside exclusively in its quality as a true record of error. Its esoteric truth is virtually cancelled, and the address to the esoteric audience goes by default. Now Bely draws a distinction between himself at the time of writing, and himself at the present moment, declaring that *Notes of an Eccentric* is intended as a satire on a certain state of mind, and that critics who are infuriated by it are experiencing exactly what its author intended. There is an obvious logical fallacy there, since the book could only be assumed to contain the intentions of the author at the time of writing; and in any case, the book is manifestly not a satire.

Bely's repudiation of the 'illness' that *Notes of an Eccentric* records takes a paradoxical form. The illness itself he calls 'mania grandiosa', the idea that the gifts of the Spirit could enter the inadequate vessel of his frail and untalented personality. In the text of the book it is really not clear whether the reader is to understand that the narrator's crisis comes about because he was not strong enough, not sufficiently prepared to bear the otherwise valid insights that were vouchsafed to him, or whether the insights were themselves illusory and the crisis stemmed from that. The parts written in 1918 tend to the former conclusion, those written in 1921 rather more (though not conclusively) to the latter. The afterword now definitively asserts the latter. Yet what does it then describe as the value of the diagnosis? 'Mania grandiosa' is an illness from which many have suffered and sunk into madness – Nietzsche, Schumann, Hölderlin – while Bely has restored himself to sanity by depicting it objectively. Moreover, it is an illness from which many now suffer, even if they are unaware of the fact. It is the illness of the age; and critics who condemn the book in ignorance of this fact need to live another couple of hundred years to find it out. The critics in question might be forgiven for finding the value of the diagnosis difficult to distinguish from the illness itself.

The apparent change in direction in the plot is probably also due to the change in Bely's attitude to the material between the two periods of composition. The ending as we have it in the Helikon edition is most likely not the ending that was envisaged in 1918. Bely had originally justified the discontinuation of its publication by the argument that it would drag on for years, and had explained to Ivanov-Razumnik in March 1919 that *Notes of an Eccentric* had 'got stuck' because of the volume of work he was doing at that time for Proletkul't.[9] He complained about the pressure of ephemeral work which was preventing him from devoting himself to his real task of writing the *Epopee* as early as the preface to *Notes of an Eccentric* in *Notes of Dreamers* No.1, and repeated the complaint at length in a later article, 'Why I cannot undertake cultural work'.[10] Yet the evidence strongly suggests that all but the final fifteen chapters as published by Helikon already existed in draft by the end of 1918. Knowing the pace at which Bely was able to work, it seems unlikely that even Proletkul't could have stood between him and the completion of fifteen chapters. It seems much more likely that at this time Bely intended *Notes of an Eccentric* to be considerably longer than the final Helikon text, and that that was why the printing was likely to go on for years. The division into two volumes, which appears to give a finality to the existing form of the book, was not introduced until the Helikon edition, and there is no break in the *Notes of Dreamers* text corresponding to the break between them. This idea is perhaps supported by Bely's mention, in his letter to Ivanov-Razumnik of 1–2 March 1927, of his completing the 'tail' (*khvostik*) of *Notes of an Eccentric* in Berlin in December 1921;[11] it possibly implies that the ending in the Helikon edition is a kind of appendage, or afterthought.

The final stages of the narrator's journey, north through Sweden and south again through Finland, along with the re-assertion of the literary pseudonym, are to be found only in the Helikon edition, and presumably constitute the part Bely wrote in Berlin at the end of 1921. In general outline there is little reason to doubt that this was the intended shape of the book's ending. The title 'Return to the Homeland' is present from the outset, and of course Bely did in fact return to Russia by this route in 1916. Yet it is not necessarily the case that his geographical and spiritual homelands were always so far apart. There is a suggestion in the later chapters of the Helikon edition that Russia might take over the role that the narrator had arrogated to himself – of being crucified and resurrected. This is an idea that played an important part in Bely's poetry of 1916 and 1917, and which also underlies his long poem *Christ is Arisen*, written in April 1918, while he was at work on *Notes of an Eccentric*.[12] This theme appears only in a muted form in *Notes of an Eccentric* (II, 215–23), and has indeed to some extent to be inferred from his other writings of the period; but it is certainly possible that it was originally intended to play a much more important part. The book would have made much better aesthetic sense in that case, since its themes would have been more fully worked out, and the narrator's personal crucifixion would have received a balancing alternative instead of a simple negation. It would, incidentally, also have given a deeper meaning to the discarded title 'Return to the Homeland'.

The rejection of the artifice of fiction entails, at least in theory and declared intention, the self-denying ordinance of abandoning literary skill and writing 'like a cobbler'. What this means in practice is that *Notes of an Eccentric*, unlike Bely's other work of this period, contains virtually no neologisms and is rhythmically uneven, reading rather like a rough draft of his usual style. The narrator repeatedly protests that language is itself inadequate to express what he has to say (I, 155, 171, 198), which in the circumstances strikes a somewhat disingenuous note, since that was precisely why Bely developed the devices that he now shuns. But he does not in fact shun them all. The recurrent image, leitmotif and pun, the principal means he has used to create plurality of meaning, are all abundantly in evidence. He even uses typographical devices to create mystical shapes on the page. As Shklovsky noted, 'cobblers don't write things like that'.[13] Stylistically the book falls between two stools and lacks any clear identity.

The generic ambiguity of *Notes of an Eccentric* is similarly unproductive. The disruption of traditional genre divisions is typical of Bely's work, both theoretical and artistic, throughout his career, from the idea of the 'Symphony' as a literary form and the approximation of literature to music, to the intrusion of the rhythmic regularity of verse into the traditional prose medium of the novel. It is part of that striving to extend the boundaries of art that is frequently encountered in Symbolist writing. But in this particular case the generic indeterminacy is the product of simple indecision; the book falls between two stools here too.

The same striving to reach beyond the confines of conventional art forms is expressed in the Symbolist idea of a transition from aesthetic to religious creation, the abandonment of art in the interests of a higher calling. In *The Silver Dove* Bely had used this as part of his subject-matter and depicted it objectively. In *Notes of an Eccentric*, however, it recurs in the idea that the abandonment of literary skill serves the interests of sincerity and thus may succeed in conveying to the reader the literal truth of what is expressed. By the time he wrote the final afterword in the autumn of 1922 Bely had evidently once more detached himself from this notion, and it never appears in his work again. But it is certainly not depicted objectively in the body of the book. In writing *Notes of an Eccentric* Bely fell for an illusion very similar to the one to which his hero Dar'yal'sky had succumbed.

In *Notes of an Eccentric*, unlike the novels of childhood, Bely was using autobiographical material that was both recent and incompletely interpreted. The intensity of the underlying experience can be sensed, despite the book's aesthetic failure, but its nature cannot easily be understood, in large part because Bely was addressing the book to an occult readership. There is, however, another source which conveys a much clearer impression of the nature of the experience. That is his intimate autobiography, compiled in the year after *Notes of an Eccentric* was completed. Here Bely gives a quite unadorned and entirely unfictionalized account of the intense occult experiences that accompanied his final decision, in the autumn of 1913, to devote himself to anthroposophy.[14] It enables the reader to understand that Bely believed quite literally that he was to undergo something akin to crucifixion, and thus be admitted to a new spiritual era. It shows that he regarded anthroposophy as destined to save the world by preparing for the second coming of Christ, and that he felt himself to be in a unique, quasi-filial relationship to Rudolf Steiner himself. Combined with what is known about Bely's later alienation from the Western anthroposophists,[15] this material makes much more comprehensible the motives that led him to write such a confused and confusing book. As a biographical document *Notes of an Eccentric* retains considerable interest.

As a literary document its interest is more limited. It has no virtues in style or structure that are not far better manifested in other works, and cannot even be claimed to occupy an illuminating transitional place in the development of Bely's techniques. Its interest lies exclusively in its material. The logic of Bely's *Epopee*, the series of autobiographical novels starting with earliest childhood, requires that they be brought up to the time of writing – or at least to the time of the mystical insight or conversion from which they all take their source. There is no logical reason for stopping at any other point, and that, evidently, is why Bely envisaged so massive a work. But the end of one cycle of development must be the beginning of the next; a spiral is always open at the end, and it is not to be imagined that Bely conceived of his whole *Epopee* as an enclosed circle. The 'Prologue' to the *Epopee* would have not only to look backwards to childhood from the point of conversion, but also forwards to the future. The recapitulation of childhood is not an end in itself, but a step towards that new spiritual condition which anthroposophy presages. The theme must therefore arise of the way in which an adult is to make that spiritual transition. *Notes of an Eccentric* approaches this theme in its anticipation of crucifixion, but then shies away from it in Bely's uncertainty as to whether that was indeed what he had experienced. The simple personal doubt on Bely's part makes it impossible to embody that theme in a form that is not unambiguously fiction.

Bely explained in a letter to Ivanov-Razumnik how the theme of his *Epopee* was later channelled into his vast philosophical treatise, *The History of the Spiritual Soul*.[16] In the process of this transition it was stripped of its personal biographical reference, and given a general historical significance. The distinction Bely makes in the letter is between two concepts which, according to the memoirs of Bely's widow, K.N. Bugayeva, are essential to the treatise. That work, in her description, rests upon the distinction between the concepts of the 'personality' (*lichnost'*) and the 'individuum' (*individuum*). The 'personality' began the process of separating itself off from the species in Ancient Greece, as is seen in the separation of individual characters from the chorus of Greek tragedy. It reached the apex of its development at the time of the Renaissance, since when it has been in decline. Meanwhile the 'individuum', which is due to succeed the 'personality', has been developing. The 'individuum' is distinguished by the fact that it does not regard itself as self-sufficient, but is the unit of a collective. Moreover, it is itself a collective in the sense that it represents the controlled harmony of the various, possibly conflicting desires of different aspects of the 'personality'.[17] Bely clearly had the word's derivation in mind: the 'in-dividuum' is that which is plural, but not divided. Bugayeva describes it in purely psychological terms, but there can be little doubt that Bely's idea went further than this. For an anthroposophist, believing in re-incarnation and karma, thinks of the individual also as a sum of re-incarnations. S. Cioran has detected this theme in *Notes of an Eccentric*.[18] Indeed Bely describes there both the experience of the inadequacy of the empirical person, and also the sense of its removal in his experience in Bergen in October 1913:

> It seemed to me: there was no *man* in *man*; and all that we call 'human' embraces only particulars, features, specializations of a human life; I felt the '*man*' in me as that point from which there shone forth the multiplicities of my human lives (it was only by chance I had selected one); I sensed in myself the collision of many people; a horde of many voices – my doubles, my trebles! – drowned out in me the specialization of poet, writer, theoretician; I sought the harmony of unrealized possibilities; and I came to a conception of '*man*' which does not exist in man; all we 'men' (with a small letter only) are the receptacles of Him, the One. (I, 72)

> ...the transformation in the point of the 'Ego' of the man in me into Man[19] occurred here in Bergen; at that moment in the history of my life all my incarnations (past and future lives), bending around, describing a circle, closed; and became for me a unity; amidst all its lives, contemplating them all, stood an immense 'Ego', conquering by immense rhythms, those of its body, soul, subconsciousness, consciousness and spirit: –
> – I was Man[19] (with a capital letter)... (II, 72)[20]

In his intimate autobiography Bely described the occult experience of 1913 as his meeting with Christ. These passages from *Notes of an Eccentric* reveal what is meant: the realization that it is in Christ, as the greater Ego, the common subject, that the disharmonies of all empirical existences are reconciled. This is the greater theme into which the misconceived spiritual autobiography of *Notes of an Eccentric* had to grow, and which he sought to develop in his subsequent work.

8

Moscow

Bely returned to Russia from Berlin in the autumn of 1923. His two years in emigration were a period of great distress, during which his relations with the anthroposophical movement in the West collapsed almost entirely. He was able to restore his own trust in and affection for Steiner himself at their last meeting in Stuttgart in March 1923,[1] and did not change in his attachment to Steiner's ideas; but he repudiated the Anthroposophical Society as an institution, and argued later that the spiritual community anthroposophy sought was incompatible with any kind of real social organization.[2] All social forms have the tendency to restrict and distort the development of the individual spirit.

That development remained his theme, both in the memoir literature where he traced it in his own personal life and the history of his generation, and in the fictional works in which it is embodied in fictional characters. It even underlies his critical studies, where his theories about the development of rhythm in literary art or of perspective in painting are based upon a conception of the spirit's increasing penetration of the secrets of nature, in parallel with its increasing liberation from the tyranny of static forms.

His *Epopee* was to be an epic of the spirit. If that is a contradiction in terms it is at all events a contradiction that corresponds to the identification of inner and outer worlds in Bely's thought, and to the experiments with genre that follow from it. It was noted, however, that already in *The Baptized Chinaman* Bely was compelled to allow the objective world a substantial degree of autonomy, and that problems of internal structure developed in the text as a result. The complete failure of *Notes of an Eccentric* persuaded him to abandon the attempt to create this new kind of epic. Nevertheless he retained the conviction that it was towards a new form of epic that literature was moving. In a reply to a questionnaire organized by an *emigré* journal in Berlin, he had written of his belief that 'we are moving towards the monumental poem – whether in verse or prose I don't know'.[3]

One of his first literary tasks on returning to Russia was the adaptation of *Petersburg* for the stage. He explained to Ivanov-Razumnik how this work brought him back to the novel form, which he had 'so hated' since 1912.[4] By the spring of 1924 the idea of the novel *Moscow* had occurred to him from a combination of the 'Moscow' of his memoirs (he was referring to the version written in Berlin that has never been published) and a fresh approach to the novel. It is principally the element of plot that distinguishes the novel form, as Bely understands the term here, from the fictionalized spiritual autobiography to which he had devoted himself since the completion of *Petersburg* in 1913. His last novels have elaborate plots, involving much suffering and cruelty, and centring upon a hero who resembles the heroes of the early novels in his combination of physical passivity with an active spiritual nature.

Like the early novels, too, *Moscow* was envisaged as part of a work in many volumes that was never completed. *The Moscow Eccentric* and *Moscow in Jeopardy* were published in 1926 as the two parts of the first volume,[5] and it was then stated that the whole work would consist of two volumes.[6] As Bely continued the writing, however, the material expanded beyond his expectations, and in the preface to the second volume, *Masks*, he declared that the entire work would comprise four volumes.[7] In the event *Masks* was Bely's last novel; the third and fourth parts were never written.[8]

Like *The Baptized Chinaman*, *Moscow* is described in the preface as 'half a historical novel'. The Moscow that it recalls is not, however, the Moscow of Bely's childhood, but rather that of the Symbolist decade. There are many satirical descriptions of society and salon life where aestheticism, mysticism and political extremism coexist amorphously. There is no attempt at historical precision; although the novel's ending coincides with the outbreak of the First World War, its action could not be specifically attributed to 1914 (a year during which Bely never even visited Russia), but takes place in a period that is broadly recognizable as falling between 1905 and 1914. *Moscow* has none of the occasional nostalgia of *The Baptized Chinaman*, since the period it recalls is evoked without regret and depicted without sympathy. Memory, in any case, is not present as an overt theme. There is no first-person narrator with a need to identify the time of writing in order to establish his perspective. In narrative attitude *Moscow* reverts to novelistic tradition; there is a single third-person narrator who does not intervene with any address on his own behalf to the reader. There is no return to the self-conscious narrator of Bely's earlier novels. Rather there is a continuation of the development that was already evident in a comparison of *Kotik Letayev* and *The Baptized Chinaman*. The narrator is subordinated to the material; he is the vehicle for its revelation; and the language of the novel serves less the function of identifying the narrator than that of re-creating the world perceived.

Objective reality thus acquires in *Moscow* an autonomy that it has not possessed in any novel of Bely's since *The Silver Dove*. This can clearly be seen in the nature and function of the novel's descriptive passages. In *Petersburg* the descriptions of the city focussed entirely upon images which acquired symbolic connotations, and the particularity of phenomena was eventually submerged in their symbolic interchangeability. In *Moscow* the function of descriptions is much closer to that of the similar passages in *The Baptized Chinaman*; they seek to capture that very particularity in language.

The novel's central hero is Professor Korobkin, a professor of mathematics at Moscow University and a mathematician of world renown. It is immediately evident that to a substantial extent this character is based upon Bely's own father, and is a development of the character of Professor Letayev in the novels of childhood. Professor Letayev was not, of course, the central character of the novels in which he appeared, but one of the poles in terms of which the child's development was charted. The confusing attempt at identifying father and son at the end of *The Baptized Chinaman* gives an indication of future developments. For Professor Korobkin, despite possessing many features that make him resemble his predecessor, is based in his inner experience much more upon Bely himself, and the ethical concerns that came to preoccupy him in later years.[9] Korobkin possesses another literary antecedent in the identically named hero of Bely's short story 'The Yogi', of 1918, a character who has been convincingly shown to be drawn in part from the philosopher Nikolay Fyodorov (1828–1903).[10] The name itself first appeared in conversation with V.Ivanov as early as

1909.[11] The resemblance between the Korobkin of 'The Yogi' and the hero of the *Moscow* novels is not great; the earlier variant of the character is marked by mystical and exalted states much closer to *Notes of an Eccentric* than to *Moscow*; and nothing further is known about the character Bely mentioned in 1909. Nevertheless the derivation of the name from *korobka* (a box), which is used symbolically in the novel, suggests a theme which probably developed through these various hypostases. The human spirit enclosed within the cranium (*cherepnaya korobka*) of the empirical individual is capable of expansion out into the universe – a theme in the story which links it to *Notes of an Eccentric* and in some measure to *Petersburg*[12] – and out into true communion with other people – the ethical theme which is more evident in the novel.

The first part of *Moscow*, *The Moscow Eccentric*, introduces all the main characters and reveals the actual relations between them, concealed beneath the apparent decorum of their domestic and social relationships. The action is reserved for the second part, *Moscow in Jeopardy*. Professor Korobkin has a wife, Vasilisa Sergeyevna, a son, Mitya, and a daughter, Nadya. His counterpart in the academic world is Professor Zadopyatov, a representative of 'inexact science', as opposed to Korobkin's 'exact science' of mathematics, and the author of four volumes of eclectic verbiage. He has a wife, Anna Pavlovna. Korobkin's true antagonist is the ostensible businessman and actual international espionage agent Mandro, whose sixteen-year-old daughter Lizasha is friendly with Mitya Korobkin. Mandro has as assistants Korobkin's neighbour across the street, Gribikov, and a syphilitic dwarf by the name of Yasha Kaval'kas. The other major character is Korobkin's friend and chess-partner, Tsetserko-Pukierko, known simply as Kierko.

Like Professor Letayev, Professor Korobkin lives in the world of mathematics. A brief summary of his biography is given early in the first chapter, describing his youth as the son of a military doctor in the Caucasus, and his reaction to the chaotic world in which he lived, his conclusion that security and clarity were only to be attained through the certainty of scientific verification (I, 14–15).[13] He is alienated from his family. His son, who receives no pocket-money because his father cannot see that he needs any, has taken to purloining his father's books and selling them to dealers in order to raise a little cash (I, 24). His wife, it transpires, has for years been carrying on an affair with Professor Zadopyatov, but with Professor Korobkin's knowledge and connivance (1, 201). His attitude to this affair is displayed when Zadopyatov's wife, who has been in ignorance of it, discovers Vasilisa Sergeyevna's love-letters to her husband and sends them to Korobkin (1, 173). He returns the packet unopened to Zadopyatov (1, 204). The only member of his family with whom he has any real communication is his daughter, and a brief scene between these two demonstrates Korobkin's need for the deep human relations he cannot find with his wife and son.

Korobkin's alienation from his family only becomes fully evident when, following an accident, he is compelled to spend all his time at home, instead of going to the university. The accident occurs when he is coming away from a lecture and a new idea comes into his head. Finding a piece of chalk in his pocket, he mistakes the side of a cab standing in the street for a blackboard, and begins to work out calculations upon it. The cab starts off, and the professor, vainly striving to keep pace with his accelerating blackboard, falls in the street (1, 69–70). This is the first instance in which his static world becomes dynamic. Forced to stay at home, he irritates everyone in the household by constantly walking round the house in search of something, and it is realized that domestic peace exists only on condition of the professor's absence (1, 91).

The reader is in a position to guess what it is that the professor is looking for. Korobkin has already noticed that some of his books have disappeared, and that some of those missing contained important notes he had made of calculations leading up to a discovery. The discovery is relevant not only to pure mathematics, but also to mechanics, and indicates the possibility of attaining speeds as high as the speed of light (1, 54–5). The discovery itself is still intact, but Korobkin is uneasy about the disappearance of the notes, and hides the discovery under the floorboards in his study (1, 95–6).

The professor's unease is fully justified. His notes are finding their way, through Gribikov, who follows his son and buys back the books he sells, to Mandro. This state of affairs is only gradually elucidated. Mitya Korobkin is a welcome guest at Mandro's house, although he is unprepossessing and less intelligent than many of his classmates who are not received. Mandro interrogates him about his father's work, but does not, at first, trouble to make his father's acquaintance. It becomes evident that Mandro already has in his possession one particularly important note of the professor's, a photographed copy of which, sent to Berlin, has enabled German scientists to deduce the military significance of Korobkin's discovery (I, 21, 79).

The details of the discovery have still to be found, and the principal interest of the plot lies in Mandro's diverse attempts to gain possession of it. He persuades Gribikov to give the dwarf Yasha a room in his apartment, and Yasha tries to acquire the discovery by ingratiating himself with the professor's servants. Mandro visits Korobkin on the initial pretext that where children are friends, parents should also be acquainted, but swiftly turns the conversation to the discovery and offers Korobkin half a million roubles for it. Korobkin replies that he has no discovery, and would not sell it if he had (I, 159). Only after this visit does the professor come to realize the full implications of the discovery he has made; he becomes doubly suspicious and pays Mandro a return visit in the hope of finding out more about him.

For no evident reason Gribikov takes some of the books back to the professor, and it seems Mitya's theft is about to be exposed. Kierko, however, who happens to be present at the time, prevents Gribikov from telling all he knows, and the identity of the thief remains undisclosed (I, 101–5). This theft is not Mitya's only misdemeanour. Owing to the fact that his father's library consists entirely of scientific works and that he has no money to buy books for himself, he is, in comparison with his classmates, extremely ignorant of literature. He is painfully aware of this, and has adopted the solution of playing truant from school and spending his days in the public library (I, 117). His forged excuse notes are revealed, and he expects to be expelled from school. However, he is forgiven for this by his headmaster, an event which is represented as a turning-point in his life. He experiences almost a rebirth, and acquires a sense of personal dignity and of purpose (I, 151). After this he ceases to visit Lizasha, to whom he had previously made half-hearted erotic advances. These advances are later explained as the substitute for the genuine communication for which both of them strove, but which they were unable to attain (I, 231).

After this point Mitya virtually disappears from the novel; the theme of his rebirth is not developed and his relationship with

Lizasha comes to an end. The interest in Lizasha comes to centre entirely upon her relationship with her father. She idolizes him, calling him '*bogushka*' (affectionate diminutive of *bog* – a god), but in the course of the first part a growing distrust of him develops in her. No sooner has she asserted to Mitya that she never lies, than she is compelled to do so in order to allay Mitya's suspicions about the note of his father's that he has discovered in Mandro's house. She is disturbed by the need to lie about dealings of her father's that she does not understand, and her latent suspicion of those dealings becomes conscious (I, 119–23). More important, however, is her unease at her father's attitude towards her; his caresses are not of a paternal nature, and the idea of kissing him provokes in her an involuntary feeling of guilt (I, 235–7).

Lizasha's growing suspicion of Mandro is not economically employed in the essentially analytical structure of *The Moscow Eccentric*. The reader learns about Mandro not through Lizasha, but independently of her. His true nature as a political intriguer is largely revealed through direct comment from the narrator early in the novel (I, 75–6). His perverse erotic leanings are revealed through the report of rumours about him that circulate in society (I, 124–5, 227). Lizasha's distrust of her father is a theme that is developed in its own right, and which derives poignancy from the fact that she comes to suspect less than the reader knows to be the case.

In *Moscow in Jeopardy* the potentially explosive situation revealed in the first part comes to realize its potential. Zadopyatov's wife prepares to avenge herself on Vasilisa Sergeyevna by throwing acid over her, but just at the moment of execution, when she is standing face to face with her intended victim, she has a stroke and collapses (II, 53–4). Professor Zadopyatov experiences a belated remorse, and is seen at his summer cottage nursing his paralysed wife, who is confined to a wheel-chair. Vasilisa Sergeyevna visits him there, and their liaison is brought to an end (II, 100–5). She and Mitya go away to Yalta (II, 111), leaving Professor Korobkin and Nadya alone at their country cottage, not far from Zadopyatov's.

Lizasha's suspicion of her father increases further when, at a meeting of the Free Aesthetic Society, they meet Kierko, who reveals knowledge of facts about Mandro's life which are not in themselves of any evident significance, but are important in that they are contrary to what Lizasha believed about her father's past. This encounter between Lizasha and Kierko is stated by the narrator to be of crucial importance for them both (II, 20–1). The relationship between Lizasha and Mandro comes to a head when Mandro's housekeeper, Madame Vulevu (Voulez-vous), pretends to go away. Taking advantage of her seeming absence, Mandro rapes Lizasha.[14] This occurrence is not actually described. What is described is a scene between them when Mandro goes to Lizasha's bedroom on the pretext of clarifying their estranged relationship, during which Lizasha drops a knife she had intended to use in self-defence. This meeting is cut short by a visit from the dwarf, Yasha (II, 141–6). The assault itself is revealed by a scream, followed by the re-appearance of Madame Vulevu, and scraps of conversation which disclose what has happened (II, 153–5). Lizasha is taken to the house of an acquaintance, Madame Evikhkayten (Ewigkeiten), and Mandro disappears. Later it is revealed that Lizasha is pregnant. She develops a friendship with Kierko, who introduces her to revolutionary ideas (II, 182–8).

Before his departure to his country cottage, Professor Korobkin's life in Moscow is interrupted by two episodes with no direct bearing on the plot. The first is the visit of the Japanese mathematician, Issi-Nissi, an admirer of Korobkin's, whom the professor exhausts by taking him round all the sights of Moscow without allowing him to rest after his journey (II, 25–37). The second is a ceremony at the university, held in his honour, during which a newly discovered star is named, after him, Kappa-Korobkin. The ceremony ends with the attempt to carry the professor shoulder-high down the stairs of the university, but in appearance this procession is said to resemble the dragging of a heretic to the cliff from which he is to be thrown (II, 60–75).

The dwarf makes an attempt to steal the professor's discovery by climbing in through the window, but is heard doing so and foiled. When it is learnt that he was the intruder, the professor takes solace in the suggested interpretation that he was merely in pursuit of one of the servants, to whom he has been paying court. He is reluctant to believe that anyone is really trying to gain possession of his discovery, and is inclined to attribute the signs of this to his own blood-pressure (II, 46–51). He tries to hold fast to this interpretation even when, at his country cottage, he becomes convinced that he is being followed (II, 120–1). It ceases to be tenable, however, when he receives from the hands of one Vish-nyakov, a tailor (who has the information from the now repentant Yasha), an anonymous letter warning him of the imminent theft of his papers (II, 125). He has already taken the precaution of remov-ing them from their hiding-place in the house, and has had them sewn into his waistcoat, but he now decides that the only adequate solution is to destroy both the discovery itself and all the papers with preliminary calculations (II, 191). He sets off back to Moscow in order to do this. On the way to the station he is approached by a stranger who asks him the way to the station and accompanies him all the way back to Moscow. He claims to be a ruined landowner in search of work and a place to sleep, and against his own better judgement, Korobkin offers him a bed for the night in his own house. Once in the house, the stranger identifies himself as Mandro, and demands the professor's discovery. When he refuses to part with it Mandro resorts to violence, ties Korobkin to a chair and burns his eye out with a candle. In the process both the torturer and his victim go mad, but the professor does not relinqu-ish his discovery. Korobkin is taken to a mental hospital and Mandro to the prison hospital, where he is said to die. The novel ends with the outbreak of the First World War.

The professor's discovery has immense implications for military technology. In its destructive power it resembles the bomb in *Petersburg*. Both have their provenance in the human mind, and both are capable of wreaking havoc on the existing world. Whereas in *Petersburg*, however, the relationship between mind and bomb was expressed in symbolic connections that could not be translated into empirical causation, that between the professor's mind and his discovery is precisely the kind of causal connection that we presume to exist in all scientific inquiry. Moreover the idea of explosion is not in any sense equated with that of spiritual transformation. The ambiguity that arose both in *Petersburg* and in *Notes of an Eccentric* because of this identification is not present in *Moscow*. Nikolay Apollonovich's attempts in *Petersburg* to prevent the bomb from exploding were due not to any positive change of heart – that is reserved for the epilogue – but merely to fear and vacillation. Professor Korobkin, by contrast, is seen throughout the novel to be undergoing a process of spiritual trans-formation, and at the end offers positive resistance, in the name of an ethical ideal, to the exploitation of his discovery. The outbreak of war is not related to the potentialities of the discovery, but parallels, as an image of suffering, of Golgotha, the professor's fate at the hands of Mandro.

Transformation by violence and transformation by spiritual discipline are thus expressly contrasted in *Moscow* in a way that was not evident in Bely's earlier work, and which undoubtedly owes much to the experience of war and revolution. His rejection of the *status quo* is, however, unchanged. The world of pre-revolutionary Moscow is likened to pre-history.[15] The city itself is evoked as a disorderly clutter of miscellaneous buildings:

Doma, domy, domiki, prosto domchonki i dazhe domchonochki: pyatietazhnyy otstroyennyy tol'ko chto, kremovyy, ves' v razgirlyandakh lepnykh; derevyanen'kiy, sinen'kiy; daleye: kamennyy, serozelyonyy, kotoryy statuilsya alyapovato frontonom... (Houses, great houses, small houses, minute ones and even diminutive houses: one of five storeys, just finished, in cream and all covered in garlands of stucco; a little blue wooden one; further a stone-built grey-green one whose ungainly pediment bristles with statues...) (I, 15)

This impression is most consistently conveyed through the leit-motif:

dom – kamenny kom; dom za domom – kom komom; fasad za fasadom – ad adom... (each house a clutter of stone; house upon house – clutter upon clutter; façade on façade – a very Hades...)

which occurs several times either in full or in part. On a number of these occasions it is accompanied by the further phrase:

a dveri – kak treshchiny...

(and the doors are like fissures)

or some mutation of it. Out of these fissures are said to emerge monsters. It is particularly in *Moscow in Jeopardy* that imagery is introduced relating to pre-history and defunct or mythical civilizations. There are recurrent mentions of the development of man from ape, of Atlantis, Easter Island and the Aztec civilization of Mexico. In the anthroposophical scheme of things savagery and barbarism arise from the failure of cultures to evolve as they are destined to do. The collapse of contemporary culture into barbarism was a topic that had figured extensively in Bely's writing both during the war and again during his period in Berlin. It is expressed most fully in *One of the Mansions of the Realm of Shadows*, published shortly after his return to Russia, in which he castigated in such terms the Western civilization he had left behind.[16] That brochure includes sections from the otherwise unpublished second volume of his travel notes on Sicily and North Africa, dating originally from 1911, which reveal a close relation between the idea of barbarism as it appears now and the use made in *Petersburg* of the image of Egypt.

The image of the city of Moscow in this novel does not acquire the pervasive symbolic force that Bely succeeded in creating in the image of Petersburg. In part this is because the symbolic value Bely does give it is derived from his anthroposophical thought-system rather than from Russian literary traditions. The older capital does not possess in Russian literature a symbolic tradition equal to that of its northern counterpart, and the tradition which does exist is evidently not appropriate to Bely's purposes. In *Eugene Onegin* or Tolstoy's long novels Moscow represents older, patriarchal values, in contrast to Petersburg, while in Chekhov's *The Three Sisters* it stands as a general symbol of nostalgia for a lost paradise; in Boborykin's *Kitay-gorod* it appears as the nation's commercial centre. None of these have anything to do with the 'horror' of Moscow, which, in a letter to Blok in 1913, Bely protested he had no words to portray.[17] But perhaps the main reason why the city does not acquire great symbolic resonance is that the descriptions in *Moscow* are not consistently directed to that purpose. The many descriptive passages that evoke particula-rized images of the city or countryside at specific times of day or year have less to do with the city's symbolic value, than with the professor's spiritual transformation, since the linguistic re-creation of the perceived world, which these passages enact, is a creative process that parallels the professor's development.

The plot leaves many ends untied. In these later years Bely resumed the reading of Dickens, but it was not plot construction that he learned from him. Nor is this inconclusiveness attributable entirely to Bely's plans for further volumes. Not only does the second volume abandon many of the characters whose fates are not concluded in the first, but it is clear from K.N.Bugayeva's account of his plans for the continuation that there was never any intention of returning to them.[18] The situation is similar to that at the end of *The Silver Dove*, with its unredeemed promise of resolution. It is not hard to see that Bely's entire approach is inimical to conclusions. An enclosed plot structure such as that in *Bleak House* is only compatible with a confidence in the finality of empirical experience which Bely never had. Nevertheless the more minor characters in *Moscow* have considerably greater independent status than the mere background figures of *The Silver Dove*. What links them to the main line of the action is a system of thematic parallels, rather than the development of real personal and social relationships.

Most of the characters of *Moscow* are associated in one way or another with the theme of transformation. The rebirth of Mitya Korobkin is one such instance, though he disappears thereafter and reappears in *Masks* in a guise which somewhat belies it. Professor Zadopyatov changes after his wife's stroke, realizing the falsity of his life and abandoning his pose of greatness. His wife, although now paralysed, is also presented as having undergone a transformation of a similar kind, as she removes the spectacles behind which she had previously hidden. Even the syphilitic dwarf rebels against his demonic master and joins the Salvation Army.

An important variant of this theme is the theme of political revolution. In *Petersburg* it had been a manifestation of Mongolism and inseparable from the destruction inherent in the bomb. In *Moscow* and *Masks* it plays quite a different role. In the two volumes together it is principally represented by Kierko, but both the theme and the character are more fully developed in *Masks* than in the earlier novel. Kierko plays no part in the main plot of *Moscow*, and is indeed apparently ignorant of Professor Korobkin's discovery. He has only a subordinate function, in that he finally destroys Lizasha's faith in her father, and befriends her after the rape and Mandro's disappearance. His own ideological leanings only become clear during his friendship with Lizasha. Kierko is evidently a character Bely introduced in the first volume in order to be able to develop him subsequently. The important features of him to emerge at this stage are his good nature, the atmosphere of relaxation but a certain unease that he brings to Korobkin's house when he visits (I, 42), and his ability to communicate easily with all sorts and conditions of men (II, 98–9, 221–2). He is, moreover, the only friend Korobkin possesses. The fact that so sympathetic a character is made the bearer of Marxist ideas reveals the attempt, which is present in most of Bely's published work after his return to Russia, to establish a form of compromise between his own essentially unchanged ideas and the dominant philosophy of the much-changed state in which he now lived. In *Moscow* the idea of revolution as a means of transforming reality is in fact borne more by Lizasha than by Kierko. She first appears as a highly-strung young lady who fancies herself as a *rusalka*, and has a vague, purely emotional sense of the inadequacy of the world in which she lives. She tries to convey this feeling to Mitya, but he fails to understand her (I, 83, 122). Gradually she comes to identify this emotional condition with ideas of revolution, and her longing for another life with a leap into the 'realm of freedom' (I, 233–4). The narrator virtually apologizes to his readers for the distorted image of social problems in Lizasha's mind. Only under the tutelage of Kierko does she come to a more 'correct' understanding, realizing that her vision of herself as a *rusalka* was a class-determined error, and that her longing for another life was in fact a longing for a classless society (II, 187). Lizasha's development as a revolutionary has no bearing upon the central plot of *Moscow*, and the essential question of the real relationship between theories of political revolution and of individual spiritual regeneration are not touched upon until the characters reappear in *Masks*.

All these peripheral characters are ultimately subordinate to Professor Korobkin. Like all Bely's heroes, he bears the novel's fundamental duality within him. The two poles of his existence are his unique mathematical ability, equalled by only a handful of people in the world, and the disorder and inadequacy of his personal life. In neither of these aspects is he a full three-dimensional being; in the mathematical world his ego lives in n dimensions, while in the empirical world he is identified with his dog Tom, living in two dimensions. From the interaction of these two aspects, however, a real man is to emerge (I, 210).[19] His division into these two conflicting extremes is the *status quo* of the outset, which the action of the novel disrupts. The internal action is the story of Korobkin's growing realization that his view of the world as rationally ordered is not adequate to the reality surrounding him. His view of the world's rationality is expressed in his favourite turns of phrase, in his opinions about marriage, which bear no relation to the reality of his own marriage (I, 30), and in the frequently mentioned bust of Leibniz which stands in his room.[20] He has a naive faith in progress, based on the conviction that the masses will follow the mathematicians, who lead them to clarity (I, 38). The event which triggers off the internal action is the professor's accident, which appears at first to be merely a humorous illustration of his absent-mindedness, but which is gradually revealed not only as the catalyst that explodes the fiction of domestic peace, but also as the source of the professor's awareness of the full importance of his discovery. The nature of the accident itself reveals the discrepancy between Korobkin's thought and the reality in which he lives; his own later recollections of it fully display its importance for the internal action (II, 120, 245).

A moving cab also runs over the professor's dog. The untimely death of his two-dimensional double clearly parallels the disruption of his static notions. The dog had already been linked, through a humorous remark of Kierko's, with the idea of evolution: 'I'm an animal too, but I'm perfecting myself; you aren't yet' (I, 43). On its death it comes to be more specifically associated with the idea of evolution through re-incarnation, as Nadya picks up the professor's mention of this idea in Hindu thought. A connection is thus made with the background imagery of defunct cultures, but it is not until much later that this association reaches the professor's awareness.

The professor's other aspect, his ego that resides in a world of n dimensions, is developed in the image of the star, Kappa-Korobkin, named after him at his jubilee. The distance between this star and the earth, a thousand light-years, comes to represent the distance between the spheres in which his thought moves and the real world that he and the other characters inhabit (II, 71). This distance is also the gulf between the technical possibilities opened up to man by his scientific discoveries and the frailty of his moral sense that must guide their employment; the autonomous reason has fatally outstripped man's ethical development, and Bely's concern is to redress that balance.

It is a series of events in the second chapter of *Moscow in Jeopardy* that finally brings home to Korobkin the complete inadequacy of his system of thought. He has a dream in which various mutations of the name Proverchenko, playing on phonetic similarities with the verbs *proveryat'* (to check) and *vertet'* (to turn), join forces with Heraclitus to teach the professor that there are no static forms, only forms of movement (II, 90–2). Shortly thereafter he visits Professor Zadopyatov at his summer cottage. He begins to express his loss of faith in progress, arguing that if the masses will not, as he had formerly supposed, follow the mathematicians to clarity, then what he had regarded as progress is in fact a regression and must lead to destruction. Without that clarity, the masses are not to be trusted with electricity. He argues that the more specialized sciences concretize the problems of less specialized ones, but that the repeated division of the object of study in this way is comparable to the constant division of a number into infinitely small parts: however small they become, the result will never be zero. So the sciences are like a hyperbola and reality like an asymptote, which approaches nearer and nearer to the hyperbola but never meets it. At this point it is clear that Korobkin is still trying to cling to the belief that his own exact science provides reliable knowledge available only to the few. But in the same section of the chapter an accident takes place in which Anna Pavlovna's wheelchair runs away down a steep incline and stops on the brink of an abyss (II, 116). The narrator uses the word 'hyperbola' to contrast this event, undreamed of in Korobkin's philosophy, with the asymptote he holds reality to be.[21]

As this occurrence then fully impinges on Korobkin's consciousness, his change of heart is expressed in a play on the word *zakon* (law). Since his accident he has been constantly aware of being followed; this sensation has become a 'law' to him (II, 120). The word is carried over into a discussion of his mathematical fame; what Korobkin says is law. This state of affairs is then contrasted with Korobkin's own realization that scientific laws depend solely upon the methods employed in research, and that they are not an expression of the nature of reality, where 'all form burns up in formlessness' (II, 121). In another work, written only shortly before the novel, Bely had spoken of law as that which restricts development, and defined revolution as 'law exploded – for all time'.[22] The restrictive nature of 'law' is expressed in the novel by its identification with the professor's sensation of being followed, and this connotation passes over into the discussion of scientific laws. The professor is then shown to realize the discrepancy between the conception of law and reality as it is, or would be if rightly understood, but he is not yet shown to be capable of thinking in the new manner required.

Throughout the novel the professor's conscious mind is shown to be gradually understanding that his interpretation of the world is inadequate. In part this is a process of perceiving things about the external world which previously had escaped his awareness. The imagery of pre-history, which conveys to the reader a conception of the world's real nature, is only towards the very end of the novel linked with the professor's mind. The 'hyperbolic' world which he hoped to refute makes an irresistible assault upon him shortly thereafter, as Vishnyakov emerges from the surrounding wood with his letter of warning. To an equal extent, however, this is a process by which Korobkin brings to awareness that which is already present inside him. The conscious mind, with which he has organized both his mathematics and his life, is but a fraction of the whole person that responds to the universe. Other kinds of response force themselves upon him as his rational control weakens. On one occasion various anagrams of Mandro's name occur to Korobkin, leading him to think of Mandro as the source of all his trouble, but also indicating that Mandro is only one hypostasis of a creature with many forms. The narrator explains: '. . .all this took place not in his forehead, but rather – in the nape of his neck, in his back. . .' (II, 209). The dream of Heraclitus with the puns on Proverchenko is a similar instance. In keeping with his penchant for rational explanation, Korobkin tries to attribute all such phenomena to his blood-pressure, and his '*pepeshki i pshishki*' becomes a recurrent image expressing his quest for empirical resolution. But this blood-pressure is closely related to the heart disease of Apollon Apollonovich, and comes similarly to express the activities of the neglected other levels of his mind.

There are a considerable number of biblical references in the novel, indicating that Korobkin's fate is to be understood as a recapitulation of the life of Christ. When the professor leaves Mandro's house after his return visit he accidentally puts Mandro's cat on his head instead of his hat, and is scratched by it (I, 252). The accident is motivated by a pun on the word '*kotikovyy*', which means 'sealskin', but is derived from a word that also means 'kitten'. The narrator's comment on this event, which forms the last words in *The Moscow Eccentric*, is: 'He put on not a cat, but – a crown of thorns' (I, 256). The biblical references are particularly concentrated in the last chapter of *Moscow in Jeopardy*, when Korobkin returns to Moscow. He says: 'If the kingdom of science were at hand, our servants would fight for us

...' (II, 192), echoing Christ's words to Pilate (John xviii, 36), and a
little later he echoes Pilate's words about Christ (John xix, 4), when
he says:

I find no fault in me. (II, 192)

Only Nadya, of the people close to him, is there; his wife and son
and his favourite student[23] have left him. He slings his knapsack on
his back 'like a cross', and sets off 'sorrowful even unto death'
(*smertel'no skorbya*, II, 192, cf. Matt. xxvi, 38). When he arrives at
the station in Moscow he mishears scraps of talk between the cab-
drivers, understanding them as references to crucifixion (II, 205),
echoing the insistence of the Jews that Barabbas should be released
and Christ crucified (John xviii, 40; xix, 6). While Korobkin and
Mandro are together in Korobkin's Moscow apartment, before
Mandro has identified himself, there are references to Christ's
agony in the garden of Gethsemane (II, 218–9; cf. Matt. xxvi, 39–
42), and to Christ's words, 'I was a stranger and ye took me not in'
(II, 220; cf. Matt. xxv, 43). The torture of Korobkin by Mandro
bears a certain resemblance to a crucifixion, in that the victim is tied
to a chair by his hands and feet. The fact that he is found to be alive,
not dead, as was expected, recalls the resurrection, and his experiences after the torture are said to resemble the Last Judgement (II,
243–4).[24]

In his delirium after the torture, in the vehicle that is taking him to
the mental hospital, Korobkin makes a number of importantly
ambiguous interpretative remarks. It is entirely consistent with the
way in which his growing awareness has been depicted throughout
the novel that his loss of ordinary sanity should be simultaneously
the acquisition of a higher awareness. He says:

I have become the way that leads beyond the borders of shattered worlds.
[...]
The Tsar is dethroned!
'We' have come to be!
[...]
I am going on a road that has not yet been trodden. (II, 245–6)

The reference to the dethroning of the Tsar relates, evidently, to the
idea of revolution as the destruction of all static forms that Bely
expressed in his 'Writer's Diary'. A particular extension of meaning
is achieved by the use of a neuter verb in the expression 'I have
become the way' (*Ya stalo putyom*). It is motivated by the fact that

Korobkin, unrecognizable after his ordeal, is referred to as 'it'; but it allows an alternative reading of his words as 'The Ego has become the way', and this then leads to the deepest anthroposophical interpretation of the novel's action.

In the memoir of 1928, *Why I became a Symbolist and never ceased to be one at all stages of my intellectual development*, Bely mentions that the novel *Moscow* raised for him the idea of karma and the problem of the relation of the lower ego to the Ego proper.[25] The doctrine of karma, taken over by both theosophy and anthroposophy from Hindu philosophy, is predicated upon the idea of re-incarnation. Into each successive existence the individual brings with him the fruits of previous lives; evil in this life is the consequence of incorrectly lived former lives, and is to be overcome only by a future succession of lives lived correctly. In *Moscow* the imagery of barbarism that expresses the world's endemic evil is rooted in anthroposophical theories of racial succession that are clearly related to the idea of karma applied collectively. The route to salvation lies through the spiritual evolution of individuals, their realization of Christ within them, which is to say, of the 'Ego proper' within the lower ego. Bely's detailed conception of what this means is evidently the content of his theory on the 'personality' and the 'individuum', and it involves a view of the nature of personality that has extensive implications for both the content and the form of his last novels.

The idea of the 'individuum' as the sum of the individual's incarnations has already been mentioned, and the connection between this and the imagery of barbarism is established pointedly in the torture scene, where it is suggested that it is not the 'personality' Mandro who is responsible, but that both he and Korobkin are the victims of one Mandloppl', 'a bloody and experienced priest' (II, 233). This Aztec bears the karma of Mandro's former incarnations. This mutation of Mandro's name also provides the interpretation of other instances where similar mutations and anagrams are employed. The affinity with the ideas of linguistic evolution in *Glossolalia* are not far to seek.

In *Why I became a Symbolist...* Bely traces something of his own biography and relations with other people. He tries to answer the charge that throughout his life he was in the habit of going back on expressed convictions and thus betraying common platforms of ideas. He sees the mutations of his own views as the

varying expressions of his 'individuum' through the partial man-
ifestations of 'personality'. Thus a 'personality' is not necessarily
constant throughout a single incarnation; indeed Bely regards it as
by no means a virtue to maintain constancy in this respect. To cling
unchangingly to a single set of convictions is to be restricted in the
world of forms. Bely had always considered that an abstract conviction is an inadequate expression of an underlying motive, and
this idea was later developed in anthroposophical terms. The
'personality' is thus expressly linked with the conscious mind and
its static forms, and the development of Korobkin shows precisely
the collapse of those things. Similarly the revelation of the developing 'individuum' must require the depiction of that which is not
yet the content of consciousness. The imagery in Bely's prose
works of all periods is designed to meet that purpose, but in the
late novels the method is greatly extended. Characters are depicted much less in terms of conscious conviction than by way of
mannerisms, gestures, and the quality of their environment.

The gestures with which Korobkin accompanies his abrupt
utterances are one of the most obvious instances of this method.
They cannot be translated into other terms; if the critic were able
to say what they 'meant' they would not be serving their intended
purpose. They are supposed to be perceived by the reader in such
a way that he comes to participate in that which is below conscious
thought and linguistic expression in the character. In *How We
Write* Bely mentions that in order to understand Korobkin in the
third volume of *Moscow* (he is presumably referring to *Masks*) he
had to read four complete histories of mathematics; but the reader
will not find them as they are all absorbed into a single gesture of
the professor's as he carves a chicken.[26] It is worth mentioning in
passing that Bely used the same method of characterization by
gesture in his memoirs, which gave rise to anger and ridicule on
the part of some of his reviewers.

Bely's use of colour in this connection is particularly interesting
in the *Moscow* cycle. The personal possessions of the characters,
their clothes and interior decorations, are described in exceptional
detail of colour. Colour-descriptions are of great importance in all
Bely's works, but they do not perform an entirely consistent function. In his essay 'Sacred Colours' Bely developed a mystical
interpretation of the spectrum, and in *The Silver Dove* and
Petersburg colours are extensively used, often in simple,

monochrome designations, with an evidently symbolic purpose – the colour red associated with lust and revolution in both novels, or the green colour of putrefaction in the river of *Petersburg*.[27] The colour designations in the *Moscow* novels are both more elaborate and more systematic than those in any previous work. K.N. Bugayeva has left an account of how Bely evolved a new method of colour observation and expression. Starting in 1924 he began to collect, during summers on the Black Sea coast, beach pebbles of as many different shades as possible, and to arrange them in trays showing the minutest gradations of colour. At other times he did the same with collections of leaves. He would then use the colours from a particular tray, within a particular range of the spectrum, to describe the possessions or environment of particular characters or particular situations. This entailed the coining of many new formulations, usually compound adjectives or compressed similes. The purpose of these descriptions is twofold. In the first place the manner of their origin confirms that they are part of Bely's continuous striving to capture in language that which exists in nature but slips through the gaps between the established concepts of speech. He had written several years before, in his Sicilian travel notes, that the real colours of nature were infinite gradations, while the notion of colour as an absolute hue was a mere abstraction.[28] Secondly, in the preface to *Masks* he claims as author the right to reveal the inner lives of his characters through the colours of their everyday objects. The relation between the range of the spectrum in which a character's environment is depicted and the inner life of that character is no more translatable into other terms than is the similar function of gesture. It seems very likely, although there is no documentary evidence, that Bely's use of colour in this psychological sense is related to the idea of the 'aura', the enveloping colours around an individual that clairvoyants claim to see, and which varies according to the character, mood and emotion of the bearer.[29] It is certainly the case that it owes much to Bely's familiarity with the colour theories of Goethe; this will be treated in more detail in Chapter 9.

The conception of personality which leads Bely to use these devices for depicting that which exists below the level of consciousness in his characters must also affect the persona of his narrator. It would not be in keeping to use an ironic narrator in the manner of *Petersburg*; the narrator's conscious mind must also be peeled off to reveal what lies beneath, and it is for this reason that the rhythm of the prose takes over from the self-conscious narrator. This development in Bely's novels, which is perceptible only faintly in a comparison of the two editions of *Petersburg*, is somewhat obscured by the first-person narrator of the novels of childhood. But with the return to a third-person narration in the *Moscow* cycle the connection between the foregrounding of rhythm and the disappearance of the narrator becomes evident.

In a letter to Ivanov-Razumnik Bely wrote that in *Moscow* he was trying to combine all the following elements from his earlier novels:

(1) The symphonism of *Kotik*
(2) The verbalism of *The Crime of Nik. Letayev*
(3) The novelism (plot element) of *Petersburg*
(4) The one-time studied 'popular' style of *The Dove* [as] the style in which words from Dal''s[30] language are introduced
(5) The skeleton of the theme: Anthroposophy.[31]

It is indeed clear that all the stylistic devices from his other novels are exploited in *Moscow*. It is closest in style to *The Baptized Chinaman*.[32] In *The Moscow Eccentric* there is a system of leit-motifs relating to the theme of time which starts as a direct borrowing from the earlier novel:

And time, a frightened hare – ran in the vestibule (1, 60).[33]

Later time is compared to a blacksmith, 'riveting the years' (1, 80), to a cannibal (1, 123), and to a camel (1, 163). The camel becomes a horse that will destroy the 'clutter of houses' that figure in the leitmotif of the city itself (1, 234), and time finally appears as a boa-constrictor (1, 255). The theme of time, and its mutations from a frightened hare to an all-devouring snake, are closely linked with the theme of the impending destruction of Moscow and the reality it represents. Leitmotifs are also used in the descriptions of times of day; evening, for instance, is on a number of occasions expressed as 'the day's hazel afterglow' (*karyaya peregar' dnya*). A further recurrent image in the novel is that of the spider, which is used specifically with reference to the relationship between Korobkin and Mandro in a manner that closely recalls its similar use in *The Silver Dove* to express the relations between Dar'yal'sky and Kudeyarov. Its implications are extended when the narrator asserts that arachnids have replaced human beings in the twentieth century (II, 132), and made ultimately to embrace the whole of the novel when the 'seven hills' of Moscow are identified with the seven (sic!) legs of the spider (II, 193).

Bely's use in *Moscow* of popular language – regionalisms and sub-literary expressions – resembles their use in *The Silver Dove* in that these two novels both contain characters to whom they can reasonably be attributed; indeed in *The Silver Dove* the Gogolian narrator is also a credible bearer of such language. Bely had in fact also had recourse to Dal''s dictionary in writing *The Baptized Chinaman*, but because there are in that novel neither characters nor a narrator to whom such vocabulary elements can be attributed in their sub-literary usage, they acquire a different quality and become indistinguishable in function from Bely's original neologisms.[34] In *Moscow* they appear both in the manner of *The Silver Dove*, when they are used by some of the characters, and also in the manner of *The Baptized Chinaman*, when they form part of the narrator's language. Examples of such words are *nevnarok* (accidentally) (I, 195), *nevpovorot'* (irreversibly) (I, 197), *vrozbezh* (crosswise) (I, 198), *vrazdray* (apart) (I, 224), or the noun *bormotun* (mutterer) (I, 171). In her memoirs Bugayeva mentions in particular the word *frolki* (for *tsvety* – 'flowers' – II, 77) as a word Bely had long since found in Dal' and stored up for future use.[35] On occasions Bely uses a word that appears in Dal' in a sense other than that which Dal' attributes to it; the word *vlazen'*, for instance, which according to Dal' is a noun, Bely employs as an adjective, by analogy with *vkhozh*: '*Viktorchik vlazen' v ikh dom*' (Viktorchik has access to their house – by crawling. . .) (II, 131). As regards true neologisms, Bely employs in *Moscow* all the varieties that are familiar from his earlier novels, and their function is very often autonomous, as in the 'verbalism' of *The Baptized Chinaman*, rather than closely motivated by context. It is noticeable that there occur in *Moscow* a small number of neologisms coined on the principle of overlapping syllables, such as *dikovyrkom* (I, 154), where the syllable *ko* is both the second of the word *diko* (wildly) and the first of *kovyrkom* (a neologism derived from *kovyryat'*, meaning here 'to pick one's nose'), or *zagrozarelo* (II, 60), where the second *za* is both the final syllable of *groza* (thunderstorm) and the first of *zarelo* (it was dawning). This manner of coinage is not at all typical of Bely's earlier neologisms, and bears strong affinities to the inventions of Khlebnikov.

K.N. Bugayeva recalls that before any other features of the character of Mandro had taken shape in Bely's mind, he already knew that he was '*dr*'.[36] The combinations *dr* and *tr* were extensively used as phonetic leitmotifs in *The Silver Dove*, and served to link an onomatopoeic rendition of a passing cart with the mention of Tartarus, and the same usage recurs here. Its recurrence in *Moscow* is a structural device of some importance. It is found not only in Mandro's name, but also in that of his imaginary mentor Dr Donner, and most nakedly in the pseudonym Mandro is said to adopt after his exposure, Dr Dro (II, 176). The subconscious significance of Mandro's name is explained in terms of its sound at the end of *The Moscow Eccentric*:

If he [Korobkin] were able to become aware of the impression from the sound 'Mandro', he would see: in 'man' there was something blue: in 'dr' was something black, as though trying to recall a dream once dreamt; 'man' – enticed; while 'dr' – ? Struck a blow. (I, 254)

The combination *dr* also occurs in two words upon which crucial thematic material is focussed: the word *dyra* (a hole), which is used as an image expressing the absence of a true Ego, or soul, in Mandro, and the word *udar* (a blow), the dominant word in the title of the second part, *Moskva pod udarom*. This word is used not only in the meaning it possesses in the title, but also in the meaning of 'a stroke'; it thus links the episode of Zadopyatov's wife's stroke, and the transformation it brings about in their lives, with the main theme of the novel, and allows their tentative rebirth to prefigure the eventual resurrection of Korobkin.

Bely's early critics in the West regarded *Moscow* as proof that he had become a Marxist and betrayed everything that he and his generation had earlier stood for.[37] With the greater knowledge that is now available about his life and work after 1923 there is scarcely any need to refute that assertion. It is true that he depicted the cultural life of pre-revolutionary Moscow in the most unflattering terms, but this was not an attitude he arrived at to please the Communist authorities; it is very clearly expressed, for instance, in some of his letters to Vyacheslav Ivanov dating from before the revolution.[38] It is also true that he made a deliberate attempt to subsume something of Marxism, and in particular the fact of the revolution, into his own scheme of ideas; but he certainly did not subordinate his own beliefs in the process. If in his early altercations over Marxism with N. Valentinov he claimed that one could proceed from Solov'yov to Marx, as from the general to the particular, but not vice versa, then very much the same relationship pertains between the constituent elements here too.[39] Indeed in the novel's ethical theme, which becomes more clearly marked in the sequel, *Masks*, Bely is taking issue with Marxism in an entirely consistent way.

It remains true that the novel's material is in some respects adapted specifically for reception in a Communist-dominated society. It is no accident that the villain of the piece is represented as a powerful capitalist. Mandro says to Korobkin during their final encounter: 'Oh, I understand who you are: in other circumstances I would be sitting in front of a bronze statue on "Korobkin square"; you must blame the system [*stroy*] where people like you fall into the jaws of sharks' (II, 225). This remark echoes the author's own assertion in the preface that in the character of Korobkin he was depicting 'the helplessness of science in the bourgeois system' and 'the struggle between science, which is essentially free, and the capitalist system'. But, as Khodasevich was quick to point out, such an undertaking can only be achieved in a novel depicting historically credible types, and *Moscow* is clearly not a realistic novel in that sense.[40] The ultimate irrelevance of the references to Marxism is perfectly demonstrated in the dedication of the novel to 'the peasant from Arkhangel'sk, Mikhail Lomonosov'. Lomonosov was regarded as the patron of the Moscow anthroposophical group, but for reasons wholly unconnected with his rustic extraction. According to Margarita Woloschin the group was dedicated to Lomonosov on the advice of Steiner himself, and she claims furthermore that Lomonosov was christened Mikhail in honour of the Archangel Michael, patron of Russia.[41] Bely mentions in *Why I Became a Symbolist* a conflict between a Lomonosov group and a Solov'yov group among the Moscow anthroposophists, where it was the Lomonosov group who particularly strove to create a free community (*obshchina*) in contrast to the rigid hierarchical structure into which the Western Anthroposophical Society had degenerated. The seven Archangels, regarded as the spirits of nations, were believed to have successive periods of dominion over the world; the seventh and last such period is the dominion of Michael, who hands his authority over to the returning Messiah himself. Asya Turgeneva, Bely's first wife, records that this theme was one of the subjects of Steiner's lectures.[42] Bely spoke of the novel's dedication to his fellow anthroposophist, the actor Mikhail Chekhov (who had played the leading role in the performance of the dramatized version of *Petersburg*), explaining that the task of the Archangel Michael was of particular importance at that time.[43] There is no doubt that the task of the Archangel, of those who recognized his hegemony, was the realization of the 'Christ impulse', which was the subject of *Notes of an Eccentric*. The novel's dedication can thus be seen to reveal, to those who understand, a meaning which is far removed from any possible Marxist interpretation. It is amusing to note that F. Stepun, one of the harshest critics of the supposed 'communism' of Bely's late novels, noted in his obituary of Bely that a rumour had reached him to the effect that Bely was working on a novel about the Archangel Michael. It evidently never occurred to him that *Moscow* and *Masks* were that very work.[44]

It has to be admitted that *The Moscow Eccentric* and *Moscow in Jeopardy* have so far encountered very few sympathetic readers. One reason is no doubt the mystification, the conflicting indicators, brought in by the introduction into an anthroposophical text of material that appears to require a Marxist interpretation. Readers are understandably confused. A second reason is the generally grotesque depiction in the novel. The fact that Bely was aware of this does nothing to modify its effect.[45] He sets out to present a reality which is cruel and horrific, but too often lapses into the merely distasteful, revealing a preoccupation with disfigurement and putrid smells. This can sometimes have a weirdly moving effect, as when two of Bely's cripples, Yasha Kaval'kas and Vishnyakov, join in the redemptive activities of the Salvation Army: a glimpse is attained of an inner spirituality that is quite beyond embodiment in any available physical form. The grotesqueness with which the parallel is established between Korobkin and Christ is similar in its effect, revealing at the same time an utter discrepancy between the potentiality for good and the limitations of the real.

Stylistically these novels show no great advance upon *The Baptized Chinaman*. What Bely has achieved here is the development of a third-person narration of a new kind, which enables him to resume the depiction of the world outside the consciousness. *Masks* will build further upon this, by testing Korobkin's transformed awareness against an unchanged world, and will also bring fresh momentum into Bely's experiments in style.

9

Masks

Masks takes up the action some two years after the ending of *Moscow in Jeopardy*, in the autumn and winter of 1916. The war forms a constant background and the explosion with which the novel culminates can best be understood as representing revolution, just as the final explosion did in the dramatized version of *Petersburg*. *Masks* thus leads up to the February revolution in much the same way that *Moscow* led up to the outbreak of war.

All the major characters of the first volume of *Moscow* reappear here in the second, but not always in the same guise. Kierko appears as Terentiy Titych Titelev and Lizasha as his wife Eleonora Leonovna, while Eduard Mandro, who was supposed to have died, re-emerges in anagrammatic form as a French journalist by the name of Drua-Domarden (Droit d'Homme Ardent). But the characters are 'masks' for a deeper reason than this, as Bely explains in his preface. The second volume is the antithesis of the first; there the characters appeared in their full egoism as 'personalities', while here they are commencing a process of transformation whose outcome will only be evident in the synthesis. It is the revolution itself that will tear the masks from them and reveal their new selves. Professor Korobkin, in particular, is said here to have rejected his former way of life, but not yet to have found his role in the events that crowd in upon him. The characters of *Masks* are depicted, Bely tells us, in semi-silence, and only in the third volume of *Moscow* will they begin to speak.[1]

The members of Korobkin's family who played a central role in *Moscow* are of little importance in *Masks*. Any spiritual transformation they had seemed to undergo is belied by their unchanged condition. Zadopyatov, following his wife's death, is now living openly with Vasilisa Sergeyevna. Mitya makes episodic appearances as a guards officer, while Nadya is dead, and her room has been let to a Futurist poetess (*poetessa-zaumnitsa*) called Zastroy-Kopyto, who appears to have some connection with

Mandro.[2] This is the environment on which Korobkin has turned his back, and it is only for purposes of contrast that these characters are introduced.

On the other hand there appears a new member of Korobkin's family, his brother Nikanor, who has come from Tashkent on learning of Korobkin's illness and makes arrangements for his release from the mental hospital where he has been a patient since the torture by Mandro. Nikanor has been told of the events in *Moscow in Jeopardy* by Titelev, who claims to be acting as the agent of other admirers of the professor's, concerned over the whereabouts of his discovery. Nikanor lives at the Titelevs' house without knowing their true identity, but it is through his naive viewpoint that their secrets are revealed to the reader.

The second major new character to appear in *Masks* is the nurse, Serafima Sergeyevna, who has been looking after Korobkin in hospital and eventually declines an offer of marriage in order to go on nursing him after his release.

In all, *Masks* has a cast of characters running into hundreds,[3] but many of them have no existence beyond a name and do not impinge upon the plot. Those that do, apart from the distinct individuals already mentioned, tend to appear in groups, each group fulfilling a single function. The principal groups are the doctors and patients at the hospital, the associates of Titelev, and the army intelligence officers who have the task of unmasking and kidnapping Mandro. This last group possess wide social connections in what is left of Moscow society, and there are a number of characters who can be taken to represent that. There is also a role in the novel for the political police, from whom the Titelevs are in hiding, but they scarcely emerge as distinct characters. It is important to the structure of the novel, however, that none of the groups is hermetic; there is considerable cross-membership, allowing the secrets of each to be eventually exposed to the others. It is clear, for instance, that the doctors have connections with the intelligence service and that an ostensible medical commission to assess the professor's condition has in part the purpose of ascertaining whether he remembers his discovery. It is also crucial to the plot that the intelligence service has leaks to the political police. Nevertheless the broad groups retain a clear independent identity, and are largely pursuing different and incompatible aims. Both at the individual level and at the group level the characters of *Masks* are manifestly at cross purposes, extracting secrets from each other which, when revealed, they either fail to understand or deliberately abuse.

There are two main strands to the plot of *Masks*. One concerns the gradual recuperation of Professor Korobkin under the therapeutic care of Serafima Sergeyevna, and his recollection and re-interpretation of the principal events of the first volume. Like all Bely's heroes he comes, through this process, to a new awareness of the world and his own role in it. The anthroposophical nature of this awareness is not overtly emphasized, but the use of the word '*samosoznaniye*' to designate it is one clear way in which it is revealed (e.g. pp. 119–21). This is the word that is used in Bely's main theoretical work on this topic to denote the stage of spiritual development which men have next to attain.[4] The other strand depends upon the revelation of the incognitos. The intelligence officers suspect that Drua-Domarden is in fact Mandro, working for the central powers, but require definitive identification of him before taking action. This can only be given by his daughter, who has her own motives for desiring his destruction, and who is persuaded without difficulty to confirm his identity. She is concealed at a social gathering to which Drua-Domarden is invited and betrays him to the intelligence officers. In so doing she has of course also to reveal her own incognito and that of her husband. The officers assure her that their quest for spies has nothing to do with exposure of the political underground, and that her secret will be honoured. Nevertheless the information is passed on, and the political police begin to close in upon Kierko/Titelev, who has both a printing-press and a supply of arms concealed in his house. When they finally storm it the whole establishment is blown sky-high.

The general bad faith and malice that inform relations between most of the characters are particularly focussed in the theme of revenge. This is the motive that leads Lizasha to betray her father. The hunting of Mandro is a reversal of the roles of the first volume, and the enactment of vengeance upon him for his earlier villainies. The idea of karma is present here. Lizasha reflects upon her own affinity to her father and comes to the conclusion that: 'Both he and she were guilty – before their birth – in a world already guilty – before creation' (p.251). The two strands of the plot are linked by the professor's attempt, once he has recovered, to break the vicious circle of reciprocal injury, in which Abel rises up to murder Cain, and to establish a new order of love.

The professor's recovery is guided by Serafima Sergeyevna, who plays Cordelia to his Lear. The relations between these two characters are presented with an unironic tenderness for which there exists no parallel in Bely's earlier work. Much is made of Korobkin's Lear-like blindness, or, to be more precise, of the contrast between his blind eye and his seeing eye, which now sees differently and more clearly as a result of the blinding of the other. The process of recovery is expressed through the re-introduction of a number of images from the first volume. In one instance Korobkin hears outside his window the sound of marching soldiers, which is represented as the sound '*dr*'. This brings to his mind the key words of the first volume, *udar* (blow) and Mandro. Through a pun on the word *drob'* which can denote both 'fraction' and the rumbling sound of a passing carriage or a marching platoon, this sound is further associated with the accident at the opening of *The Moscow Eccentric*, when Korobkin tried to write formulae on the side of a moving cab (pp.125–27). The 'two-dimensional' dog, with the rag in its mouth that recalls the professor's gag, reappears in association with a cat that develops from the closing scene of *The Moscow Eccentric*, where Korobkin inadvertently enacted a pun on *kotik* and put a cat on his head, a 'crown of thorns', instead of his sealskin hat. Cat and dog face each other in the world of two dimensions and stand for the conflict between Mandro and the professor. At an early stage of his recuperation Korobkin sings some verses of his own composition, ending with the lines:

> Basically, doggie,
> Don't go fight the cat. (p.120)

The star, Kappa-Korobkin, which represented the *n* dimensions of the professor's thought, first recurs as no more than an indication that his memory is returning, and recalls his discomfiture at the ceremony where the star was named (p.127). Since that ceremony, however, was in part an anticipation of his later 'crucifixion', it is fitting that the star comes to be associated with the burning of his eye, and ultimately with the new insight derived from it:

> Thus 'Kappa', the star –
> > – descended like a comet
> into his eye. (p.240)

This image is also redolent of many in the novels of childhood, where astral forces enter the child's skull in a similar manner, and expresses the transformation of the professor's mode of thinking.

The chief psychiatrist at the hospital adopts a mechanistic approach to the patients which is entirely at variance with the intuitive methods by which Serafima treats her protégés and coaxes Korobkin back to health. The most essential medicament at her disposal is colour; she teaches her patients to practise the concentrated perception of colours, and tells them:

...Collect them, examine them; the shades that are poured out into your eyes fly forth from your eyes as a science of seeing, so that without the history of painting you can learn for yourselves what is more important, so that you can understand exactly, for what purpose knowledge is needed. (p.63)

Here Bely has turned into part of the novel's subject-matter the ideas that underlay his own use of colour as a device in his later novels. The source of these ideas can be found in the colour theory of Goethe. Bely had studied Goethe's scientific theories extensively during his period in Dornach, and a long chapter in *Rudolf Steiner and Goethe* is devoted specifically to the *Farbenlehre*.[5] There are other references in *Masks* itself, and other later works of Bely's, that leave no doubt about his continued interest in it.[6] Goethe opposed Newton's idea that the colours of the spectrum could be defined as seven in number, and argued that they consisted of an infinite variation. He wrote at length on the moral impression created by particular colours and on the balance of colours in natural phenomena. What Serafima Sergeyevna is instilling in her patients through this form of therapy is a manner of perceiving nature, through concentration upon colour, in which the knowledge attained is immediately suffused with moral significance. Goethe writes:

It has been circumstantially shown above, that every colour produces a distinct impression on the mind, and thus addresses at once the eye and feelings. Hence it follows that colour may be employed for certain moral and aesthetic ends.

Such an application, coinciding entirely with nature, might be called symbolical, since the colour would be employed in conformity with its effect, and would at once express its meaning.[7]

Goethe makes no distinction between moral and aesthetic ends here, nor between the colours in nature and the colours in art.

Both the direct observation that Serafima induces in the patients, and the linguistically mediated observation that Bely, as author, induces in his readers, are designed to produce an effect which is simultaneously aesthetic and moral. This use of colour in *Masks* can be seen to be not peripheral, but absolutely central to the main theme of the novel, which might precisely be defined as the moral significance of knowledge.[8]

The city of Moscow, in which the action takes place, is not the same as the city of the first volume. All Bely's previous depictions of the city of his birth, from the *Second Symphony* through the childhood novels to *Moscow in Jeopardy*, are essentially the same: observations of a particular region around the Arbat where he lived virtually the whole of his first thirty years. The Moscow of *Masks* is the rambling, ramshackle outskirts, a city of random houses and disorderly lanes, bounded by broken wooden fences. Its metropolitan character and cultural traditions are emphasized much less than previously, and it feels more like an extension of the Russian provinces, bearing perhaps a distant affinity to Dostoyevsky's Skotoprigon'yevsk in *The Brothers Karamazov*. True, there are a number of scenes in the houses of the wealthy, or in the Pall-Mall Hotel where Mandro is finally cornered, but here the descriptive emphasis is upon the interiors, which could be anywhere in the world. Moscow too, it seems, is a mask of its former self, engaged in a process of transformation.

The war is present in a number of ways. Bely points out in his preface the importance of perceiving the different focal lengths of his various descriptions. Many of the scenes in long focus are depictions of the fighting at the front. But the war impinges upon most aspects of the novel. It is, of course, the reason for the presence of so many men in uniform, from officers in the drawing-rooms to platoons passing in the street. It is as an image of suffering that it functions particularly, and in this capacity it is especially associated with Professor Korobkin, thereby developing a connection that was asserted by juxtaposition at the end of *Moscow in Jeopardy*. Chapter 3 opens with a section entitled 'Brother Ivan', which describes the bringing of a mutilated, but still living body to the hospital; once patched up it is allowed to go walking along Kuznetsky Most to the horror of passers-by (pp.113–14). 'Brother Ivan' is the way in which Nikanor usually refers to his brother, and many of the images in this short section repeat verbatim passages from the closing sections of *Moscow in Jeopardy*. Others, however, refer to the war and to injuries which the professor has not received; and his name is not mentioned in the text at all. A little later Professor Korobkin is introduced in the hospital to a wounded soldier called Ivan Khampauer (pp.134–5). The identity of the suffering the two have undergone is clear, but in the identity of their names, and in the sympathy the professor feels for the other, a further theme becomes apparent: that the professor's recovery is a process of overcoming his own individual suffering, making of it a route to the suffering of others and establishing a new relationship of brotherhood with all of suffering mankind. In a later scene, which distantly recalls the behaviour of the Korobkin in Bely's story 'The Yogi', Professor Korobkin identifies himself simply as Ivan, saying he was once a professor (p.172), and later again he speaks of himself as 'Ivan to all Ivans' (p.192).

The culmination of the professor's recovery comes in Chapter 7, as he re-visits his old home for the last time and sees the place where he was tortured. Again soldiers are heard marching past, and the sound that impinges upon Korobkin's consciousness is the officer's voice giving the order: '*raz – pravo*' (left, right) (p.301, see also p.90). It is understood as the word *rasprava* (reprisal, retribution) and the pun is continued in the professor's thought: '*rasprava – nepravaya*' (reprisal is wrong). In this way the themes of the professor's recovery, the war and revenge are all linked at this crucial point of the novel. Korobkin is, as it were, resurrected, and proceeds to put into effect the ethical insight that his illness and recovery have brought him.

In the first place this concerns the fate of his discovery. It has fallen into the hands of Kierko, who, however, has not told the party he has it (p.249). His intention is to persuade the professor that it is his moral duty to put the discovery, and the power its possession confers, at the party's disposal. This would mean conniving at the Marxist morality of revolutionary expediency which Bely had himself repudiated many years before.[9] Korobkin is not persuaded; to all Kierko's blandishments he replies:

To give the discovery would mean to shrug at murder; but I...

...

don't shrug. (p.347)

Asked then by Kierko how he proposes to 'warm the constellations', he replies, 'by love' (p.350). He has already reached the conviction that the very existence of the discovery makes him as guilty of violence and destruction as anyone else, and he finally destroys it by tearing up the paper on which it is written (p.351).

The other way in which Korobkin's new ethics impinge upon the plot is in his relations with Mandro and his attempt to stop the cycle of retribution. Once he has arrived at Kierko's house in Chapter 8 he learns the remaining details about Lizasha and Mandro, and sets out for the Pall-Mall Hotel to fetch Mandro, hoping to reconcile him with Lizasha, as well as with himself. He achieves this aim, and the reconciliation takes place. However, in any practical sense the outcome of his action is disastrous. Nikanor, on learning who the visitor is, seizes a poker and makes off to take revenge on his brother's behalf. The professor tries to restrain him, and the brothers fight a grotesque battle with poker and broom, in the course of which Serafima also receives an inadvertent blow. The encounter between Lizasha and Mandro completes the alienation between Lizasha and Kierko, whose relations have been strained throughout the novel, on account of their conflicting preoccupations, hers with her father, his with the discovery. Furthermore the removal of Mandro from the hotel, where he was surrounded by enemies who however could not touch him in so public a place, makes possible his kidnap and murder. And finally the political police are also led to Kierko's hideout with the direct consequence of its total destruction. The practical application of Korobkin's ethics leads to utter calamity.

It was noticed that after the total internalization of valuable experience in *Kotik Letayev* and *Notes of an Eccentric* Bely's novels began to turn once more towards the external world. The importance of plot as a structural element in the *Moscow* cycle is one piece of evidence for this. It is in keeping with this development that the issues raised by the plot, and the nature of the spiritual development to which the hero is brought, have a specifically ethical character. It was of course part and parcel of Bely's ideas about Symbolism, and a necessary element in the spiritual pilgrimage of all his heroes, that the right transformation of attitudes to the world would bring with it a complete regeneration of human relations. But it is only in the *Moscow* novels, and particularly in *Masks*, that the ethical moment has priority. Dar'-yal'sky was concerned to establish a new form of human community, but for him the cultic took precedence over other aspects of human relations, and the reader is not invited to apply ethical judgements to his behaviour.

The external reality to which Korobkin applies his ethical insight also possesses an autonomy that was not in evidence in most of Bely's earlier work. Where previously it had seemed that, barring malign influences, if men made the necessary spiritual adjustments, the world would follow, it is evident here that the world does no such thing. Objective reality is unmoved by Korobkin's behaviour, and he is not only powerless to prevent the disaster, but actually helps bring it about. Bely faces here the problem of what happens when one man acts in accordance with a new ethical code while others do not. Korobkin's failure to transform the world is not an indication that he was wrong, but it is an acknowledgement that the evil and barbarism of the world, its karma, are not to be overcome so easily. One is tempted to draw comparisons with Dostoyevsky's *The Idiot*, but it has to be borne in mind that Bely is still not accepting the full extent of Dostoyevsky's tragic vision; his anthroposophical evolutionism still insists that such change is ultimately possible.

The theme of *Masks* has also a specifically political dimension, which Bely clearly indicates in the role of Titelev and the party. While on the plane of individual ethics the professor's solution of destroying the discovery is probably the only solution possible, it has to be admitted that the attendant political problem would not be solved thereby. A discovery once made cannot be unmade – not even by the discoverer except in the very short term – and the political power to use it is always wielded by someone. The professor's solution, in effect, is to unthink the discovery until such time as men have grown spiritually to the point where they can be trusted with it. An interesting comparison can be drawn with Karl Jaspers' *Die geistige Situation der Zeit*, also published in 1932, where he similarly recommends an abstention from political activity until men are spiritually worthy to wield political power. The political vacuum left by those who are perfecting themselves is soon occupied by those who are not. There is no knowing what Bely might have done with this theme had he written further volumes, but the ending we have strongly indicates that he was not unaware of the problem, and that his views should not be too easily identified with his hero's.

In her memoirs Klavdiya Nikolayevna Bugayeva, Bely's widow, has left the only account we possess of Bely at work. The method she describes was the one that he used in the writing both of the first volume of *Moscow* and of *Masks*,[10] but never before; Bugayeva follows Bely himself in calling it a 'mosaic' method. The first stage was a process of selection. For this purpose he used special strips of paper on which he compiled lists under a variety of headings. The heading might be the name of a character, or it might be one of the novel's major themes, such as 'Russia' or 'War'. The items on the list might then consist of particular characteristics, gestures, fragments of conversation, habits, ways of dressing, or of specific landscape features, street scenes or domestic trivia. Other headings might refer to larger or smaller units: the gestures of Nikanor might require a list to themselves; the relations of Kierko and the professor could become a separate section. But Bugayeva stresses that there was nothing stable or mechanical in this process; the lists could multiply and change character incessantly, some falling into disuse while others came into prominence. The process of gathering material at this level was performed mainly while walking; Bely would have with him special preparatory notebooks in which he would jot down anything that occurred to him, for transference to the official lists when he came home.

The development from this accumulation of raw material to the production of a finished text went through several stages of refinement, for each of which Bely had his own designation; but it was impossible for anyone else to know what exactly was the difference, for instance, between a 'semi-list' (*polu-rubrika*) and a 'pre-rough-copy' (*predchernovik*); and his nomenclature became much more complex than that. The general outline of the process, however, could be observed. Bely would go through his lists, or those of them which related to the themes to be touched upon in the section he was about to write, and would select the particular items that were needed at this point. Then began the gradual process, through anything up to six or more revisions, of turning that selection of material into a continuous text. As the writing of the novel progressed the material on the lists would gradually be either exhausted or transferred elsewhere, and at the end of each major section Bely would 'review his troops' and re-arrange the remaining lists and items.

It is important to realize that it was not simply details or decorative elements that were filtered through this process, but the entire text. There is no skeleton of direct narration to which other features are attached. Bugayeva mentions that sometimes in the early stages of drafting Bely would write in an extremely simple style, and would laugh at its 'fearless naivety' and the imagined response of his critics: 'There you see, I do know how to write simply. It's all comprehensible: he said, she stood up, the professor entered. People should hear what Andrey Bely is capable of. There now – he's writing like a human being... Bravo!.. He's come to his senses.'[11] But such passages are hardly to be found in the final text. It is even harder than in the preceding novels to identify the voice of a narrator in any conventional sense. What Bely has sought to do here is to dispense as completely as possible with the narrator, understood as a fixed point of reference (however ambiguously related to the author), or as a limited mediating consciousness.[12] The essence of the anthroposophical vision that *Masks* is meant to convey is the limitless multiplicity of possible meaning, the inadequacy of all fixed or partial viewpoints and the abhorrence of all forms of abstraction. This affects every level of the text, from the telling of the story, through all descriptions to the rhythm and euphony of the language.

The ten chapters of *Masks* are divided, on the same basic principle that operates in all Bely's novels, into short sections of two or three pages. There is no frequent alternation between different scenes; often half a chapter will develop continuously a series of scenes that follow the progress of a particular group of characters through a specific segment of the action. But the reader has to make many of the connections himself. In passages of dialogue, which is invariably given in short snatches rather than continuous speeches of any length, Bely usually omits to identify the speakers, so that what is presented to the reader's perception is a *mélange* of disjointed utterances, attributable mainly through particular quirks of diction. In the narration of actions Bely frequently omits the subject of the verb, so that the action stands out independently, and has, rather like the dialogue, to be attributed by the reader on the basis of context or other indications. On the other hand actions are very frequently rendered, with or without direct identification of the subject, not by an ordinary finite verb, but by what Nabokov, speaking of Pushkin, has called the 'interjectional' verb.[13] These are either monosyllabic words derived from the root of a verb, such as '*torch*' (p.206), '*shamk*' (p.224), '*bod*' (pp.242,424), '*bros*' (p.208), '*porkh*' (p.201), or compounds derived from the addition of a prefix to such a root. Examples of the latter are '*vstryas*' (p.358), '*vyyurk*' (pp.45,106) or '*nakhmur*' (p.26). In general it is clear that while *Masks* is rich in neologisms of all the types Bely has employed previously, this particular kind occurred little in his earlier novels and is used with great frequency here.[14] Of course by no means all such words are neologisms, since the derivation of nouns from verbs in this manner is perfectly natural. For instance the expression '*Plesk i tresk*' (p.97) is used in very much the same way, while both words are standard lexical nouns. The general naturalness of such usage in Russian is attested by the example from Pushkin, but the frequency and variety of such words in Bely's text makes for a very specific and unusual effect. The actions and gestures of the characters, presented through words that are morphologically nouns rather than verbs, acquire an independence, almost an ontological status of their own, regardless of the performer.

This loosening of the relationship between actor and action that is implicit in normal syntax is one instance of a principle that seems to operate also at other levels. It can be used to explain the unifying principles of the chapter sections. In the case of some of the earlier novels, notably *Kotik Letayev*, critics have successfully shown a clear relationship between, say, imagery and rhythm.[15] With the introduction of a large element of external description that is not subordinate to the functioning of the hero's mind such relationships become more complex, and the connections between the elements cannot be perceived in the same way. The speech and gestures of the characters, the colouration of internal settings, or the outdoor scenes in the street or at the battle front, all are presented in a juxtaposition that gives no priority to one or another and asserts no relations of dependence. The connections between them can thus be imagined in an almost infinite variety of ways. This, clearly, is in keeping with the anthroposophical quest for plurality of interpretation. Each separate section, besides serving to advance the action, functions as a vignette, or tableau, in its own right.

In his preface Bely writes of his endeavour to suffuse meaning (*smysl*) with colour and sound, so that colour and sound should in .

their turn become 'eloquent' (p.11). If we take 'meaning' to refer to any notion or concept that might be abstracted from the text, it is not difficult to see how closely this statement relates to his argument, following Steiner, about the many possible 'moods' or 'tones' in which an abstract conviction can be clothed.[16] The creative method that Bugayeva has described was evidently designed to establish at the very earliest stage of composition, the stage of selecting the material, which colours, sounds, gestures and meanings properly, as Bely imagined them, belonged together.

The avoidance of abstraction can well be exemplified by a sentence of description:

i – ser': skryla rot razodranstvom platka (p.27)

This sentence might be re-written into standard Russian as something like:

razodrannyy seryy platok skryl rot

(a tattered grey cloth concealed his mouth)

First it may be observed that the object and its quality are dissociated and presented separately: not 'a grey cloth', but an independent noun to denote the grey colour. Moreover the noun employed does not have the common abstracting suffix *-ost'* (*serost'* – greyness), but is of a form that is more concrete in connotation; this greyness is a particular thing, not an abstraction from many things. The sentence as re-written would be the logical sentence resulting from the assimilation and interpretation of all the phenomena observed; the effect produced by the sentence Bely wrote is the re-creation of the process of perception itself in its original sequence. The first impression is the colour grey (*ser'*); the second is the position of this colour – where the mouth should be (*skryla rot*); the third is the appearance of the object bearing this colour (*razodranstvom*); and only finally is this appearance attached to the object and the object itself identified (*platka*). Instead of referring the reader, as the re-written sentence would, to the established concepts derived from past perceptions, Bely sets out to present this little scene as though all its elements were being perceived for the first time.

This concern to achieve unprejudiced perception extends beyond the textural level to Bely's entire descriptive method. In this respect it is illuminating to look at his book *Gogol''s Craftsmanship*, a study of Gogol''s style and technique on which he started work shortly after completing *Masks*.[17] Bugayeva notes that he summarized there a theory of perspective which he developed in much greater detail in his diary.[18] What is perhaps of greater importance is that he links this theory of perspective both with his theories about colour and also with his ideas about the metaphorical nature of the basic sounds of language.[19]

Bely had already in *Glossolalia* asserted affinities between certain sounds and certain colours. Now he argues the connection on the basis of synaesthesia. An expression such as 'a warm colour' is entirely justified by the fact that the range of visible colours is only one segment of known radiation; beyond visible red are the infra-red rays which consist precisely of warmth. There is thus, it must be inferred, no difference of kind, but only of degree, between the phenomena perceived by the different senses. This relates also to sound. Taking up again the ideas about sound expressed in 'Aaron's Rod' Bely declares that 'the acoustic metaphor posits colour beyond the limits of the spectrum'. Radiation beyond the visible range can be perceived at the very edge of consciousness by means of 'coloured hearing', which in ordinary, everyday perception is obscured. Thus it is apparent that the euphonic patterns of a text may supplement the sensory images created by the semantic meaning of the words. If colour is inseparable from moral attributes, then it follows (though Bely does not say so) that the same is true of sound. It is apparent that the ideas Bely developed in relation to Gogol' may also be applied to his own practice. The 'acoustic metaphor', with its attached but untranslatable implications of colour and associated moral character, can then be seen to underlie the numerous instances in *Masks* where phonetic elements clearly predominate over conceptual meaning. This is the case with many of the names, particularly of those characters who make only a single appearance. The English baronet, Sir Ranger, for instance, derives all his attributes and his very name from an alliterative pattern which, in Bely's intention, synaesthetically conveys his qualities:

ser Ranzher, –
  – s oranzhevoy bakoy, –
    – v oranzhevom smokinge –
    – orang-utangom –
    – otplyasyval
    tango!

(Sir Ranger – with orange sideburns – in an orange dinner-jacket – like an orang-outang – was dancing the tango!) (p.112)

Madame Kuboa, who is equally unimportant in the plot, is a similar example:

I zhdala – yubka kubovaya pod boa: v kuby kubovyye; il' – madam Kuboa, – iz Baku.
(And there waited – an indigo skirt beneath a boa, to enter the indigo cubes; or – Madame Kuboa, – from Baku.) (p.191)

Perhaps the most striking instance of this device is the rhyming list of third-form children taking part in a political demonstration (p.370).

The theory of perspective is based upon the argument that perspective is created by the movement of the eye, and that there are not three dimensions to be considered, but four angles of vision: length, breadth, height and depth. Depth is usually neglected, because the perspective of the Italian masters is regarded in the West as canonical. That is achieved by placing the object in front of the observer and viewing it statically, from below upwards. But there are in truth as many possible perspectives as there are 'circles of movement of a body', that is to say, sequences in which the moving eye can encompass the whole scene. The perspective of Japanese painting is created on quite different principles from the Italian, and the 'spherical perspective' of Petrov-Vodkin also shows other forms of perspective to be equally possible. Different kinds of perspective give predominance to different ranges of colour, because of the different background hues that follow from different angles of vision.

The synaesthetic connection is made through the dual function of the ear, which is not only the organ of hearing, but also the organ of balance. The sense of space, however, within which balance is established, is created by the eye. Thus the functions of ear and eye are inseparable in the creation of perspective, and it can moreover be seen that in discussing the data available to the senses of hearing and vision Bely makes no distinction between sense-data in the customary understanding and data of an extra-sensory or moral nature. He proposes a kind of perceptual continuum embracing perspective, colour, sound and moral qualities.

It is difficult to say with any certainty whether the theory of perspective itself is embodied in *Masks*, since the novel contains very few descriptive passages that are long enough for a dynamic angle of vision, such as it requires, to be developed. Bely emphasizes in his preface, however, the importance of the reader's appreciating the changes of focus in the different scenes of the novel (p.8). It would follow from his theory that different systems of colouration would imply different kinds of perspective, and therefore that the particular perspective of a given scene could be inferred from its other features. Since the descriptions almost always form one element in the complex vignettes that are the separate sections, there is no way of detaching the perspective as a distinct feature to be observed.

Whether the reader of *Masks* is actually able to perceive all that Bely's theory tells us is there to be perceived must remain very much a moot point. It is an essential premise of Bely's anthroposophy that the world as traditionally perceived is inadequate, and that new forms of perception have to be developed. His last novel is quite clearly designed to serve that purpose. At all events this theory makes possible a deeper understanding of the reasons for the creative method that Bugayeva describes, and provides an explanation of the kind of connection that is intended between the various elements that go to make up the individual sections of the text.

In the preface Bely declares roundly that *Masks* is written not in prose, but in verse, and that its publication in a prose layout is solely for the purpose of economizing on paper (p.11). This declaration has never been taken with the seriousness it deserves. Critics have for the most part complained about the monotony of the ternary rhythm in which *Masks*, like all the late novels, is composed. Bely describes the rhythm as anapaestic, though G. Janecek, who has performed the most detailed analysis of the rhythmic patterns in Bely's novels, considers that it is in fact closer to the dactylic.[20] In his own statements about prose rhythm (in essays dating from a decade earlier) Bely laid emphasis upon its greater rhythmic flexibility in comparison with verse. Had he been attempting to write prose in the definition implicit there, he would presumably have heeded his own statement.[21]

The most commonly accepted approach to the theoretical question of rhythm in prose is to examine various forms of parallelism in rhythmic and syntactic units, while clearly distinguishing such regular recurrence of forms perceived as similar from the regularly recurring ictus of verse. Zhirmunsky, exemplifying this approach, specifically excludes Bely's late prose from consideration on the grounds that it is 'a hybrid poetic form'.[22] And indeed, although such rhythmic and syntactic parallelisms are a common enough feature of Bely's style, it is clear that they are overridden by rhythm in the most literal sense. Tomashevsky defines the difference between prose and verse by arguing that while in prose the rhythm is the result of the meaning and the expressive quality of the discourse, in verse rhythm is itself the determining feature, within whose framework both meaning and expression have to be accommodated.[23] *Masks* is not prose in this definition, but it is not clear that it is verse either. For the rhythmic patterns of verse are normally understood as being organized into units of line and stanza, in other words as comprising recurrent forms substantially larger than the foot. It is when these larger units are not perceptible that a regular rhythm comes to be experienced as simply an accumulation of more and more of the same, and the accusation of monotony appears appropriate.

Bely would not have been in the least dismayed to hear his prose described as a hybrid form. In all his later writings about rhythm he was concerned to do away with the conventional distinction between prose and verse. He argues historically that metre as it comes to be established in verse is originally nothing more than the most commonly employed rhythms of speech. The canonization of certain metrical forms is a process of increasing artificiality, and strict metrical form is a straitjacket from which true poetry seeks constantly to liberate itself. Bely's concern with flexibility of rhythm leads him naturally from a consideration of verse to an examination of artistic prose. He argues that it appears later in the history of literature because it is harder to write, and that free verse is a natural transitional form between the two.[24] What Bely is positing here is a kind of unbroken spectrum of possible forms in terms of their rhythmic character which is similar in principle to the unbroken spectrum he allows on the time-space axis in his early definition of the forms of art.[25] He specifically abandons normative definitions in favour of a system that allows the maximum of flexibility.

These arguments found their most complete form in Bely's book *Rhythm as Dialectics*, published in 1928, the year he started work on *Masks*.[26] He re-iterates there the basic conception of rhythm as the direct expression of the artist's creative impulse that underlay his earliest definitions. All other features of a text develop out of rhythm, and the final meaning is never wholly adequate to the original impulse. Rhythm is the deepest level of language, as he had declared in 'Aaron's Rod', and if the reader seeks to penetrate beyond the inadequate surface to the original impulse, it is the rhythm of poetry that he must examine. The idea of metre as a form of coercion from which expression seeks to liberate itself gives rise to the notion of a desirable new condition where rhythm 'consciously governs the variety of metrical modifications'.[27] It is to the identification and interpretation of such modifications of metre that all Bely's prosodic analyses are devoted. What he has in mind here is a new poetic canon in which the original impulse, 'rhythm' in its psychological sense, will be less encrusted in the rigid shell of metre, and the final form of the utterance will thus be more adequate to the impulse.

Bely's discussion in *Rhythm as Dialectics* centres upon poetry, not prose, and specifically upon the iambic tetrameter of Pushkin's *Bronze Horseman*. By far the greatest part of Bely's work on the rhythmic analysis of poetry, throughout his career, is devoted to the iambic tetrameter. In *Rhythm as Dialectics* he outlines the method that was devised by the circle of poets and scholars that he gathered around him in the years immediately following the publication of his first analyses in *Symbolism*, for defining gradations of stress, as distinct from the simple establishment of their presence or absence.[28] This makes possible a much subtler rhythmic analysis than had previously been possible. He uses it upon *The Bronze Horseman* and seeks to demonstrate in conclusion how the varying rhythmic tension of different passages of the poem can be seen to modify the semantic meaning of the words.

Ternary rhythms in Russian poetry have never been analysed with the same detail as binary metres, since the distinctive feature of the absent, or reduced metrical stress, so common in binary verse, does not occur in ternary forms. As M.L. Gasparov has pointed out, rhythmic variety in these forms is created by the positioning of the word-boundaries and by the presence of additional subsidiary stresses.[29] Gasparov proceeds to offer a method of defining such subsidiary stresses, which, though different in many details, is in principle similar to that which Bely and his circle devised and which Bely employed in his analysis of

Pushkin's iambic tetrameter. There is thus no reason in principle why a modification of Bely's method should not be used for demonstrating the rhythmic variability of a ternary form. If it can be used for ternary verse, it can also be used for Bely's own hybrid ternary prose. And although Bely himself did not use it for that purpose, it stands to reason that someone who could subject binary metres to such close analysis of rhythmic variations would perceive ternary forms in similar terms.

This then leads to the conclusion that the rhythm of Bely's last novels needs to be examined with methods that have never yet been applied to it. The charge of monotony rests upon two assumptions. One is that the ratio of stressed and unstressed syllables is absolutely constant; a subtler definition of stress, such as Bely surely had in mind, would remove that premise. The reader who wishes to perceive the rhythmic variations would, indeed, need to sharpen his perception, but that is exactly what is required of him in all other respects too. It is worth noting that the rhythmic patterns of Indian music, for example, make similarly unwonted demands upon Western ears. The second assumption is that the larger units, corresponding to line and stanza in poetry, are not perceptible. The incorrectness of that is easier to observe. Janecek concedes that a relative rhythmic variety is created in *Masks*, in contrast to *Moscow*, by the generally shorter length of the 'lines'. He concludes from this that 'the result is a rather tortured, halting style, but one in which the predominant ternary rhythm is somewhat hidden by the fragmentation'.[30] This is not a satisfactory conclusion. If one looks further, at the larger units that correspond to the stanzas of poetry, it can be seen that the text is built up of longer sections, consisting of up to a dozen or so 'lines' of varying length, which are held together as units not by simple rhythmic repetition, but by a complex intonational pattern and a cadence that is not difficult to perceive. All the euphonic effects of alliteration, assonance and rhyme, as well as syntactic parallelisms, play their part in the establishment of what is, in the end, a rhythmic form of great subtlety. It is not ultimately a form that corresponds to Tomashevsky's definition of verse, since the rhythmic structure is not rigid enough for us to say with certainty that the other features are subordinate to it. It is precisely a hybrid form, as Zhirmunsky stated, but one which Bely devised with the greatest deliberateness in order to accommodate both the flexibil-

ity of prose and the structural cohesion of verse. All Bely's theoretical statements on the subject tend towards the abolition of
traditional genre-definitions, and it is not in the least surprising
that his own culminating artistic work should defy generic cate-
gorization.

Masks makes exceptional demands upon its readers. They are
required to perceive every level of the language in a hitherto
unfamiliar way, and concomitantly to attain a new awareness of
the nature of the reality that the language represents. It is a mode
of perception to which Bely himself came only after a lifetime of
intense intellectual activity, and it is not surprising if few can
follow him. He was aware that he could not expect much sympathetic response from the readership to whom it was available in
1932. The Symbolists were either dead or in emigration; the
anthroposophists were disbanded and exiled; and the literary
order of the day was to enthuse over the building by forced labour
of the White Sea canal. But in no circumstances could such a novel
have found a wide readership. Bely admitted in a letter to
Ivanov-Razumnik that he felt he might be writing only for two or
three people, Klavdiya Nikolayevna, Ivanov-Razumnik himself,
and a handful of close friends.[31] He realized that the novel would
be found incomprehensible by practically everyone who picked it
up. Not many have picked it up. As John Malmstad has recently
written: 'Probably few will agree with Klavdia Nikolaevna's belief
that *Maski* is Bely's finest novel; few, however, have read it.'[32] To
this one might add that fewer still have read it with sympathy and a
genuine desire to understand what Bely was attempting.

A description of the novel such as has been essayed here is
necessarily a description of what Bely intended the novel to
express, and how he wished it to be read. There is no other way of
approaching so rebarbative a text, unless it be simply to dismiss it.
To identify the author's intentions is not, of course, to judge the
work, but it can provide a key to the code, as it were, and make
judgement ultimately possible. It may well be that *Masks* is destined to remain forever inaccessible, as readers and critics are
unable or unwilling to follow its author into regions beyond ordinary habitation.

There is nevertheless one form of assessment that can be made
at once, and that is to examine the coherence and consistency of

the aesthetic system Bely has employed. It can then be seen that he has created a work of remarkable aesthetic unity. Every level of this text, from the individual word as a semantic unit through the euphonic patterning and the rhythm of the sentences, to the structure of larger sections and ultimately the plot of the whole novel, is consistent. There is an exact correlation between matter and manner; colour as a therapeutic device to heal the professor is indistinguishable from colour as a literary device to enlighten the reader. *Masks* is, moreover, largely free of the lapses of taste that marred *Moscow*, and also of the ponderousness of its style. In its treatment of the theme of suffering it shows distance and true compassion, in contrast to the touches of hysteria and self-pity that could be detected in its predecessor. It avoids the confusion of fiction and memoir that to a greater or lesser extent affected all his work since *Kotik Letayev*. It shows developments beyond *Moscow* in stylistic ingenuity, particularly in the use of neologisms and the refinement of rhythm. It should not be forgotten, either, that the theme of this novel, apparently so distant from the pressing historical concerns of the public he addressed, is now seen clearly as one of the most pressing concerns of men anywhere: the morality of knowledge, the disproportion between the practical possibilities opened to man by his exploitation of nature, and the frailty of his moral sense that must guide their use. *Masks* does, after all, show us Bely at a zenith of achievement; nothing could be further from the truth than to regard this novel as the work of a waning talent.

Conclusion

Between the completion of *Masks* in late 1930 and his death in January 1934 Bely devised plans for a number of further novels that were destined to remain unwritten. The *Moscow* cycle itself was intended to run to a further two volumes; according to Bely's preface to *Masks* the first of these was to cover the period of revolution and civil war, while the second would carry on through NEP to the subsequent period of reconstruction.[1] K.N. Bugayeva has left in her memoirs an account in different terms of these novels' intended content. The professor was to suffer a relapse after the explosion and wander around Moscow making speeches to such as might listen; he was to be adopted by a group of anarchists and eventually rescued from them by Kierko, who would take him, along with Serafima Sergeyevna, to the Caucasus. There he would once more recover his health, and begin to establish around himself a new community of local people.[2] This plot carries echoes both of the story 'The Yogi', and also of events from Bely's own life in his later years, when the Caucasus acquired great importance for him as a source of fresh stimulus and a place where he was able to establish new relationships. The plot as Bugayeva outlines it sounds perilously close to a repetition of what has gone before, though a further relapse and recovery would presumably have been presented as a higher cycle of development. No mention is made in her account of the professor's discovery, and it remains possible that Bely's rather cavalier dismissal of it in *Masks* would have been the unsatisfactory end of the matter. Nevertheless it is also the case that in the process of writing Bely's novels usually turned into something quite different from the original plan, and very probably the same would have happened here.[3]

There is no contradiction between Bely's own description in terms of Russian history and Bugayeva's in terms of individual fates. Historical events would no doubt have continued to play the kind of background role that they perform in the existing novels. Nevertheless the fact that those events were projected beyond 1917 would have compelled Bely to confront the central historical issue which in *Masks* he could still avoid. He would have had to redeem his promise of showing the characters acquiring a new selfhood, 'beginning to speak', in the revolution. He had written in 1924 that the revolution as he envisaged it had still not come about, but it is hard to believe he would have said the same a decade later. The tendency towards compromise with the official Soviet interpretation of events begins to be apparent in his work by the end of the 1920s. His travel notes, *A Wind from the Caucusus*,[4] for instance, had somewhat soured his relations with Ivanov-Razumnik, who felt he should not have praised the construction of the 'new life' without mentioning the human cost involved.[5] There existed another idea for an unwritten novel which seems to indicate a similar leaning. He developed an immense interest in the projected construction of a railway line through one of the passes in the Caucasus, and spent much of 1933 considering how he might write his own kind of five-year-plan novel on this theme.[6] Presumably he would have placed the emphasis upon the development of personalities and relationships in the collective labour of the enterprise; but some compromise with the political methods adopted in the five-year-plan period would surely have been inevitable.

Perhaps the most interesting of his unachieved plans was the idea of a novel about the rise of Fascism in Germany, based in part upon his own experiences there during the inflationary period of the early 1920s – experiences that had already been recorded in his strident little volume *One of the Mansions of the Realm of Shadows*.[7] A contract was signed for this novel in October 1931 and its appearance announced for the end of that year, but Bely never got further than a plan.[8] This plan shows that the novel's plot was to hinge upon the conflict of two tendencies in German culture, roughly characterized as the classical tradition of Goethe and the imperialism of Bismarck. The central hero was to embody this conflict in himself and eventually fall a victim to the growing social unrest that it engendered. In the relationship between inner life and external reality, in the element of political adventure and intrigue that the plot was to contain, this novel can easily be seen as a successor to other novels of Bely's, most of all to *Petersburg*.[9]

It is a plan that Bely could well have realized with a minimum of compromise.

There exists, of course, no information about the stylistic qualities these novels might have shown. Saddened though he was by the inaccessibility of *Masks*, it seems unlikely that Bely would willingly have reverted to a radically simpler style. It is, after all, in his view the style of the language that carries the deepest meaning of the words. In his critical study *Rhythm as Dialectics* Bely had reached the ingenious conclusion that the rhythmic characteristics of Pushkin's *The Bronze Horseman* give the poem a politically subversive meaning for its time which could not be expressed at the semantic level. Something similar happens in *Masks*, where the surface elements of political compromise are absorbed into a greater system of meaning, carried by the entirety of the novel as a linguistic unity. The continuation of the *Moscow* cycle, or the five-year-plan novel, could have been written along the same lines, acquiring through their stylistic qualities a meaning quite at variance with a politically orthodox surface, though one which hardly any of their readers would have perceived. At the same time it has to be remembered that the year of Bely's death was also the year in which Socialist Realism was officially canonized. If Bely had continued to write in a style similar to that of *Masks*, it is extremely unlikely, to say the least, that his novels would have seen the light of day.

Petersburg has always been regarded as Bely's finest novel. It is one of those rare works which are increasingly seen, as their historical moment recedes, to embody the quintessence of their time. For its formal originality alone it would stand apart from any other prose work in the immediate pre-revolutionary period; but it combines that quality with a vision of Russian history that equally has no rivals for breadth and penetration. It absorbs into its charmed circle two centuries of political and intellectual history, and becomes a kind of meta-novel to the Russian literary tradition of the nineteenth century. In its juxtaposition of history's eternal recurrence and the threat – or promise – of an apocalyptic transformation it expresses the endemic mood of a generation, a mood which helped pave the way, as a self-fulfilling prophecy, for the transformations that were shortly to take place. The moment of its writing – just after the end of a literary movement that had seen art as a path to brotherhood, and just before a war that was to turn most men into fratricides – was itself unique, and it is tempting to think that *Petersburg* could not have been written at any other time.

It is natural enough that its influence was both immense and short-lived. For a brief period there was hardly a writer who did not succumb to it in one way or another, be it at the stylistic level in the exuberant cacophony of Pil'nyak's *Naked Year*, or at the thematic level in the hermetic and geometrical city that reappears in Zamyatin's *We*. In 1922 Mandel'shtam wrote that Russian prose would not move forwards until there appeared a writer who was free from Bely's influence.[10] But he need not have worried: the pressures of Soviet literary politics saw to it that Russian prose moved forwards quite soon. In any case the end of civil war and chaos brought with it the realization that even after the apocalypse the sun still rose and set, and that literature had to find new paths to follow. No later work of Bely's exerted any substantial influence.

The peculiar combination of individual genius and historical moment which created *Petersburg* could never be repeated. What is remarkable is that Bely did not burn himself out in its achievement, but turned immediately to fresh tasks. He had in effect outgrown the novel even before he put the finishing touches to it at the end of 1913, and had embarked upon a course that was to provide him with a purpose for the rest of his life, but was to take him further and further away from his country's history as commonly understood. The immediate artistic result was *Kotik Letayev*, a novel which is in no way aesthetically inferior. Indeed it is the most tightly organized and homogeneous of any of Bely's novels, and on aesthetic criteria alone would have to be regarded as his greatest attainment in the genre. Its aesthetic unity is bought at the price of the internalization of all meaningful experience, but that experience is evoked with such delicacy and complexity that the compensation is ample. *Kotik Letayev* sets out to re-create the world in language, and it is at this point in his career that Bely achieved the finest balance between linguistic inventiveness and general accessibility. For however much it outraged its earliest readers,[11] the language of *Kotik Letayev* is not particularly difficult to understand, and the mythic interpretation of early consciousness that it embodies is not now thought nearly as obscure as it was at the time.

Of Bely's lesser achievements *The Silver Dove* still occupies a place of great importance in the prose of the first decade of the twentieth century, and can well stand comparison with Bunin's *The Village* or Remizov's *The Pond* for its depiction of rural Russia. It is only in comparison with the greater power of Bely's own subsequent novels, or with the more sustained achievement of Sologub's *Petty Demon* that it pales. After *Kotik Letayev* Bely struggled to move outwards again from that novel's total internalization, and encountered aesthetic problems in trying to combine inner experience and outer world, self and history, that proved very hard to solve. *Notes of an Eccentric* is a maverick work whose failure closed off one unproductive line of development, while the unresolved dualism of *The Baptized Chinaman* showed that this combination could only be attained by reverting to third-person narration and reinstating plot. *The Moscow Eccentric* and *Moscow in Jeopardy* are too nearly a re-working of themes and devices that Bely had fully exploited before, but in *Masks* he reached a new level of attainment.

Masks is, along with *Petersburg* and *Kotik Letayev*, the third high point of Bely's novelistic career. Its qualities, however, are of a different order. Its geographical and historical setting are not genuinely specific, as was the case with *Petersburg*, and the external world that the hero confronts is not a world of history in any generally accepted sense. On the other hand the images representing that world do not interlock and overlap as they did in *Petersburg*, and do not reduce its phenomena to ultimate identity as happens there. *Masks* is not a symbolist novel in the sense in which *Petersburg* has come to be regarded as the paradigm of that type.[12] Nor is it illustrative of pre-existing mythic schemes, as *Kotik Letayev* can in one sense be said to be. It is a work, to borrow Bely's own favourite Latin phrase, that is entirely *sui generis*. As a genre it is as different from the traditional novel as Indian music is from Beethoven. In fact such a comparison can help in the understanding of the peculiar demands Bely's last novel makes upon its readers, requiring them to perceive something as culturally unfamiliar as the quarter-tones and extended rhythmic units that occur in Indian music. The language of *Masks* can be learnt, but it is not a language anyone understands unaided.

The Symbolists' quest for an organic religious culture could only be sustained in the long run by the creation of an esoteric society like that of the anthroposophists. Of all the Symbolists it was Bely who clung most tenaciously to that dream, and his allegiance to

Steiner's ideas shows the consistency of his intellectual development. From a different viewpoint one might say that it showed the
most obstinate refusal to learn from experience, but that would
not be just. The priority of inner experience, as that which gives
form to the outer world, was an axiom to which Bely always held,
and the historical experience from which he may be thought to
have declined tuition could never disprove that tenet. In his
anthroposophy, too, this rule holds good. Although some of his
theoretical utterances are afflicted by that ponderous silliness that
makes so much esoteric writing unreadable, his artistic work never
sinks to the level of received wisdom. It is always the original inner
experience, re-generated in the reader by the action of the aesthetic form, that governs Bely's novels. In this understanding of
Symbolism Bely did, as he constantly claimed in later years,
remain entirely faithful to it, and *Masks*, in its lack of dogma and
total reliance on aesthetic effect, observes that principle more
thoroughly than any of its predecessors.

Abbreviations

L.	Leningrad
M.	Moscow
M.-L.	Moscow–Leningrad
N.Y.	New York
Pb.	Petersburg
Pg.	Petrograd
Spb.	Saint Petersburg
TsGALI	Tsentral'nyy gosudarstvennyy arkhiv literatury i iskusstva (Central State Archive of Literature and Art)
IRLI	Institut russkoy literatury (Institute of Russian Literature)
GBL OR	Gosudarstvennaya biblioteka imeni Lenina. Otdel rukopisey (Lenin Library Manuscript Department)
ASEER	*American Slavic and East European Review*
SEER	*Slavonic and East European Review*
SEEJ	*Slavic and East European Journal*
FILLM	Fédération Internationale des Langues et Littératures Modernes

Notes

Introduction

1 For further details see the Select Bibliography, pp.246–9.
2 A.Hönig, *Andrej Belyjs Romane*, Munich 1965, p.101.
3 A.Bely, *Mezhdu dvukh revolyutsiy*, L. 1934, p.354.
4 J.D.Elsworth, *Andrey Bely*, Letchworth 1972.

1. Bely's theory of symbolism

1 *Epopeya* 1, Berlin 1922, p.225 footnote. The 'Argonauts' were a group of friends in Moscow in the early years of the century.
2 *Mezhdu dvukh...*, p.208.
3 *Simvolizm*, M. 1910; *Arabeski*, M. 1911; *Lug zelyonyy*, M. 1910.
4 *Mezhdu dvukh....*, p.377.
5 The essay 'O granitsakh psikhologii', *Simvolizm* pp.31–48, is a particular example.
6 F.Stepun, *Vstrechi*, Munich 1962, p.166.
7 *Arabeski*, p.161.
8 *Mezhdu dvukh...*, p.397.
9 *Arabeski*, pp.207, 219, 220; *Simvolizm*, p.24.
10 *Arabeski*, p.163.
11 The matter is further complicated by the fact that on one or two occasions the terms 'individualism' and 'subjectivism' are positively distinguished from one another: *Simvolizm*, p.515; 'Printsip sovremennoy estetiki', *Zori*, vyp.6, 20 March 1906, p.1.
12 *Arabeski*, p.167.
13 'Kumir na glinyanykh nogakh', *Pereval*, 1907 No.8–9, pp.70–5.
14 *Arabeski*, p.175.
15 N.Valentinov, *Dva goda s simvolistami*, Stanford, Calif., 1969, pp.65–6.
16 *Pereval*, 1907 No.8–9, p.72.
17 Valentinov, p.165.
18 Stepun, p.167.
19 *Simvolizm*, p.3.
20 ibid., p.10.
21 ibid., p.453.
22 'O nauchnom dogmatizme', *Simvolizm*, pp.11–19.

23 cf. F.Überweg, *Geschichte der Philosophie*, 12. Auflage, Berlin 1923, 4. Teil, pp.310–11, 416–17, 449–67; E.v.Aster, *Geschichte der Philosophie*, Stuttgart 1947, pp.372–3; W.Brock, *An Introduction to Contemporary German Philosophy*, Cambridge 1935, Ch.1 section 1.

24 H.Rickert, *Der Gegenstand der Erkenntnis*, 2. Auflage, Tübingen and Leipzig 1904, p.165.

25 ibid., p.169.

26 ibid., p.170–1 (Rickert's italics).

27 ibid., pp.201–2.

28 ibid., p.208.

29 *Arabeski*, p.178.

30 The quotation marks are Rickert's; op. cit., p.221.

31 ibid., p.222–3.

32 '...dass die letzte Basis des Wissens ein *Gewissen* ist'. ibid., p.231.

33 ibid., p.235.

34 F.Stepun, *Mystische Weltschau*, Munich 1964, p.290.

35 A.Bely, *Nachalo veka*, M.-L. 1933, p.115.

36 *Simvolizm*, pp.12–13.

37 ibid., p.56.

38 ibid., p.467.

39 *Nachalo veka*, p.115.

40 *Simvolizm*, pp.4, 107–8.

41 ibid., p.129.

42 ibid., p.67.

43 ibid., p.6.

44 cf. *Arabeski*, p.108: 'Symbolization is, so to speak, the objectivization of experience.'

45 *Simvolizm*, p.70.

46 ibid., p.433.

47 ibid., p.76.

48 ibid., p.67.

49 ibid., p.8.

50 ibid., pp.213–17.

51 'Formy iskusstva', 'Printsip formy v estetike', ibid., pp.149–94.

52 ibid., p.178.

53 ibid., p.181.

54 ibid.

55 ibid., p.179. The word *vidimost'*, used here and above, is a synonym for 'nature' or 'objective reality' in the sense of unformed raw material.

56 ibid., p.178.

57 ibid., pp.204–5.

58 ibid., pp.26, 539.

59 V.Zhirmunsky, *Introduction to Metrics*, transl. C.F.Brown, The Hague 1966, p.47.

60 *Simvolizm*, p.176.
61 ibid., p.202.
62 ibid., p.223: 'The content is the form of the creative process.'
63 ibid., pp.73, 80.
64 A.Bely, 'S nami Bog', *Grif* No.3, M. 1905, p.193.
65 *Lug zelyonyy*, p.58.
66 *Arabeski*, p.391.
67 A.Bely, 'Material k biografii (intimnyy), prednaznachennyy dlya izucheniya tol'ko posle smerti avtora', TsGALI fond 53 opis'2 yed. khr.3.
68 V.Zen'kovsky, *Istoriya russkoy filosofii*, vol.2 Paris 1950, pp.11–72.
69 *Simvolizm*, p.76.
70 ibid., p.105. J.Holthusen has objected that this capitalized Symbol is a concept that does not appear in any other of Bely's essays and is never fully clarified; J.Holthusen, *Studien zur Ästhetik und Poetik des russischen Symbolismus*, Göttingen 1957, p.27. It does in fact occur in Bely's 'Printsip sovremennoy estetiki', *Zori*, vyp.9–10, 17 April 1906, p.2, in exactly the same form, while the same idea is expressed elsewhere in such formulations as 'symbolic Unity' or 'world symbol'; see 'O pessimizme', *Svobodnaya sovest'* No.1, M. 1906, p.177; 'Okno v budushcheye', *Vesy*, 1904 No.12, p.8.
71 *Lug zelyonyy*, pp.222–47; originally published in *Vesy*, 1905 No.4.
72 *Arabeski*, p.21.
73 ibid., p.216.
74 ibid., p.21.
75 This is a somewhat brutal summary of the ideas Ivanov expressed in a number of essays, most of which were re-published in his collected volume *Po zvyozdam*, Spb.1909. For greater detail see J.West, *Russian Symbolism*, London 1970, Ch.2.
76 *Vesy*, 1908 No.10, p.47.
77 These points are argued in three essays: 'Iskusstvo i misteriya', *Vesy*, 1906 No.9; 'Simvolicheskiy teatr', *Utro Rossii*, 16, 28 Sept. 1907; 'Teatr i sovremennaya drama', *Teatr. Kniga o novom teatre*, Spb. 1908. All three were re-published in *Arabeski*.
78 V.Ivanov, 'Estetika i ispovedaniye', *Vesy*, 1908 No.11, pp.45–50. This essay, also re-published in *Po zvyozdam*, was a reply to Bely's 'Simvolizm i sovremennoye russkoye iskusstvo', *Vesy*, 1908 No.10 (and *Lug zelyonyy*).
79 *Lug zelyonyy*, p.28.
80 A.Bely, *Tragediya tvorchestva. Dostoyevskiy i Tolstoy*, M.1911.
81 It is particularly in evidence in *The Silver Dove* and *Notes of an Eccentric*.
82 A.Bely, 'Sotsial-demokratiya i religiya', *Pereval*, 1907 No.5, pp.23–35.
83 A.Bely, 'Ibsen i Dostoyevskiy', *Vesy*, 1905 No.12, pp.47–54 (also in *Lug zelyonyy*).

84 *Tragediya tvorchestva*, passim.
85 A.Bely, 'Pravda o russkoy intelligentsii. Po povodu sbornika "Vekhi"', *Vesy*, 1909 No.5, pp.65–8.
86 A.Bely, 'Kamennaya ispoved'. Po povodu stat'i N.A.Berdyayeva "K psikhologii revolyutsii"', *Obrazovaniye*, 1908 No.8, pp.28–38. The development of Bely's attitude towards Dostoyevsky and the idea of revolution in these years is described in Valentinov, op.cit., pp.173–200.
87 *Simvolizm*, p.429.
88 ibid., p.440.
89 ibid., p.429.
90 ibid., p.440.
91 ibid., pp.446–7.
92 ibid., p.74.
93 ibid., pp.447–8.
94 A.Bely, 'Mysl' i yazyk', *Logos* No.2, M. 1910, p.250.
95 *Vesy*, 1908 No.7, p.75.
96 In his essay 'Dve stikhii v sovremennom simvolizme', *Zolotoye runo*, 1908 Nos.3–5 (and in *Po zvyozdam*).
97 *Vesy*, 1908 No.5, pp.59ff.
98 *Vesy*, 1908 No.7, p.76.
99 ibid., p.75.
100 ibid., p.77.
101 N.Berdyayev, 'Russkiy soblazn', *Russkaya mysl'*, 1910 No.11, p.112.
102 *Vstrechi*, p.165.
103 The expression is Mandel'shtam's; he writes of the 'lazy omnivorousness' of theosophy. See 'O prirode slova' in O.E.Mandel'shtam, *Sobraniye sochineniy*, vol.2, New York 1966, p.285.
104 He specifically interpreted Nietzsche in terms of theosophy in an article written in 1907: 'Fridrikh Nitsshe', *Vesy*, 1908 Nos.7–9 (re-published with date of composition in *Arabeski*).
105 This feature is played down in Bely's published memoirs, but emerges very clearly in the unpublished 'Material k biografii (intimnyy)...', TsGALI.
106 *Lug zelyonyy*, p.34.

2. Bely and anthroposophy

1 N.A.Berdyayev, 'Teosofiya kak raznovidnost' russkoy religioznoy mysli', *Russkaya mysl'*, 1916 No.11, quoted in *Byulleteni literatury i zhizni*, 1916–17 No.7–8, pp.368ff.
2 Bely himself noted the affinity between Solov'yov and Steiner; A.Bely, 'Vospominaniya ob A.A.Bloke', *Epopeya* No.1, Berlin 1922, p.163.
3 A.Bely, *Na rubezhe dvukh stoletiy*, izd. 2-oye, M.-L. 1931, pp.354–5.

More fully in 'Material k biografii (intimnyy)...', TsGALI f.53, op.2, yed.khr.3.

4   see also *Nachalo veka*, pp.54–60, 'Vospominaniya ob A.A.Bloke', *Epopeya* No.4, Berlin 1923, p.138.

5   Spiritus (= A.Bely), 'Sem' planetnykh dukhov', *Vesy*, 1909 No.9, pp.68–71.

6   *Simvolizm*, p.624.

7   ibid., p.505.

8   *Arabeski*, p.286, *Simvolizm*, p.624.

9   Bely's letter to Blok of 1/14 May 1912 in A.Blok i A.Bely, *Perepiska*, M.1940, pp.293–301; A.Bely, 'Iz vospominaniy', *Beseda* No.2, Berlin 1923, pp.83–106; J.D.Elsworth, *Andrey Bely*, Letchworth 1972, pp.82–4.

10 J.Hemleben, *Rudolf Steiner in Selbstzeugnissen und Bilddokumenten*, Rowohlt, Reinbek bei Hamburg 1963, p.60.

11 N.A.Berdyayev, *Samopoznaniye*, Paris 1949, p.206.

12 R.Steiner, *Occult Science: an Outline*, London 1963 (many other editions); see also A.P.Shepherd, *A Scientist of the Invisible*, London 1964.

13 *Samopoznaniye*, p.210.

14 F.Stepun, *Mystische Weltschau*, p.290.

15 Andrej Belyj, *Verwandeln des Lebens*, aus dem russischen von Swetlana Geier, Basel 1975, passim.

16 'Material k biografii (intimnyy)...'

17 *Notes of an Eccentric* and *Glossolalia* are perhaps the most opaque.

18 R.Steiner, *Die Philosophie der Freiheit*, 1893 (usually known in English translation as *The Philosophy of Spiritual Activity*); *Goethes Weltanschauung*, 1897.

19 This is a summary of the argument in Chapters 3–5 of *Die Philosophie der Freiheit*.

20 A.Bely, *O smysle poznaniya*, Pb. 1922.

21 A.Bely, *Na perevale*, Berlin–Pb.–M. 1923, p.26.

22 A.Bely, *Simfoniya (Vtoraya, dramaticheskaya)*, *Sobraniye sochineniy*, vol.4, M.1917, p.240.

23 A.Bely, *Serebryanyy golub'*, M.1910, vmesto predisloviya.

24 See, for instance, A.Bely, 'O zlobodnevnom i vechnom', *Birzhevyye vedomosti*, 23 June 1916, No.15635, p.2.

25 See below, Ch.5.

26 A.Bely, *Ofeyra. Putevyye zametki*, chast.1, M.1921; A.Bely, *Putevyye zametki*, t.1, *Sitsiliya i Tunis*, Berlin 1922. A.Bely, *Istoriya stanovleniya samosoznayushchey dushi*, unpublished; see J.Crookenden, 'The chapter "Simvolizm" from Bely's "Istoriya stanovleniya samosoznayushchey dushi"', *Andrey Bely. Centenary Papers*, ed. Boris Christa, Amsterdam 1980, pp.39–51.

27 *Na perevale*, p.53.

28 ibid., p.135.

29 ibid.
30 ibid., p.14.
31 ibid., pp.69ff.
32 This is argued somewhat more fully in: J.D.Elsworth, 'The Concept of Rhythm in Bely's Aesthetic Thought', *Andrey Bely. Centenary Papers*, pp.68–80.
33 *Na perevale*, p.97.
34 *O smysle poznaniya*, p.48.
35 ibid.
36 ibid., p.42. He squares each of the figures before multiplying them together.
37 ibid., pp.58, 73–4.
38 See below, Ch.7.
39 R.Steiner, *Christianity as Mystical Fact*, London 1948, Ch.7.
40 Bely asserted similarities between them, however; see above, Ch.1 n.104.
41 A.Bjely, 'Die Anthroposophie und Russland', *Die Drei*, 4.Heft, 1922, pp. 320–1.
42 A.Bely, 'Myortvyye goroda', *Birzhevyye vedomosti*, 17 August 1916, No.15745, p.2.
43 A.Bely, *Revolyutsiya i kul'tura*, M.1917.
44 A.Bely, *Sirin uchonogo varvarstva*, Berlin 1922. See also: H.Stammler, 'Belyj's Conflict with Vyačeslav Ivanov over War and Revolution', SEEJ, vol.18 No.3, 1974, pp.259–70.
45 *Die Drei*, 5.Heft, 1922, p.378.
46 *Na perevale*, p.162.
47 A.Bely, 'Dnevnik pisatelya', *Rossiya*, 1924 No.2 (11), p.140.
48 See below, Ch.7.
49 A.Bely, 'O ritme', *Gorn*, 1920 No.5, p.47.
50 A.Bely, 'Zhezl Aarona', *Skify* No.1, 1917, p.161.
51 A.Bely, *Glossolaliya*, Berlin 1922, p.9.
52 ibid., p.115.
53 'Zhezl Aarona', p.200.
54 A.Bely, 'O khudozhestvennoy proze', *Gorn*, 1919 No.2–3, pp.49–55.
55 See above, p.22.
56 'Zhezl Aarona', p.181.
57 ibid., p.184.
58 *Arabeski*, p.391.

3. The Silver Dove

1 A.Bely, *Simfoniya (Vtoraya, dramaticheskaya)* M.1902; Boris Bugayev, 'Formy iskusstva', *Mir iskusstva*, 1902 No.12, pp.343–61.
2 In the original edition and the edition of 1917 (p.125) he speaks of three meanings, but in his memoirs he reflects that it would have been better to speak of three aspects; *Nachalo veka*, p.121.

3 A.Bely, *Kubok meteley. 4-aya Simfoniya*, M.1908, p.1.
4 *Simfoniya (Vtoraya...)*, M.1917, p.125.
5 E.Szilard, 'O strukture *Vtoroy Simfonii* A.Belogo', *Studia Slavica Hungarica* XIII, 1967, p.320.
6 *Simfoniya (Vtoraya...)*, M.1917, p.129.
7 ibid., pp.144,146.
8 E.Szilard, 'O vliyanii ritmiki prozy F.Nitsshe na ritmiku prozy A.Belogo', *Studia Slavica Hungarica* XIX, 1973, pp.289–313.
9 G.Janecek, 'Literature as Music: Symphonic Form in Andrei Belyj's *Fourth Symphony*', *Canadian-American Slavic Studies* VIII No.4 (Winter 1974), p.510.
10 Szilard, 'O strukture...', p.313.
11 Janecek, 'Literature as Music'.
12 O.A.Maslenikov, 'Andrej Belyj's Third "Symphony"', ASEER 1948 vol.7, pp.78–92.
13 Even on its re-publication in 1922 it was found to be dated; K.Loks, 'Bely. – Vozvrat. Povest'', *Pechat' i revolyutsiya*, 1923 No.1, p.223.
14 One critic, however, finds words of judicious praise for it; S.A. Askol'dov speaks of the *Fourth Symphony* as 'the most enigmatic, most inexplicable, and at the same time the most captivating of Bely's Symphonies'; S.A.Askol'dov, 'Tvorchestvo A.Belogo', *Literaturnaya mysl'* 1, Pg.1923, p.86.
15 A.Kovač, *A.Belyi. The Symphonies, 1899–1908*, Bern 1976; G.Janecek, 'Literature as Music'.
16 *Mezhdu dvukh revolyutsiy*, p.138.
17 A.M.Shane, 'Remizov's *Prud*: From Symbolism to Neo-Realism', *California Slavic Studies* VI, Berkeley 1971, pp.71–82.
18 S.Karlinsky, 'Symphonic Structure in Andrej Belyj's "Pervoe svidanie"', *California Slavic Studies* VI, pp.61–70; A.Bely, 'Lettre autobiographique à Ivanov-Razumnik', *Cahiers du monde russe et soviétique*, vol.XV 1–2, 1974, p.74.
19 A.Bely, 'Adam. Zapiski, naydennyye v sumasshedshem dome', *Vesy* 1908 No.4, pp.15–30. C.Douglas, '"Adam" and the Modern Vision', *Andrey Bely. A Critical Review* (ed. G.Janecek), Lexington, Ky 1978, pp.56–70.
20 A.Bely, 'Kust', *Zolotoye runo*, 1906 No.7–8, pp.129–35. See also *Mezhdu dvukh...*, p.138.
21 These short stories, as well as two others that Bely wrote later, are examined in detail in: R.Peterson, *Andrei Bely's Short Prose*, Birmingham Slavonic Monographs No.11, Birmingham 1980.
22 *Mezhdu dvukh...*, pp.354, 376.
23 Full publication details are given in the Bibliography.
24 *Literaturnoye nasledstvo* 27–8, p.604.
25 Stepun, *Vstrechi*, p.178.
26 Page references in the text are to the Skorpion edition, Moscow 1910. The Berlin edition, although reprinted and generally more accessible,

contains a certain number of misprints; see J.D.Elsworth, 'The Silver Dove: An Analysis', *Russian Literature* IV No.4 (1976), pp.378, 384, 392 (notes 16 and 17).

27 K.Mochul'sky, *Andrey Bely*, Paris 1955, p.165.

28 S.Adrianov, 'Kriticheskiye nabroski', *Vestnik Yevropy*, 1910 No.7, pp.389ff.

29 The idea is most closely associated with Vyacheslav Ivanov, but was also at one time an intimate concern of Sergey Solov'yov, who served in part as a model for Dar'yal'sky; *Mezhdu dvukh...*, p.88.

30 Sergey Musatov, a character in the *Second Symphony*, had dreamt 'of uniting the skeleton of the West with the blood of the East'; 1917 edition, p.240.

31 A.Bely, 'Apokalipsis v russkoy poezii', *Lug zelyonyy*, p.230.

32 'Nastoyashcheye i budushcheye russkoy literatury', ibid., p.61.

33 ibid., p.60.

34 A.Bely, 'Vospominaniya ob A.A.Bloke', *Epopeya* No.4, Berlin 1923, p.130; N.A.Berdyayev, 'Russkiy soblazn', *Russkaya mysl'*, 1910 No.11, p.104; K.Mochul'sky, *Andrey Bely*, p.158.

35 R.Ivanov-Razumnik, *A.Blok. A.Bely*, Pb.1919, pp.95–6; K.Mochul'sky, *Andrey Bely*, p.167.

36 ibid.

37 V.Stanevich, 'O Serebryanom golube', *Trudy i dni*, 1914 No.7, pp.141–50.

38 A.Bely, *Pepel*, Spb. 1909.

39 R.Ivanov-Razumnik, *A.Blok. A.Bely*, pp.92–3; K.Mochul'sky, *Andrey Bely*, pp.157–8; S.Adrianov, 'Kriticheskiye nabroski', p.389; see also: A.Bely, *Masterstvo Gogolya*, M.-L. 1934, pp.297–302.

40 Mochul'sky, *Andrey Bely*, loc.cit.; see also T.R.Beyer, 'Belyj's *Serebrjanyj golub'*: Gogol' in Gugolevo', *Russian Language Journal*, xxx No.107, Fall 1976, pp.79–87.

41 Beyer, pp.83–4.

42 D.S.Mirsky, *A History of Russian Literature*, New York 1949 (reprinted 1960), p.469.

43 For example: 'No ni starushka, ni gusary eyo nezabvennoy pamyati, ni lyubeznyye serdtsu dubrovy s baryshney, eshcho boleye yemu lyubeznoy, ne segodnya vozbuzhdali sladkikh vospominaniy' (p.6); 'Vsyo zhe bylo stranno, chto na Dar'yal'skogo roptavshaya i Katinu Dar'yal'skim zagryzayushchaya zhizn' starushka v glubine dushi glukhoy uzhe krepko i tsepko uspela pozhalet' nepriglyadnogo na eyo vzglyad vnuchkina zhenikha' (p.95).

44 A.Hönig confirms that it is rhythmically the freest of Bely's novels; *Andrej Belyjs Romane*, p.28.

45 For example: 'Kogda zapad raz''yal svoyu past' i tuda utekal dnevnoy plamen' i dym' (p.36); 'Yastrebinyy u golubya vyshel v tom rukodelii klyuv' (p.199).

46 Perhaps the best example is: 'kak vostok tyomnyy istochal tok, i tuda – v tyomnogo toka techen'ye-uvodila doroga'. (p.37)
47 J.L.Rice, 'Andrej Belyj's *Silver Dove*: The Black Depths of Blue Space, or Who Stole the Baroness's Diamonds?', *Mnemozina. Studia Literaria Russica in Honorem Vsevolod Setchkarev*, Munich 1974, p.302.
48 V.Ivanov, 'Zavety simvolizma'; A.Blok, 'O sovremennom sostoyanii russkogo simvolizma', *Apollon*, 1910 No.8.
49 *Tragediya tvorchestva*, M.1911.

4. Petersburg

1 The fullest discussion of the history of the novel is contained in the notes and commentary to the recent Moscow edition: L.K.Dolgopolov, 'Tvorcheskaya istoriya i istoriko-literaturnoye znacheniye romana A. Belogo "Peterburg"', in A.Bely, *Peterburg*, M.1981, pp.525–623.
2 *Literaturnoye nasledstvo* 27–8, p.600.
3 *Nachalo veka*, p.326; V.Ivanov, 'Vdokhnoveniye uzhasa', *Rodnoye i vselenskoye*, M.1918, p.92.
4 Details in: L.K.Dolgopolov, 'Andrey Bely v rabote nad "Peterburgom"', *Russkaya literatura*, 1972 No.1, pp.157–67.
5 R.Ivanov-Razumnik, *Vershiny. A.Blok. A.Bely*, Pb.1923, p.92. Most probably this text was among the materials destroyed in Ivanov-Razumnik's house during the German invasion. The fate of his archive is summarized in: Roger Keys, 'The Bely–Ivanov-Razumnik Correspondence', in G.Janecek (ed) *Andrey Bely. A Critical Review*, p.202.
6 *Literaturnoye nasledstvo* 27–8, p.601; Ivanov-Razumnik, *Vershiny*, loc.cit.
7 TsGALI, fond 53, opis' 1, yed.khr. 18.
8 Translated by Nadya Strasser and published by Georg Müller, Munich.
9 *Literaturnoye nasledstvo* 27–8, pp.602–3. This second is extant in the form of a copy of the 1916 edition with corrections in the author's hand. See also Dolgopolov, 'Tvorcheskaya istoriya...', p.576.
10 Details of all these editions are given in the Bibliography.
11 TsGALI f.53, op.1, yed.khr.19, 20. There is a handwritten note of Bely's on the title-sheet of the typescript to the effect that the version performed was the less successful, and a reading of both versions confirms this view.
12 *Literaturnoye nasledstvo* 27–8, p.604.
13 All references in the text are to the 1916 edition, which was printed exactly as the journal edition of 1913–14, and therefore has three separate sets of page-numbers.
14 A.Bely, *Stikhotvoreniya*, Berlin 1923, p.299.

15 Helene Hartmann argues that Dudkin can be seen as Nikolay Apollo-novich's 'Astral body'; *Andrej Belyj and the Hermetic Tradition*, unpublished Ph.D. thesis, Columbia University, N.Y., 1969, p.39.

16 ibid., p.38.

17 E.Starikova, 'Realizm i simvolizm', *Razvitiye realizma v russkoy literature*, t.III, M. 1974, pp.223–4.

18 N.Pustygina, 'Tsitatnost'' v romane Andreya Belogo "Peterburg"', *Uchonyye zapiski Tartuskogo gosudarstvennogo universiteta, Trudy po russkoy i slavyanskoy filologii*, XXVIII, Tartu 1977, vyp.414, p.82.

19 T.G.West has revealed that in Mongolian the word *Av* means 'father' and *lai* means 'plague' or 'pestilence'; T.G.West, *The Novel in Transition*, unpublished Ph.D. thesis, University of Manchester, 1979, p.399.

20 This feature of the novel has been the subject of a number of studies. In addition to those already mentioned, see: D.Burkhart, 'Leitmotivik und Symbolik in Andrej Belyjs Roman "Peterburg"', *Die Welt der Slaven*, Jahrg. IX, Heft 3, 1964, pp.277–323.

21 L.K.Dolgopolov first drew attention to this; 'Andrey Bely v rabote. . .'

22 A.Bely, *Masterstvo Gogolya*, M.-L. 1934, p.305.

23 Starikova, op.cit., and Pustygina, op.cit. are among the critics who have noted this; see also A.Steinberg, *Word and Music in the Novels of Andrey Bely*, CUP 1982, pp.162–91.

24 Starikova, p.243.

25 Burkhart, pp.311ff.

26 ibid., p.310.

27 *Glossolaliya*, p.109.

28 *Na perevale*, p.142.

29 TsGALI f.53, op.1, yed.khr.20.

30 Steinberg, *Word and Music in the Novels of Andrey Bely*, pp.185–91.

31 Hartmann, *Andrej Belyj and The Hermetic Tradition*, p.97.

32 T.G.West, *The Novel in Transition*.

33 Starikova, p.239.

34 A. Bely, 'Yegipet. (Iz puteshestviya)', *Sovremennik*, 1912 Nos. 5–7.

35 A.Lavrov, 'Andrey Bely i Grigoriy Skovoroda', *Studia Slavica Hungarica*, XXI, 1975, pp.395–404.

36 T.G.West, *The Novel in Transition*.

37 This period of Bely's life is most fully described in 'Material k biografii (intimnyy). . .'

38 *Masterstvo Gogolya*, pp.306–7; Ivanov-Razumnik quotes an unpublished note of Bely's to the same effect from 31 August 1921: *Vershiny*, pp.109–10.

39 *Glossolaliya*, pp.102,113.

40 H.Hartmann-Flyer, 'The Time Bomb', G Janecek (ed.) *Andrey Bely. A Critical Review*, pp.121–6.

41 *Serebryanyy golub'*, M.1910, pp.278–95.

42 Pustygina, p.88 fn.23.

43 *Vershiny*, pp.115–125.

44 G.Janecek, 'Rhythm in Prose: The Special Case of Bely', *Andrey Bely. A Critical Review*, pp.90, 96.
45 *Vershiny*, pp.130–7.
46 J.Holthusen, 'Andrej Belyj und Rudolf Steiner', *Festschrift für Max Vasmer*, Berlin 1956.
47 They corresponded little during this time; see R.Keys, 'The Bely–Ivanov-Razumnik Correspondence' p.197.
48 Janecek, 'Rhythm in Prose', p.96.
49 *Literaturnoye nasledstvo* 27–8, p.602.
50 From a copy held in Pushkinsky dom (IRLI), Leningrad, fond 79, opis'.3, yed.khr.81.
51 The first version of his 'Vospominaniya ob A.A.Bloke' was written before he left Russia in the autumn of 1921 and published in *Zapiski mechtateley* No.6, 1922. This was then expanded into the version published in four issues of *Epopeya*, Berlin 1922–3, and further into the initial draft of *Nachalo veka*, written in Berlin but never published. See also his *Stikhotvoreniya*, Berlin 1923.
52 A.Bely, *Stikhotvoreniya*, Bibl. poeta, malaya seriya, L.1940; A.Bely, *Stikhotvoreniya i poemy*, Bibl. poeta, bol'shaya seriya, M.–L.1966.
53 This view is not shared by B.Christa: *The Poetic World of Andrey Bely*, Amsterdam 1977, p.11.
54 Western critics tend to make the distinction between the *Sirin* edition and the Berlin edition, rather than between the *Sirin* (first) edition and the 1928 (last lifetime) edition, on the grounds that the removal of religious imagery from the latter was probably not a voluntary act of Bely's. That the Soviet censors were concerned about its mysticism is borne out by Bely's letter to Ivanov-Razumnik of 8 February 1928,quoted by R.Keys, 'The Bely–Ivanov-Razumnik correspondence' p.198. R.Maguire and J.Malmstad chose to translate the Berlin text partly on aesthetic, and partly on textological grounds; A.Bely, *Petersburg*, translated by R.Maguire and J.Malmstad, Bloomington, Indiana and Hassocks, Sussex, 1978, pp.xxiv–xxv.
55 Janecek, 'Rhythm in Prose', p.96.
56 *Vershiny*, pp.96ff.
57 'Tvorcheskaya istoriya...', pp.577ff.

5. Kotik Letayev

1 See above, Ch.2.   2 See above, Ch.1 and 3.
3 Starikova, op.cit.
4 It is very much in evidence in his articles for *Birzhevyye vedomosti* during 1916, but underlies all his theoretical works of this period.
5 *Literaturnoye nasledstvo* 27–8, p.605.
6 *Skify* No.1, Pb.1917.
7 Cited in *Literaturnoye nasledstvo* 27–8, p.604.
8 *Zapiski mechtateley* No.4, 1921, pp.21,24.

9 *Zapiski mechtateley* No.1, 1919, p.11; see also 'Vmesto predisloviya' in A.Bely, *Zapiski chudaka*, M.1922.
10 *Zapiski mechtateley* No.1, 1919, unnumbered (p.9).
11 Apart from the edition that appeared in *Skify* Nos. 1 and 2,
   1917–18, there has been only one edition of *Kotik Letayev*,
   Pb.1922. All references in the text are to that edition.
12 A.Belyj, *Verwandeln des Lebens*, p.339; A.Turgenieff, *Erinnerungen an Rudolf Steiner*, Stuttgart 1972, p.78.
13 This is one instance of an image of Bely's derived from 'Am
   farb'gen Abglanz...' A similar example can be found in A.Bely,
   Rudol'f Shteyner i Gete v mirovozzrenii sovremennosti, M.1917,
   p.77.
14 See further: G.Janecek, 'Anthroposophy in Kotik Letaev', *Orbis
   Litterarum* (1974), XXIX, pp.245–67; also his 'The Spiral as Image
   and Structural Principle in Andrej Belyj's *Kotik Letaev*', *Russian
   Literature*, 1976, IV, No.4, pp.357–64.
15 R.Steiner, *Christianity as Mystical Fact*, London 1948, pp.93–126.
16 ibid., p.115.
17 ibid., p.113.
18 The epigraph to the first chapter is taken from Tyutchev:
                'Chas toski nevyrazimoy...
                Vsyo – vo mne... I ya – vo vsyom.'
19 This is fully recounted in A.Turgenieff, *Erinnerungen...*
20 For instance '*stroyevaya sluzhba*' (p.85); at another point Kotik's
   Auntie Dotya is 'upset' – '*rasstroyena*' (p.68).
21 *Glossolaliya*, p.10.
22 Bely speaks of his own experience of the Dornach period in these
   terms in 'Material k biografii (intimnyy)...'
23 C.Anschuetz, *Word Creation in 'Kotik Letaev' and 'Kreščenyj
   kitaec*', unpublished Ph.D. thesis, Princeton University 1972,
   pp.22–3.
24 See above, p.34.
25 This is argued more fully in: J.D.Elsworth, 'The Concept of
   Rhythm in Bely's Aesthetic Thought', in B.Christa (ed.), *Andrey
   Bely. Centenary Papers*, pp.68–80.
26 G.Janecek, 'Rhythm in Prose...', *Andrey Bely. A Critical Review*,
   pp.90, 97.
27 G.Janecek, 'An Acoustico-Semantic Complex in Belyj's *Kotik
   Letaev*', SEEJ, vol.18 No.2 (1974), p.157.
28 Bely had in fact used a very similar device and employed the same
   sounds for the purpose, in describing the mysterious emergence of
   Kudeyarov from darkness in *The Silver Dove*: '*Sam stolyar stroil-
   sya iz t'my*' (p.63); but there it was still isolated and unsystema-
   tized.
29 For further discussion see: C.Anschuetz, *Word Creation...*,
   pp.56, 57, 59, 74.

30 An earlier study of the neologisms throughout Bely's prose was: L.Hindley, *Die Neologismen Andrej Belyjs*, Munich 1966.
31 G.Janecek, 'An Acoustico-Semantic Complex...'; C.Anschuetz, 'Recollection as Metaphor in *Kotik Letaev*', *Russian Literature*, 1976, IV, no.4, pp.345–55.
32 *Cahiers du monde russe...*, vol.XV No.1–2, 1974, p.74.
33 G.Janecek, 'Anthroposophy...', p.246.
34 A.Bely, 'Predisloviye k "Kotiku Letayevu"', *Novyy zhurnal* No.101, 1970, p.70.
35 P.Hart, 'Psychological Primitivism in *Kotik Letaev*', *Russian Literature Triquarterly* No.4, Fall 1972, pp.319ff.; S.Cioran, *The Apocalyptic Symbolism of Andrej Belyj*, The Hague 1973, p.167.
36 Hart, p.329 fn.7.
37 V.Shklovsky, 'Andrey Bely', *Russkiy sovremennik*, 1924 No.2, p.232.
38 C.Anschuetz, 'Recollection as Metaphor...', p.352.

6. The Baptized Chinaman

1 *Literaturnoye nasledstvo* 27–8, p.605.
2 *Zapiski mechtateley* No.4, 1921, pp.21–165. This was also published in *Sovremennyye zapiski* Nos.11–13, 1922.
3 A.Bely, *Kreshchonyy kitayets*, M.1927; all references in the text are to this edition. The 'crime' in question was a period of truancy from school, which was put to the purpose of reading contemporary literature; see *Na rubezhe...*, p.334. T.R.Beyer has recently suggested that the crime can better be understood as 'filial guilt', a theme which runs through Bely's other novels as well; 'Andrej Belyj's *The Christened Chinaman* – Resolution of the Conflict of Filial Guilt', *Russian Literature* X (1981), pp.369–80.
4 *Zapiski mechtateley* No.4, p.23.
5 *Na rubezhe...*
6 'Arbat', *Sovremennyye zapiski* No.17, 1923, pp.157–82; 'Otkliki prezhney Moskvy'. *Sovremennyye zapiski* No.16, 1923, pp.190–209, also in *Dni* No.202, 1 July 1923. Compare *Kreshchonyy kitayets*, p.186.
7 A.Bely, *Pervoye svidaniye*, Pb.1921.
8 A.Bely, *Stikhotvoreniya*, Pb.–Berlin 1923.
9 See note 51 to Chapter 4.
10 A.Veksler, '*Epopeya* A.Belogo. Opyt kommentarii', *Sovremennaya literatura* (sbornik), L.1925, pp.48–75.
11 ibid., p.59.
12 ibid., pp.57–8.
13 By analogy with *letopis'* (chronicle); the description of 'years' (*leta*) is replaced by the description of static existence (*byt*).

14 Bely recalled that the novel had its origins in Schumann's *Kreisleriana; Kak my pishem*, L.1930, p.17. Presumably the principal reason is mnemonic, as Bely's mother used to play Schumann; but a general structural resemblance between the two works, in the way in which their themes are developed, is not difficult to detect, and might repay further study.

15 Bely's father wrote an essay on this subject. It is translated into English in: Louis J.Shein (ed. and transl.), *Readings in Russian Philosophical Thought*, The Hague 1968; N.V.Bugayev, 'Basic Principles of Evolutionary Monadology'.

16 *Simvolizm*, p.494; Bely cites Blavatskaya's *Secret Doctrine*. The reference is to the pre-classical languages of Mesopotamia.

17 A.Besant and C.W.Leadbeater, *Talks on the Path of Occultism*, Madras 1926, p.386.

18 V.F.Khodasevich, 'Andrey Bely, "Kreshchonyy kitayets"', *Sovremennye zapiski* No.32, 1927, p.454.

19 Bely refers to *Glossolalia* in several letters to Ivanov-Razumnik dating from the autumn of 1917; IRLI, fond 9, opis'3, No.81.

20 For instance, on p.60 Veksler speaks of the aerial '*n*', while on pp.110–11 of *Glossolalia* Bely associates '*n*' with depth and water; Veksler speaks of '*pf*' as 'the sound of swelling' (p.72), while Bely writes 'in "*p-f*" flesh disintegrates' (p.113).

21 *Glossolaliya*, p.102.

22 ibid., p.61.

23 ibid., p.109.

24 ibid., p.113.

25 ibid., p.112.

26 ibid.

27 ibid., p.71.

28 He writes of this interest in a letter to Asya Turgeneva, dating from approximately the time of writing; Ms. Dept. of Lenin Library (GBL), f.25, papka 30, yed.khr.19.

29 'Zhezl Aarona', pp.186–7.

30 *Cahiers du monde russe...*, vol.xv No.1–2, 1974, p.81.

31 C.Anschuetz, *Word Creation...*, pp.138ff.

32 V.Shklovsky, *O teorii prozy*, M.1929, p.219.

33 Anschuetz, *Word Creation...*, p.64.

34 ibid., pp.81, 101–3.

35 G.Janecek, 'Rhythm in Prose...'; C.Anschuetz raises the objection that Bely sometimes employs neologisms for no other evident reason than to preserve the rhythm of the prose; *Word Creation...*, pp.62,83.

36 Veksler, '*Epopeya* A.Belogo...,' p.49.

37 'Zhezl Aarona', p.200; see above, Ch.2.

38 G.Janecek, 'Rhythm in Prose...', p.100; A.Bely, 'O khudozhestvennoy proze', *Gorn* No.2–3, 1919, pp.49–55; 'O ritme', *Gorn* No.5, 1920, pp.47–54.

39 Anschuetz, *Word Creation...*, p.140.
40 Quoted in V.Markov, *Russian Futurism: A History*, London 1969, p.130.
41 ibid., p.127.
42 Anschuetz, *Word Creation...*, p.33.
43 *Zapiski mechtateley* No.4, p.24.

7. Notes of an Eccentric

1 K.N.Bugayeva, *Letopis' zhizni i tvorchestva A.Belogo*, Ms. dept. of Leningrad Public Library, fond 60, yed.khr.107; *Cahiers du monde russe...*, vol. xv No.1–2, p.76.
2 Bely himself later wrote of it as a failed experiment from which he had learnt valuable lessons; *Kak my pishem*, L.1930, p.15.
3 Details of publication are given in the Bibliography. All references in the text of this chapter are to the Helikon edition.
4 *Letopis' zhizni i tvorchestva...*
5 The passage in square brackets is omitted from the Helikon edition, and is quoted from *Zapiski mechtateley* No.2–3, p.25.
6 *Zapiski mechtateley* No.4, p.24.
7 A similar assertion is made in the preface to '"Ya" (Sumasshedsheye)', where Bely invites the mass of readers to approach the work as they would Gogol''s *Diary of a Madman*, but addresses 'the few' with the claim that it is a depiction of real facts of consciousness that will shortly be encountered in life; *Moskovskiy al'manakh*, Berlin 1922, pp.175–6.
8 The attempt is made to trace this parallel in a fuller version of this chapter: '"A Diary in Story Form": *Zapiski chudaka* and some problems of Bely's biography' (to be published shortly)
9 IRLI f.79, op.3, No.81. Bely worked for Proletkul't between September 1918 and August 1919; *Letopis' zhizni i tvorchestva...*
10 *Zapiski mechtateley* No.1 pp.11–12; A.Bely, 'Pochemu ya ne mogu kul'turno rabotat'', *Zapiski mechtateley* No.2–3, pp.113–31.
11 *Cahiers du monde russe...*, vol.xv No.1–2, p.76.
12 *Literaturnoye nasledstvo* 27–8, p.594.
13 V.Shklovsky, *O teorii prozy*, M.1929, p.210.
14 'Material k biografii (intimnyy)...'
15 This is recorded by various memoirists, but see particularly V.F.Khodasevich, *Nekropol'*, Brussels 1939, pp.61–99; see also B.Christa, 'Andrey Bely's Connections with European Occultism', *Russian and Slavic Literature*, ed. R.Freeborn et al., Cambridge Mass. 1976, p.220.
16 *Cahiers du monde russe...*, vol.xv No.1–2, pp.81–2.
17 K.N.Bugayeva, *Vospominaniya*, Berkeley, Calif. 1981, pp.155ff.
18 S.Cioran, *The Apocalyptic Symbolism of Andrej Belyj*, The Hague 1973, p.193.

19 Here Bely not only capitalizes the word for man, *Chelovek*, but also divides it into its apparent components, *Chelo veka*, meaning 'the brow of the age'.

20 Misprint in the Helikon edition corrected from *Zapiski mechtateley* No.2–3, p.91.

8. Moscow

1 *Cahiers du monde russe...*, vol.xv No.1–2, p.80.

2 A.Bely, *Pochemu ya stal simvolistom i ne perestal im byt' vo vsekh fazakh moyego ideynogo i khudozhestvennogo razvitiya*, TsGALI f.53, op.1, yed.khr,74.

3 A.Bely, 'My idyom k predoshchushcheniyu novykh form', *Veretyon-ysh*, 1922 No.1, p.2.

4 *Cahiers du monde russe...*, vol.xv No.1–2, p.81.

5 Details are given in the Bibliography. All references in the text of this chapter are to the 1926 edition; *Moskovskiy chudak* is designated as I, *Moskva pod udarom* as II.

6 *Moskva pod udarom*, M.1926, vmesto predisloviya.

7 A.Bely, *Maski*, M.1932, p.5.

8 There also exist in manuscript two dramatized versions of *Moscow*. On one of these there is a handwritten note of Bely's, explaining that a production of it was planned by Meyerkhol'd in 1928, but that despite three years' efforts, his attempts to bring it to the stage met with no success. Neither version has ever been either performed or published. TsGALI f.53, op.1, yed.khr.35; op.3, yed.khr.3. See also: F.D. Reeve, 'A Geometry of Prose', *Kenyon Review*, Winter 1963.

9 K.N.Bugayeva, *Vospominaniya*, Berkeley, Calif., 1981, p.148.

10 A.Bely, 'Yog. (Rasskaz)', *Sirena* No.2–3, Voronezh 1918, pp.17–30; S.S.Grechishkin and A.V.Lavrov, 'Andrey Bely i N.F.Fyodorov', *Tvorchestvo A.A.Bloka i russkaya kul'tura dvadtsatogo veka. Blo-kovskiy sbornik* III, Tartu 1979, pp.147–64.

11 *Kak my pishem*, L.1930, p.13.

12 R.Peterson, *Andrey Bely's Short Prose*, Birmingham 1980, p.65.

13 In externals this description corresponds to Bely's father's biography; *Na rubezhe*, p.26.

14 Stepun has interpreted this event as a final cynical comment by Bely on the Sophia cult of the early Symbolists. There is no evidence to support this reading; *Mystische Weltschau*, p.351.

15 Both Mochul'sky (*Andrey Bely*, p.264) and Stepun (*Mystische Welt-schau*, p.350) take this to mean that Bely now saw 1917 as the beginning of Russian history.

16 A.Bely, 'Myortvyye goroda', *Birzhevyye vedomosti* No.15745, 17 Aug. 1916; 'O "Rossii" v Rossii i o "Rossii" v Berline', *Beseda* No.1, Berlin 1923, pp.211–36; *Odna iz obiteley tsarstva teney*, L.1924.

17 A.Blok i A.Bely, *Perepiska*, M.1940, p.325.

18 K.N.Bugayeva, *Vospominaniya*, p.152.

19 Zh.El'sberg, 'Tvorchestvo Andreya Belogo – prozaika', in his *Krizis poputchikov i nastroyeniya intelligentsii*, M.–L.1930, p.212.

20 In the reference to 'the best of all possible worlds' (I, 12) Korobkin's Leibniz recalls Voltaire's satire in *Candide*, but there is another parallel which Bely no doubt intended. In *Rhythm as Dialectics* he speaks of Leibniz as the inventor of calculus, which made possible the creation of machinery of immense power: *Ritm kak dialektika*, M.1929, p.10.

21 Since the Russian word *giperbola* means both 'hyperbola' and 'hyperbole' Bely uses it for a pun; in the latter meaning of a rhetorical figure it gives rise to 'symbol', which contrasts with the 'allegory' of which the professor had recently spoken.

22 'Dnevnik pisatelya', *Rossiya*, 1924 No.2 (11), pp.137, 140.

23 Korobkin's favourite student is not mentioned anywhere else in the novel, and is clearly introduced here only to stress the professor's solitude.

24 The section describing these experiences of Korobkin's is numbered 48, while those on either side are numbered 24 and 25. Bely evidently uses a geometrical progression instead of an arithmetical progression to indicate that the experiences take place in another dimension, as it were.

25 *Pochemu ya stal simvolistom...*, see note 2 above.

26 *Kak my pishem*, L.1930, p.21.

27 A.Bely, 'Svyashchennyye tsveta', *Arabeski*, pp.115–129; S.Cioran, 'A Prism for the Absolute: the Symbolic Colours of Andrey Bely', in G.Janecek (ed.), *Andrey Bely. A Critical Review*, pp.103–14; A.Steinberg, *Word and Music in the Novels of Andrey Bely*, pp. 203–36.

28 A.Bely, *Putevyye zametki. Sitsiliya. Tunis*, M.–Berlin 1922, pp.147ff.

29 See, for instance, A.Besant and C.W.Leadbeater, *Thought-Forms*, London & Benares 1905.

30 V.I. Dal''s dictionary of Russian, which was first published in 1863–6, has a unique standing in Russian lexicography as a record not only of the literary language but also of the widest variety of dialectal and popular usage from all over Russia.

31 *Cahiers du monde russe...*, vol.XV No.1–2, p.81.

32 Khodasevich considered that the 'complex and delicate devices' used in *The Baptized Chinaman* had been debased and vulgarized ('*dovedeny do lubka*') in *Moscow*; *Sovremennyye zapiski* No.XXXII, Paris 1927, p.455.

33 *Kreshchonyy kitayets*, p.49.

34 This feature was noted by A.Veksler; '*Epopeya Belogo...*'

35 K.N.Bugayeva, *Vospominaniya*, p.164.

36 ibid., p.143.

37 Principally Mochul'sky and Stepun; see notes 14 and 15 above.

38 GBL OR f.25 p.30 yed.khr.5.

39 N.Valentinov, *Dva goda s simvolistami*, p.66.

40 V.F.Khodasevich, 'Ableukhovy – Letayevy – Korobkiny', in his *Literaturnyye stat'i i vospominaniya*, New York 1954, pp.191f.

41 M.Woloshin, *Die grüne Schlange. Lebenserinnerungen*, Stuttgart 1954, p.276.

42 A.Turgenieff, *Erinnerungen...*, pp.24–5.

43 M.Chekhov, 'Zhizn' i vstrechi', *Novyy zhurnal* No.9, 1944, p.13.

44 F.Stepun, *Vstrechi*, Munich, 1962, p.160.

45 K.N.Bugayeva, *Vospominaniya*, p.165.

9. Masks

1 A.Bely, *Maski*, M.1932, p.6. Page references in the text of this chapter are to this edition.

2 Bely combines a dig at the Futurists' 'metalogical' language with a reminiscence of Sobakevich's deceased peasant, Neuvazhay-Koryto.

3 A.Hönig has counted over four hundred; *Andrej Belyjs Romane*, p.98.

4 Usually referred to as *Istoriya stanovleniya samosoznayushchey dushi*, this work is also sometimes known as *Istoriya stanovleniya samosoznaniya*; see *Literaturnoye nasledstvo* 27–8, p.622, *Mezhdu dvukh...*, p.114.

5 *Rudol'f Shteyner i Gete...*, Ch.3.

6 *Maski*, p.389; *Masterstvo Gogolya*, p.116.

7 *Goethe's Theory of Colours*, translated by Charles Lock Eastlake, reprinted 1967 from the edition London 1840, p.350.

8 See also A.Steinberg, *Word and Music in the Novels of Andrey Bely*, pp.213–36.

9 'Kumir na glinyanykh nogakh', *Pereval*, 1907 No.8–9. See above, Ch.1.

10 K.N.Bugayeva, *Vospominaniya*, Berkeley, Calif., 1981, p.186.

11 ibid., p.206.

12 There are occasional direct addresses to the reader (pp.96, 159, 177, 441), but these are untypical and do not form part of a system.

13 A.S.Pushkin, *Eugene Onegin, A Novel in Verse*, trans. & ed. by V.Nabokov, London 1964, vol.2, p.405. The particular instance from Pushkin is the line: 'Tatyana *pryg* v drugiye seni'.

14 See L.Hindley, *Die Neologismen Andrej Belyjs*, Munich 1966, pp.24ff. Although the author is not concerned to establish the frequency of particular types of neologisms in particular novels, it can be seen that nearly all her examples of this type are from *Maski*.

15 G.Janecek, 'An Acoustico-Semantic Complex...', in SEEJ, vol.18, No.2 (1974), pp.153–9.

16 See above, Ch.2.

17 For dates of composition, see *Literaturnoye nasledstvo* 27–8, pp.609, 627.

18 K.N.Bugayeva, *Vospominaniya*, p.109.
19 *Masterstvo Gogolya*, pp.115–19.
20 'Rhythm in Prose...', p.100.
21 See above, Ch.6 note 38.
22 V.Zhirmunsky, 'O ritmicheskoy proze', *Russkaya literatura*, 1966 No.4, p.105.
23 B.Tomashevsky, *Teoriya literatury. Poetika*, M.–L. 1928, p.73.
24 A.Bely, 'O khudozhestvennoy proze', *Gorn*, 1919 No.2–3, pp.49–55.
25 See above, Ch.1.
26 A.Bely, *Ritm kak dialektika i "Mednyy vsadnik"*, M.1929.
27 ibid., p.25.
28 S.S.Grechishkin and A.V.Lavrov, 'O stikhovedcheskom nasledii Andreya Belogo', *Trudy po znakovym sistemam* 12, 1981, pp.97–146.
29 M.L.Gasparov, *Sovremennyy russkiy stikh*, M.1974, p.126. In the chapter from which this is taken Gasparov analyses the rhythm of an extensive passage from *Maski* (ib., p.141); but it is as a control sample from prose that it is used, and its use does not therefore affect the argument above about its generic definition.
30 'Rhythm in Prose...', p.99.
31 Letter of 3 October 1927.
32 J.E.Malmstad, 'Introduction' to K.N.Bugayeva, *Vospominaniya*, p.25.

Conclusion

1 *Maski*, p.5.
2 K.N.Bugayeva, *Vospominaniya*, p.152.
3 ibid., p.143.
4 A.Bely, *Veter s Kavkaza*, M.1928.
5 *The Memoirs of Ivanov-Razumnik*, translated by P.S.Squire, London 1965, p.104.
6 *Literaturnoye nasledstvo* 27–8, pp.609–10.
7 *Odna iz obiteley tsarstva teney*, L.1924.
8 *Literaturnoye nasledstvo* 27–8, pp.609, 637.
9 S.S.Grechishkin and A.V.Lavrov, 'Neosushchestvlyonnyy zamysel Andreya Belogo (Plan romana "Germaniya")', *Russkaya literatura*, 1974 No.1, pp.197–200.
10 O.Mandel'shtam, 'Literaturnaya Moskva. Rozhdeniye fabuly', *Rossiya*, 1922 No.3, p.26.
11 TsGALI, f.53 op.1 yed.khr. 21 includes a selection of readers' letters, sent to the editor of the newspaper *Russkiye vedomosti* after the publication in the paper in 1916 of extracts from *Kotik Letayev*. One of them describes it as "a totally meaningless collection of words, which not only lack all connection between themselves, but simply do not exist in the Russian language".
12 This view of the novel is best expressed by E.Starikova, op.cit.

Select bibliography

What follows is not a complete bibliography of work either by or about Bely. It is concentrated specifically upon his prose fiction and aesthetic theory, and upon recent research.

The section on Bely's works lists all editions in Russian of his novels and shorter prose works, as well as all English translations of them. Apart from those, it lists only theoretical and critical works that were published in separate editions. Further reference to other works, both published and unpublished, is made in the notes to the chapters. The fullest existing bibliography of Bely's published works is:

Georges Nivat, 'L'oeuvre polémique, critique et journalistique d'Andrej Belyj', *Cahiers du monde russe et soviétique*, 1974 No. 1–2, pp.22–39.

With minor exceptions, however, this lists only works published during Bely's lifetime. Some further items are included in Zakharenko and Serebryakova (see below).

The critical bibliography includes only major items from the critical literature published before Bely's death. It has greater claims to completeness in the period since, but here, too, is restricted in the main to work with a direct bearing on the subject of this book. General histories of Russian literature or of the Russian novel, works on contemporary writers that make reference to Bely, or works specifically devoted to other aspects of Bely's output, have largely been omitted.

Fuller bibliographical information is to be found in the following:

Vladislavlev, I.V., *Russkiye pisateli*, M.–L. 1924.

Nikitina, Ye., *Russkaya literatura ot Simvolizma do nashikh dney*, M.1926.

Muratova, K.D., *Russkaya literatura kontsa XIX–nachala XX veka. Bibliograficheskiy ukazatel'*, M.1963.

Sovetskoye literaturovedeniye i kritika. Bibliograficheskiy ukazatel', M.1966.

Zakharenko, N.G., Serebryakova, V.V., *Russkiye sovetskiye pisateli. Poety. Bibliograficheskiy ukazatel'*, tom 3, chast' 1, M.1979.

Works of Andrey Bely

1. Novels.

Serebryanyy golub', *Vesy*, M.1909, Nos.3, 4, 6, 7, 10–11, 12.

Serebryanyy golub', M.1910.

246

Serebryanyy golub', Berlin 1922.
Serebryanyy golub', Nachdruck der Ausgabe Berlin 1922 mit einer Einleitung von Anton Hönig, Munich 1967.
Serebryanyy golub', Ann Arbor 1979.
The Silver Dove, translated by George Reavey, N.Y. 1974.
Peterburg, Ch. 1–2, *Sirin* No.1, M.1913, pp.1–148; Ch.3–5, *Sirin* No.2, M.1913, pp.1–209; Ch.6–8, *Sirin* No.3, M.1914, pp.1–276.
Peterburg, M.1916.
Peterburg, Berlin, 1922.
Peterburg, M.1928.
Peterburg, M.1935.
Peterburg, Nachdruck der Ausgabe Moskau 1928 mit der endgültigen Fassung, eingeleitet von Dmitrij Tschiževskij, Munich 1967.
Peterburg, Letchworth 1967.
Peterburg, M.1978.
Peterburg, 'Literaturnyye pamyatniki', M.1981.
St. Petersburg, translated by John Cournos, N.Y. 1959.
Petersburg, translated, annotated and introduced by Robert A. Maguire and John E. Malmstad, Bloomington, Indiana 1978; Hassocks, Sussex 1979.
Kotik Letayev, Ch. 1–4, *Skify* No.1, Spb.1917, pp.9–94; Ch. 5–6, *Skify* No.2, Spb.1918, pp.37–103.
Kotik Letayev, Pb. 1922.
Kotik Letayev, Nachdruck der Ausgabe 1922, mit einer Einleitung von D. Tschiževskij und A. Hönig, Munich 1964.
Kotik Letaev, translated by Gerald Janecek, Ann Arbor 1971.
Prestupleniye Nikolaya Letayeva. ('Epopeya', tom pervyy). Kreshchonyy kitayets, glava pervaya, Zapiski mechtateley No.4, 1921, pp. 21–165.
Prestupleniye Nikolaya Letayeva, in *Sovremennyye zapiski* Nos. 11–13, Paris 1922.
Kreshchonyy kitayets, M.1927.
Kreshchonyy kitayets, M.1928.
Kreshchonyy kitayets, Nachdruck der Ausgabe Moskau 1927 mit einer Einleitung von Anton Hönig und Dmitrij Tschiževskij, Munich, 1969.
Zapiski chudaka, M.–Berlin 1922.
Zapiski chudaka, Slavica Reprints, Lausanne 1973.
Moskovskiy chudak, pervaya chast' romana 'Moskva', M.1926.
Moskva pod udarom, vtoraya chast' romana 'Moskva', M.1926.
Moskovskiy chudak, M.1927.
Moskva pod udarom, M.1927.
Moskva I and II, Nachdruck der Ausgabe Moskau 1926, Munich 1968.
Maski, M.1932.
Maski, Nachdruck der Ausgabe Moskau 1932, Munich 1969.

2. Extracts from novels
Serebryanyy golub', Ch. 1–4, A.Bely, *Sobraniye sochineniy*, tom VII, M.1917.
'Knizhnaya ("nekrasovskaya") redaktsiya dvukh pervykh glav romana *Peterburg*', In A.Bely, *Peterburg*, M.1981, pp.420–92.
'Otryvki iz detskikh vpechatleniy, (iz povesti "Kotik Letayev")', *Birzhevyye vedomosti* No.15533, 2 May 1916.
do., *Russkiye vedomosti*, Nos. 263, 280, 298, 13 Nov., 4 Dec., 25 Dec. 1916.
Extracts from *Kotik Letayev, Literaturnaya Rossiya, sbornik 1*, pod redaktsiyey Vl. Lidina, M.1924, pp.17–24.
Extracts from *Kotik Letayev*, translated by George Reavey and Marc Slonim, in their *Soviet Literature. An Anthology*, London 1933, pp.54–67.
'Dnevnik chudaka. Pisatel' i Chelovek, (otryvok iz povesti)', *Nash put'* No.2, May 1918, pp.9–18.
'Zapiski chudaka (dva otryvka). 1. London. 2. Fantasmagoriya', *Put'* No.6, Oct.–Dec. 1919, pp.27–34.
'"Ya". Epopeya. Tom pervyy. "Zapiski chudaka", chast' pervaya, "Vozvrashcheniye na rodinu"', *Zapiski mechtateley* No.1, 1919, pp.9–71.
'"Ya". Epopeya. (Prodolzheniye)', *Zapiski mechtateley* No. 2–3, 1921, pp.5–95.
Vozvrashcheniye na rodinu (otryvki iz povesti), M.1922.
'"Ya" (Sumasshedsheye)', *Moskovskiy al'manakh*, Berlin 1922.
'Tomochka-pyosik (Otryvok iz romana "Epopeya")', *Dni*, Berlin, 24 Dec. 1922; also published in: *Russkiy al'manakh*, ed. Z.Shakhovskaya, Paris 1981, pp.9–14, with afterword by G.Nivat, pp.15–20.
Moskva. Roman, chast' 1, glava 1, 'Den' professora', *Al'manakh arteli pisateley "Krug"*, IV, M.–L. 1924, pp.19–71.
Moskva. Roman, chast' 1, glava 2, 'Dom Mandro', *Al'manakh arteli pisateley "Krug"*, V, M.–L. 1924, pp.27–91.
'Lektsiya professora Korobkina', *Volya Rossii* No.7–8, Prague 1925, pp.254–8.
Extracts from *Moskovskiy chudak, Dni*, Berlin, 8 Aug. 1926.
Extracts from *Moskva pod udarom, Dni*, Berlin, 26 Sept. 1926, also in *Versty* No.2, Paris 1926.
'Salony' (from Ch.2 of *Maski*), *Vechernyaya Moskva*, 5 Dec. 1932.

3. Shorter works of fiction.
Severnaya simfoniya (Pervaya, geroicheskaya), M.1904.
Simfoniya (Vtoraya, dramaticheskaya), M.1902.
These two republished together in: A.Bely, *Sobraniye sochineniy*, tom IV, M.1917.
Vozvrat. Tret'ya simfoniya, M.1905.
Vozvrat. Povest', Berlin 1922.

Kubok meteley. Chetvyortaya simfoniya, M.1908.
Die vier Symphonien, Nachdruck mit einer Einleitung von D. Tschiżewskij, Munich 1971.
'Otryvki iz chetvyortoy simfonii', *Al'manakh 'Grif*, M.1903, pp.52–61.
'Prishedshiy. Otryvok iz nenapisannoy misterii', *Severnyye tsvety* No.3, M.1903, pp.2–25.
'Past' nochi. Otryvok iz zadumannoy misterii', *Zolotoye runo*, 1906 No.1, pp.62–71.
'Svetovaya skazka (Rasskaz)', *Al'manakh 'Grif* No.2, M.1904, pp.11–18.
'Kust. Rasskaz', *Zolotoye runo*, 1906 No.7–8, pp.129–135.
'My zhdyom yego vozvrashcheniya', *Svobodnaya sovest'. Literaturno-filosofskiy sbornik*, kn.1, M.1906, pp.160–3.
'Gornaya vladychitsa. (Rasskaz)', *Pereval*, 1907 No.12, pp.20–5.
'Adam. Zapiski, naydennyye v sumasshedshem dome', *Vesy*, 1908 No.4, pp.15–30.
'Adam' translated by Charlotte Douglas, *Russian Literature Triquarterly* No.4 Fall 1972, pp.81–92.
'Yog. (Rasskaz)' *Sirena* No.2–3, Voronezh 1918, pp.17–30.
'Chelovek. Predisloviye k povesti "Chelovek", yavlyayushchey soboy khroniku xxv veka', *Znamya truda. Vremennik* No.1, Jun.1918, pp.22–4.
Rasskazy, Gesammelt und eingeleitet von Ronald E. Peterson, Munich 1979.
Complete Short Stories, translated by Ronald Peterson, Ann Arbor 1979.

4. Theoretical and critical works in separate editions.
Lug zelyonyy, M.1910.
Simvolizm, M.1910.
Arabeski, M.1911.
Tragediya tvorchestva. Dostoyevsky i Tolstoy, M.1911.
Revolyutsiya i kul'tura, M.1917.
Rudol'f Shteyner i Gete v mirovozzrenii sovremennosti. Otvet Emiliyu Metneru na yego pervyy tom 'Razmyshleniy o Gete', M.1917.
Na perevale i *Krizis zhizni*, Pb. 1918.
Na perevale ii. *Krizis mysli*, Pb. 1918.
Na perevale iii. *Krizis kul'tury*, Pb. 1920.
Na perevale. 3 chasti, Pb.–Berlin 1923.
Glossolaliya, poema o zvuke, Berlin 1922. (Misprinted as *Glossaloliya*).
O smysle poznaniya, Pb. 1922.
Poeziya slova, Pb. 1922.
Sirin uchonogo varvarstva, Berlin, 1922.
Ritm kak dialektika i 'Mednyy vsadnik', M.1929.
Masterstvo Gogolya, M.–L. 1934.

Select bibliography

Critical bibliography

Abramovich, N.Ya., 'Kriticheskiye nabroski, V. *Serebryanyy golub'* A. Belogo', *Studencheskaya zhizn'*, 1910. Sept. 12., No.28(4).

Alexandrov, V.E., 'Unicorn impaling a knight: the transcendent and man in Andrei Belyi's *Petersburg'*, *Canadian-American Slavic Studies*, 16, No.1 (Spring 1982), pp.1–44.

Amfiteatrov, A.V., 'Novyy narod i yego pevtsy', *Sochineniya*, vol.xv, pp.211–261, Spb. 1910–1914.

Andreyev, V., *Istoriya odnogo puteshestviya*, M.1974.

Anichkov, E., 'Zapadnichestvo i slavyanofil'stvo v novom oblike', *Gaudeamus*, 1911 No.1.

Annenkov, Yu., *Dnevnik moikh vstrech. Tsikl tragediy*, 2 vols., N.Y. 1966.

Anschuetz, C., *Word Creation in Belyj's 'Kotik Letaev' and 'Kreščeny kitaec'*. Unpublished Ph.D. thesis, Princeton 1973.

'Recollection as Metaphor in *Kotik Letaev*', *Russian Literature* IV, 1976, pp.345–355.

Antsiferov, N.P., *Dusha Peterburga*, Pg. 1922.

Askol'dov, S.A., 'Tvorchestvo A. Belogo', *Al'manakh Literaturnaya mysl'* kn. 1, Pg. 1923, pp.73–90.

Asmus, V., 'Filosofiya i estetika russkogo simvolizma', *Literaturnoye nasledstvo* 27–28, M.1937, pp.1–53.

Avramenko, A.P., '"Simfonii" Andreya Belogo', *Russkaya literatura XX veka (dooktyabr'skiy period)*, Sbornik 9, Tula 1977, pp.55–72.

Bakhrakh, A., '*Epopeya* 1922 No.3', *Novaya russkaya kniga*, 1923 No.1.

'Po pamyati, po zapisyam: Andrey Bely', *Kontinent* 3, 1975, pp. 288–321.

Bebutov, G., *Otrazheniya*, Tbilisi 1973.

Bel'kind, Ye., 'A. Bely i A.A. Potebnya (k postanovke voprosa)', *Tezisy I vsesoyuznoy (III) konferentsii 'Tvorchestvo A.A. Bloka i russkaya kul'tura XX veka'*, Tartu 1975, pp.160–164.

Berberova, N., 'A note on Andrey Biely', *The Russian Review* vol.10 No.2, April 1952, pp.99–105.

Kursiv moy, Munich 1972.

Berdyaev, N., 'Russkiy soblazn', *Russkaya mysl'*, 1910 No.11, pp.104–15. *Samopoznaniye*, Paris 1949.

Berkovsky, N., 'O *Moskve* Andreya Belogo', *Zhizn' iskusstva*, No.49, 1926.

Beyer, T.R., 'Andrej Belyj's *The Christened Chinaman* – Resolution of the Conflict of Filial Guilt', *Russian Literature* X, 1981, pp.369–80.

Andrej Belyj's 'The Magic of Words' and *The Silver Dove*', SEEJ XXII, 1 (1978), pp.464–72.

'Belyj's *Serebrjanyj golub'* : Gogol' in Gugolevo', *Russian Language Journal*, 1976 No.107, pp.79–88.

Select bibliography

Andrej Belyj's real'nyj criticism: Precursor of Russian Formalism, Unpublished Ph.D. dissertation, University of Kansas 1974.

Bitsilli, P.M., 'A. Bely. *Ritm kak dialektika'*, *Sovremennyye zapiski* No.43, 1930, pp.501–3.

'O nekotorykh osobennostyakh russkogo yazyka. Po povodu *Moskvy pod udarom* Andreya Belogo'. *Rossiya i slavyanstvo* No.155, 14 Nov. 1931.

Blagoy, D.D., 'A Bely. *Na rubezhe dvukh stoletiy'*, *Russkiy yazyk v sovetskoy shkole*, 1930 No.2.

Blok, A., 'A. Bely. *Simfoniya vtoraya, dramaticheskaya'*, *Novyy put'*, 1903 No.4.

Blok, A. and Bely A., *Perepiska*. M.1940.

Bobrov, S., 'Andrey Bely. *Poeziya slova'*, *Pechat' i revolyutsiya*, 1923 No.4, pp.253–4.

'A. Bely. *Glossolaliya. Poema o zvuke'*, *Lef* No.2, 1923, pp.156–7.

Bolotnikov, A., 'Neudavshiysya maskarad', *Literaturnyy kritik*, 1933 No.2, pp.81–97.

Bryusov, V.Ya., 'A.Bely. *Vozvrat. Tret'ya simfoniya'*. *Vesy*, 1904 No.12, pp.59–60.

'Al'manakh knigoizdatel'stva "Grif" Moskva 1905', *Vesy*, 1905 No.4, p.60.

'V zashchitu ot odnoy pokhvaly. Otkrytoe pis'mo A.Belomu', *Vesy*, 1905 No.5, pp.37–9.

'Andrey Bely. *Urna*. Stikhotvoreniya, Moskva 1909', *Russkaya mysl'*, 1909 No.6, p.135.

'O rechi rabskoy; v zashchitu poezii', *Apollon*, 1910 No.9.

'Ob odnom voprose ritma', *Apollon*, 1910 No.11.

Dalyokiye i blizkiye, M.1912.

Za moim oknom, M.1913.

'A. Bely. *Glossolaliya'*. *Pechat' i revolyutsiya*, 1923 No.3, pp.245–6.

Dnevniki 1891–1910, M.1927.

'Pis'ma k P. Struve', *Literaturnyy arkhiv* 5, 1960.

'Pis'mo Bryusova k P. Struve', *Voprosy literatury*, 1973 No.6, pp. 314–8.

Bugayeva, K.N., Petrovsky, A.S., 'Literaturnoye nasledstvo A. Belogo', *Literaturnoye nasledstvo* 27–8, M.1937, pp.575–638.

Bugayeva, K.N., *Vospominaniya o Belom*, edited, with introduction and notes, by John Malmstad, Berkeley, Calif., 1981.

Burkhart, D., 'Leitmotivik und Symbolik in Andrej Belyjs Roman *Peterburg'*, *Die Welt der Slaven*, Jahrg. IX, Heft 3, Dec. 1964, pp.277–323.

Byalik, B.A. (ed.), *Literaturno-esteticheskiye kontseptsii v Rossii kontsa XIX–nachala XX v.*, M.1975.

Byalik, B.A., Tager, Ye. B., Shcherbina, V.R. (eds.), *Russkaya literatura kontsa XIX–nachala XX v. Devyanostyye gody*, M.1968, *1901–1907*, M.1971, *1908–1917*, M.1972.

Select bibliography

Cassedy, S., 'Mallarmé and Andrej Belyj: Mathematics and the Phenomenality of the Literary Object', *Modern Language Notes*, vol.96, 1981, pp.1066–83.

Catteau, J., 'A propos de la littérature fantastique: André Belyj héritier de Gogol et de Dostoïevski', *Cahiers du monde russe et soviétique*, vol.III No.3, 1962, pp.327–73.

Chekhov, M.A., 'O postanovke *Peterburga* A. Belogo v MKhAT 2', *Novaya Rossiya*, 1926 No.1, pp.75–8.

'Zhizn' i vstrechi', *Novyy zhurnal*, 1944 No.9.

Christa, B., 'Andrey Bely's Connections with European Occultism', *Russian and Slavic Literature*, ed. R. Freeborn, R.R. Milner-Gulland, C.A. Ward, Cambridge Mass. 1976, pp.213–23.

'Music as Model and Ideal in Andrej Belyj's Poetic Theory and Practice', *Russian Literature* IV, 1976, pp.395–413.

The Poetic World of Andrey Bely, Amsterdam 1977.

Christa, B. (ed.), *Andrey Bely. Centenary Papers*, Amsterdam 1980.

Cioran, S., *The Apocalyptic Symbolism of Andrey Bely*, The Hague 1973.

Deppermann, M., *Andrej Belyjs ästhetische Theorie des schöpferischen Bewusstseins. Symbolisierung und Krise der Kultur um die Jahrhundertwende*, Munich 1982.

Doležel, L., 'The Visible and the Invisible Petersburg', *Russian Literature* VII, 1979, pp. 465–90.

Dolgopolov, L.K., 'Andrey Bely v rabote nad *Peterburgom*', *Russkaya literatura*, 1972 No.1, pp.157–167.

'Obraz goroda v romane A. Belogo *Peterburg*', *Izvestiya Akademii Nauk. Seriya literatury i yazyka*, 1975, vol. 34 No.1, pp.46–59.

'Simvolika lichnykh imyon v proizvedeniyakh Andreya Belogo', *Kul'turnoye naslediye drevney Rusi. Istoki. Stanovleniye. Traditsii*, M.1976, pp.348–54.

'Roman A. Belogo *Peterburg* i filosofsko-istoricheskiye idei Dostoyevskogo', *Dostoyevsky: Materialy i issledovaniya* 2, L.1976, pp.217–24.

'A. Bely o postanovke "Istoricheskoy dramy" *Peterburg* na stsene MKhAT-2', *Russkaya literatura*, 1977 No.2, pp.173–6.

Na rubezhe vekov, L.1977.

'Tvorcheskaya istoriya i istoriko-literaturnoye znacheniye romana A. Belogo *Peterburg*', in A. Bely, *Peterburg*, M.1981 pp.525–623.

Donchin, G., 'A Russian Symbolist Journal and its links with France', *Revue de littérature comparée*, 1956 No.3.

The Influence of French Symbolism on Russian Poetry, The Hague 1958.

Ellis (=L.L. Kobylinsky), *Russkiye simvolisty*, M.1910.

El'sberg, Zh., *Krizis poputchikov i nastroyeniya intelligentsii*, M.1930.

El'sberg, Ya. Ye., 'Realizm i modernizm', *Realizm i yego sootnosheniya s drugimi tvorcheskimi metodami, sbornik statey*, M.1962, pp.245–70.

Select bibliography

Elsworth, J.D., *Andrey Bely*, Letchworth 1972.
'Bely in English: A Review Article', *Irish Slavonic Studies* No.2, 1981, pp.74–8.
Erenburg, I., *Portrety sovremennykh poetov*, M.1923.
Lyudy. Gody, Zhizn', kn.1, 2, M.1961, kn.3, 4, M.1963.
Erlich, V., *Russian formalism*, The Hague 1955.
Eykhenbaum, B., 'Mig soznaniya', *Knizhnyy ugol*, 1921 No.7.
Skvoz' literaturu, L.1924.
Farber, L.M., *Sovetskaya literatura pervykh let revolyutsii 1917–1920 gg.*, M.1966.
Florensky, P.A., 'Pis'ma P.A. Florenskogo B.N. Bugayevu', *Vestnik russkogo khristianskogo dvizheniya*, No.114, June 1974.
Forsh, O., 'Propetyy gerbariy', *Sbornik 'Sovremennaya literatura'*, L.1925.
Sumasshedshiy korabl', Washington 1964.
Gerigk, H-J., 'Belyjs "Petersburg" und Nietzsches "Geburt der Tragödie"', *Nietzsche–Studien*, Bd.9 1980, pp.356–73.
Gershenzon, M., *Mudrost' Pushkina*, M.1919.
Gippius, Z.N., *Zhivyye litsa*, 2 vols., Prague 1925.
Sinyaya kniga, Belgrade 1929.
Gloshka, V., 'Elementy fantasticheskogo v tvorchestve Andreya Belogo', *Zborník pedagogickej fakulty v Banskej Bystrici* XVII, Bratislava 1969, pp. 145–88.
'Muzykal'nyye osnovy tvorchestva Andreya Belogo', *Zborník pedagogickej fakulty v Banskej Bystrici* XVII, Bratislava 1969, pp.189–206.
'Simfoniya (2-aya, dramaticheskaya)', *Zborník pedagogickej fakulty v Banskej Bystrici* XVII, Bratislava 1969, pp.207–36.
'Intonatsionnyye znaki v arkhitektonike stikha i prozy, ikh smysl v esteticheskoy sisteme Andreya Belogo', *Zborník pedagogickej fakulty v Banskej Bystrici* XVII, Bratislava 1969, pp.237–60.
Goncharov, B.P., 'Andrey Bely – stikhoved', *Nauchnyye doklady vysshey shkoly. Filologicheskiye nauki*, No.4, 1980, pp.20–8.
Gornfel'd, A., 'Nauchnaya glossolaliya (Ob A. Belom)', *Parfenon* sb.1, 1922, pp.61–70.
Grechishkin, S.S., Lavrov, A.V., 'Neosushchestvlyonnyy zamysel Andreya Belogo (Plan romana "Germaniya")', *Russkaya literatura*, 1974 No.1, pp.197–200.
'Vstupitel'naya stat'ya k perepiske Bryusova s A. Belym', *Literaturnoye nasledstvo* 84, M.1976, pp.327–48.
'Andrey Bely i N.F. Fyodorov', *Tvorchestvo A.A. Bloka i russkaya kul'tura XX veka. Blokovskiy sbornik* III, Tartu 1979, pp.147–64.
'O stikhovedcheskom nasledii Andreya Belogo', *Trudy po znakovym sistemam*, 12, Tartu 1981, pp.97–146.
Griftsov, B., 'Roman A. Belogo', *Sofiya*, 1914 No.3, pp.99–100.
Grigor'yan, K., 'Andrey Bely ob Armenii', *Literaturnaya Armeniya*, 1967 No.1, pp.76–91.

Select bibliography

Gromov, V., *Mikhail Chekhov*, Moscow, 1970.

Guenther, J. v., *Ein Leben im Ostwind. Zwischen Petersburg und München. Erinnerungen*, Munich 1969.

Gul', R., *Pol v tvorchestve. Razbor proizvedeniy Andreya Belogo*, Berlin 1923.

Odvukon', N.Y. 1973.

Gurevich, L., 'Ot "byta" k "stilyu"', *Russkaya mysl'*, 1911 No.11, otdel 2, pp.84–103.

Gurian, W., 'The memoirs of Bely', *Russian Review*, vol.3 No.1, 1943, pp.95–103.

Hart, P., *Andrej Belyj's 'Petersburg' and the Myth of the City*, Unpublished Ph.D. thesis, University of Wisconsin 1969.

'Psychological Primitivism in *Kotik Letaev*', *Russian Literature Triquarterly* No.4, 1972, pp.319–30.

Hartmann, H., *Andrej Belyj and the Hermetic Tradition: A Study of the Novel 'Petersburg'*, Unpublished Ph.D. thesis, Columbia University 1969.

Hindley, L., *Die Neologismen Andrej Belyjs*, Munich 1966.

Holthusen, J., 'Andrej Belyj und Rudolf Steiner', *Festschrift für Max Vasmer zum 70. Geburtstag*, Berlin 1956.

Studien zur Ästhetik und Poetik des russischen Symbolismus, Göttingen 1957.

'Die Bedeutung des Stils bei Andrej Belyj', *Russian Literature* v, 1973, pp.65–78.

'Erzähler und Raum des Erzählers in Belyjs *Serebrjanyj golub''*, *Russian Literature* IV, 1976, pp.325–344.

Hönig, A., *Andrej Belyjs Romane*, Munich 1965.

Ivanov, G., *Peterburgskiye zimy*, N.Y. 1952.

Ivanov, V.I., 'Vdokhnoveniye uzhasa', *Utro Rossii* 148, 28 May 1916, pp.5–6; also in Ivanov, V.I., *Rodnoye i vselenskoye*, M.1918, pp.89–101.

Ivanov-Razumnik, R., 'Vostok ili zapad?' *Russkiye vedomosti*, 4 May 1916, No.102.

'Dve Rossii', *Skify* No.2, Spb. 1918, pp.201–31.

A. Blok. A. Bely, Pb. 1919.

Vershiny. A.Blok. A.Bely, Pb.1923.

Memoirs, translated by P.S. Squire, London 1965.

'Letter to A. Bely (Dec. 1927)', *Glagol* No.1, Ann Arbor, 1977, pp.195–8.

Janecek, G., 'Anthroposophy in *Kotik Letaev*', *Orbis Litterarum*, (1974), XXIX, pp.245–267.

'An Acoustico-Semantic Complex in Belyj's *Kotik Letaev*', SEEJ, vol. 18, No.2, (1974), pp.153–9.

'Literature as Music: Symphonic Form in Andrei Belyi's *Fourth Symphony*', *Canadian-American Slavic Studies*, VIII.4 (Winter 1974), pp. 501–12.

Select bibliography

'The Spiral as Image and Structural Principle in Andrej Belyj's *Kotik Letaev*', *Russian Literature* IV, 1976, pp.357–63.

Janecek, G. (ed.) *Andrey Bely. A Critical Review*, Lexington, Kentucky 1978.

Johnson, D.B., 'Belyj and Nabokov: A Comparative Overview', *Russian Literature* IX, (1981), pp. 379–402.

Karlinsky, S., 'Symphonic Structure in Andrej Belyj's "Pervoe svidanie"', *California Slavic Studies* vol.VI., Berkeley 1971, pp.61–70.

Keys, R., 'Pis'ma Andreya Belogo k A.S. Petrovskomu i Ye. N. Kezel'man' *Novyy zhurnal* 122, 1976, pp.151–66, 124, 1976, pp.163–72.

Khmel'nitskaya, T.Yu., 'Poeziya Andreya Belogo', in *Andrey Bely, Stikhotvoreniya i poemy*. M–L. 1966, pp.5–66.

Khodasevich, V.F., 'A. Bely. *Kreshchonyy kitayets*', *Sovremennyye zapiski* No.32, 1927, pp.453–5.

'Tri pis'ma A. Belogo', *Sovremennyye zapiski*, No.55, 1934, pp.256–70.

Nekropol', Brussels 1939.

Literaturnyye stat'i i vospominaniya, N.Y. 1954.

Khovin, V., *Na odnu temu*, Pb. 1921.

Knebel', M., 'Vospominaniya', *Teatr* 1, 1971 No.6, pp.94–102.

Knigge, A., *Die Lyrik Vl. Solov'evs und ihre Nachwirkung bei A. Belyj und A. Blok*, Amsterdam 1973.

Kolobayeva, L.A., 'Chelovek i yego mir v khudozhestvennoy sisteme Andreya Belogo', *Nauchnyye doklady vysshey shkoly. Filologicheskiye nauki* No.5, 1980, pp.12–20.

Koshevaty, N., 'Vstrechi s Andreyem Belym', *Grani* No.17, 1953, pp.91–8.

Kovač, A., *Andrej Belyi: The "Symphonies" (1899–1908). A Re-Evaluation of the Aesthetic-Philosophical Heritage*, Bern 1976.

Kozlik, F.C., *L'Influençe de l'anthroposophie sur l'oeuvre d'Andrei Bielyi*, 3 volumes, Frankfurt am Main, 1981.

Krutikova, N.Ye., *V nachale veka. Gor'ky i simvolisty*, Kiev 1978.

Kuleshova, Ye., *Polifoniya idey i simvolov. Stat'i o Belom, Bloke, Bryusove i Sologube*, Toronto 1981.

Lane, A.M., *Nietzsche in Russian Thought 1890–1912*, Unpublished Ph.D thesis, University of Wisconsin, Madison 1976.

Lavrov, A.V., 'Andrey Bely i Grigoriy Skovoroda', *Studia Slavica Hungarica* XXI, 1975, pp.395–404.

'Andrey Bely i Kristian Morgenshtern', *Sravnitel'noye izucheniye literatur. Sbornik statey k 80-letiyu Akademika M.P. Alekseyeva*, L.1976, pp.466–72.

'Mifotvorchestvo "Argonavtov"', *Mif-Fol'klor-Literatura*, L.1978, pp. 137–170.

'Rukopisnyy arkhiv Andreya Belogo v Pushkinskom Dome', *Yezhegodnik rukopisnogo otdela Pushkinskogo doma*, L.1978, pp.23–63.

Levitsky, S., 'Genial'nyy neudachnik (Ob Andreye Belom)', *Grani* No.59, 1965, pp.142–67.

Likhachev, D.S., 'Printsip istorizma v izuchenii yedinstva soderzhaniya i formy literaturnogo proizvedeniya', *Russkaya literatura*, 1965 No.1.

Loks, K., 'Bely – *Vovzrat*', *Pechat' i revolyutsiya*, 1923 No.1, pp.223–4.

Ljunggren, M., *The Dream of Rebirth. A Study of Andrej Belyj's Novel "Peterburg"*, Stockholm, 1982.

'O spornom i besspornom', *Krasnaya nov'*, 1926, No.11, pp.238–40.

Lottridge, S., 'Andrej Belyj's *Peterburg*: The City and the Family', *Russian Literature* IV, (1978), pp.175–96.

Lunacharsky, A.V., 'O *Peterburge* A. Belogo vo vtorom khudozhestvennom teatre', in A.V.L. *Sobraniye sochineniy v 8 tt.*, t.3 M.1964, pp.279–80.

Makovsky, S., *Portrety Sovremennikov*, N.Y. 1955.

Na parnase serebryanogo veka, Munich 1962.

Maksimov, D., 'O tom, kak ya videl i slyshal Andreya Belogo. Zarisovki izdali', *Zvezda*, 1982 No.7, pp.167–78.

Malkina, Ye., 'A. Bely', *Literaturnyy sovremennik*, 1940 No.5–6, pp.214–16.

Mandel'shtam, O., 'Literaturnaya Moskva. Rozhdeniye fabuly', *Rossiya*, 1922 No.3.

'A. Bely. *Zapiski chudaka*', *Krasnaya nov'*, 1923 No.5, pp.399–400.

Maslenikov, O.A., 'Andrej Belyj's Third "Symphony"', ASEER, 1948 No.VII, pp.78–92.

The frenzied poets. A. Biely and the Russian symbolists, Berkeley, Calif., 1952, N.Y. 1968.

'Ruskin, Bely, and the Solov'yovs', SEER, vol.XXXV, No.84, Dec.1956.

'Russian Symbolists: The Mirror Theme and allied motifs', *Russian Review*, Jan. 1957, pp.42–52.

Meyerkhol'd, V.Ye., *Perepiska 1896–1939*, M.1976.

Mikhaylovsky, B.V., *Russkaya literatura XX veka*, M.1939.

['O romane A. Belogo *Peterburg*'] in *B.V.M. Izbrannyye stat'i o literature i iskusstve*, M.1969, pp.448–62.

Mints, Z.G., 'O nekotorykh "neomifologicheskikh" tekstakh v tvorchestve russkikh simvolistov', *Tvorchestvo A.A. Bloka i russkaya kul'tura XX veka. Blokovskiy sbornik* III, Tartu 1979, pp.76–120.

Mochul'sky, K.V., 'Literaturnyye besedy. *Moskva pod udarom*', *Zveno* No.196, 31 Dec 1926, pp.1–2.

'*Moskva* A Belogo', *Zveno* No.177, 26 June 1926.

Andrey Bely, Paris 1955.

Andrei Bely: His Life and Works, translated by Nora Szalavitz, Ann Arbor 1977.

Murav'yov, L., 'Dva pis'ma N. Berdyayeva k A. Belomu s poslesloviem F. Stepuna', *Mosty* No.XI, Munich 1965, pp.359–68.

Nevadovskaya, R., 'Andrey Bely', *Novosel'ye*, 1944 No.12.

Nilsson, N.A., *Ibsen in Russland*, Stockholm 1958.

Nivat, G., 'A. Blok et A. Belyj: étude sur la correspondance des deux poètes', *Revue des études slaves*, No.45, 1966, pp.145–64.

'Le "jeu cérébral". Étude sur *Pétersbourg*', in Andréi Biély, *Pétersbourg*, traduit par Jacques Catteau et Georges Nivat, Lausanne 1967, pp.321–67.

'Le palimpseste de l'enfance', in Andréi Biély, *Kotik Letaiev*, traduit par Georges Nivat, Lausanne, 1973, pp.241–89.

'"Ultima Thule", ou l'itinéraire du symbolisme russe', *Cahiers du monde russe et soviétique*, vol.xv No.1–2, 1974, pp.7–16.

'Eléménts pour une biographie d'Andrej Belyj', *Cahiers du monde russe et soviétique*, vol.xv No.1–2, 1974, pp.17–21.

'L'oeuvre polémique, critique et journalistique d'Andrej Belyj', *Cahiers du monde russe et soviétique*, vol.xv No.1–2, 1974, pp. 22–39.

'Ostrovok v sumyatitse zhizni: rasskaz o Tomochke-pyosike', *Russkiy al'manakh*, Paris 1981, pp.15–20.

Orlov, V., *Puti i sud'by*, M.–L. 1963.

Pereput'ya, M.1976.

Otsup, N., *Sovremenniki*, Paris 1961.

Peterson, R.E., *Andrej Belyj's Short Prose*, Birmingham Slavonic Monographs No.11, Birmingham 1980.

Pustygina, N., 'Tsitatnost' v romane Andreya Belogo *Peterburg*', *Uch. zap. Tartuskogo gos. univ.*, vyp. 414. *Trudy po russkoy i slavyanskoy filologii* XXVIII, 1977, pp.80–97; vyp. 513, XXXII, 1981.

Pyast, V., *Vstrechi*, L.1929.

Pyman, A., *The Russian decadents, 1890–1905, with special reference to D.S. Merezhkovsky*, unpublished Ph.D. thesis, Cambridge, 1959.

Reavey, G., 'A Note on Andrei Biely', *The New Review*, No.4, Jan. 1932.

Reeve, F.D., '"Vesy": A Study of a Russian Magazine', SEER, vol.37, 1958–9, pp.221–235.

'A Geometry of Prose', *Kenyon Review*, Winter 1963, pp.11–25.

Rice, J.L., 'Andrej Belyj's *Silver Dove*: the Black Depths of Blue Space or Who Stole the Baroness's Diamonds?' *Mnemozina. Studia literaria russica in honorem Vsevolod Setchkarev*, Munich 1974, pp.301–16.

Sapir, B., 'An Unknown Correspondent of Andrey Bely', SEER, vol. XLIX No.116, July 1971, pp.450–2.

Shaginyan, M., 'Epopeya Belogo (Morfologicheskiye zametki)', *Letopis' doma literatury*, 1921 No.1

Shklovsky, V., 'Andrey Bely', *Russkiy sovremennik*, 1924 No.2, pp.231–45.

O teorii prozy, M.–L. 1925.

Shpet, G., *Esteticheskiye fragmenty*, vyp 1–3, Pb. 1922.

Smirnov, I.P., *Khudozhestvennyy smysl i evolyutsiya poeticheskikh sistem*, M.1977.

Solov'yov, S., 'A. Bely. *Kubok meteley. Chetvyortaya simfoniya M.1908*', *Vesy*, 1908 No.5, pp.73–5.

Select bibliography

Stammler, H.A., 'Belyj's Conflict with Vjačeslav Ivanov over War and Revolution', SEEJ, vol.18 1974, pp.259–70.
Stanevich, V., 'O serebryanom golube', Trudy i dni, 1914 No.7, pp.141–50.
Starikova, E., 'Realizm i simvolizm', Razvitiye realizma v russkoy literature, t.III. M.1974, pp.165–246.
Steinberg, A., 'On the structure of Parody in Andrej Belyj's Peterburg', Slavica Hierosolymitana, vol.1 1977, pp.132–157.
'Colour and the Embodiment of Theme in Bely's "Urbanistic" novels, SEER, vol.57, No.2, Apr. 1979, pp.187–213.
Word and Music in the Novels of Andrey Bely, Cambridge 1982.
Stepun, F., Vergangenes und Unvergängliches. 1. Teil 1884–1914, Munich 1949.
Vstrechi, Munich 1962.
Mystische Weltschau, Munich 1964.
Stojnić-Caričič, M., Simbolistička doktrina Andreja Belog, Belgrade 1971.
Struve, G., 'Andrej Belyj's experiments with novel technique', Stil- und Formprobleme in der Literatur, FILLM, Heidelberg 1959, pp.459–67.
'K biografii Andreya Belogo. A. Bely i A.A. Turgeneva', Annali dell'Istituto Universitario Orientale. Sezione Slava, 13, Naples 1970, pp.47–67.
'K biografii Andreya Belogo', Novyy zhurnal 124, Sept. 1976, pp.152–162.
Szilard, Ye., 'O strukture Vtoroy simfonii A. Belogo', Studia Slavica Hungarica, XIII 1967, pp.311–22.
'O vliyanii ritmiki prozy F. Nitsshe na ritmiku prozy A. Belogo', Studia Slavica Hungarica, XIX 1973, pp.289–313.
Tarasenkov, A., 'Tema voyny v romane Andreya Belogo Moskva', Lokaf (=Znamya), 1932 No.10, pp.170–83.
Timofeyev, L., 'O Maskakh A. Belogo', Oktyabr', 1933 No.6, pp.212–17.
Tomashevsky, B., 'Andrey Bely i khudozhestvennaya proza', Zhizn' iskusstva, 1920 Nos.454, 458–9, 460.
Trotsky, L., Literatura i revolyutsiya, M.1923.
Tsvetayeva, M.I., Proza, N.Y. 1953.
Turgeneva, A., 'Po povodu "Instituta istorii iskusstv"', Mosty No.12, 1966, pp.358–362.
'Andrey Bely i Rudol'f Shteyner', Mosty No.13–14, 1969, pp.236–51.
Turgenieff, A., Erinnerungen an Rudolf Steiner und die Arbeit am ersten Goetheanum, Stuttgart 1973.
Turgenieff-Pozzo, N.A., Zwölf Jahre der Arbeit am Goetheanum, Dornach 1942.
Valentinov, N., Dva goda s simvolistami, Stanford, Calif. 1969.
Veskler, A., 'Krizis tvorchestva A. Belogo', Zhizn' iskusstva, Nos.276–7, 280–1, 1919.
'Epopeya Belogo', Sbornik 'Sovremennaya literatura', L.1925, pp.48–75.

Select bibliography

Woloshin, M., *Die grüne Schlange. Lebenserinnerungen*, Stuttgart 1954.

West, J.D., *Russian Symbolism*, London 1970.

'Neo-Romanticism in the Russian Symbolist Aesthetic', SEER, vol.51. No.124, 1973, pp.413–27.

West, T.G., *The Novel in Transition. A Study of J.-K. Huysmans' "A Rebours", R.M. Rilke's "Malte Laurids Brigge" and A. Bely's "Petersburg"*, Unpublished Ph.D. thesis, University of Manchester, 1979.

Woronzoff, A., 'Andrej Belyj's *Peterburg*, James Joyce's *Ulysses*, and the Stream-of-Consciousness Method', *Russian Language Journal*, 1976, No.107, pp.101–07.

Andrej Belyj's "Petersburg", James Joyce's "Ulysses" and the Symbolist Movement, Berne, Frankfurt am Main 1982.

Yampol'sky, I., 'Valeriy Bryusov o *Peterburge* Andreya Belogo', *Voprosy literatury*, 1973, No.6, pp.317–18.

Zamyatin, Ye., *Litsa*, N.Y. 1955.

Zaytsev, B.K., 'Andrey Bely (vospominaniya, vstrechi)', *Russkiye zapiski*, July 1938.

Moskva, Paris 1939.

'Molodost' – Bely', *Mosty* No.10 1963, pp.6–17.

Dalyokoye, Washington 1965.

Zelinsky, K., *Na rubezhe dvukh epokh*, M.1959.

Zhirmunsky, V., 'Po povodu knigi *Ritm kak dialektika*', *Zvezda*, 1929, No.8, pp.203–18.

Gete v russkoy literature, L. 1937.

'O ritmicheskoy proze', *Russkaya literatura*, 1966 No.4, pp.103–14.

Index

Index

261

Index

Index

OPERA BEFORE MOZART

Music
———

Editor
SIR JACK WESTRUP
Heather Professor of Music
in the University of Oxford